kburn

Developing Your Counselling and Psychotherapy Skills and Practice

Developing Your Counselling and Psychotherapy Skills and Practice

Ladislav Timulak

Los Angeles | London | New Delhi
Singapore | Washington DC

First published 2011

SAGE Publications Ltd
1 Oliver's Yard
55 City Road
London EC1Y 1SP

SAGE Publications Inc.
2455 Teller Road
Thousand Oaks, California 91320

SAGE Publications India Pvt Ltd
B 1/I 1 Mohan Cooperative Industrial Area
Mathura Road
New Delhi 110 044

SAGE Publications Asia-Pacific Pte Ltd
33 Pekin Street #02-01
Far East Square
Singapore 048763

Library of Congress Control Number: 2010925814

British Library Cataloguing in Publication data

A catalogue record for this book is available from the British Library

ISBN 978-1-84860-623-4
ISBN 978-1-84860-624-1 (pbk)

Typeset by C&M Digitals (P) Ltd, Chennai, India
Printed and bound in Great Britain by TJ International Ltd, Padstow, Cornwall
Printed on paper from sustainable resources

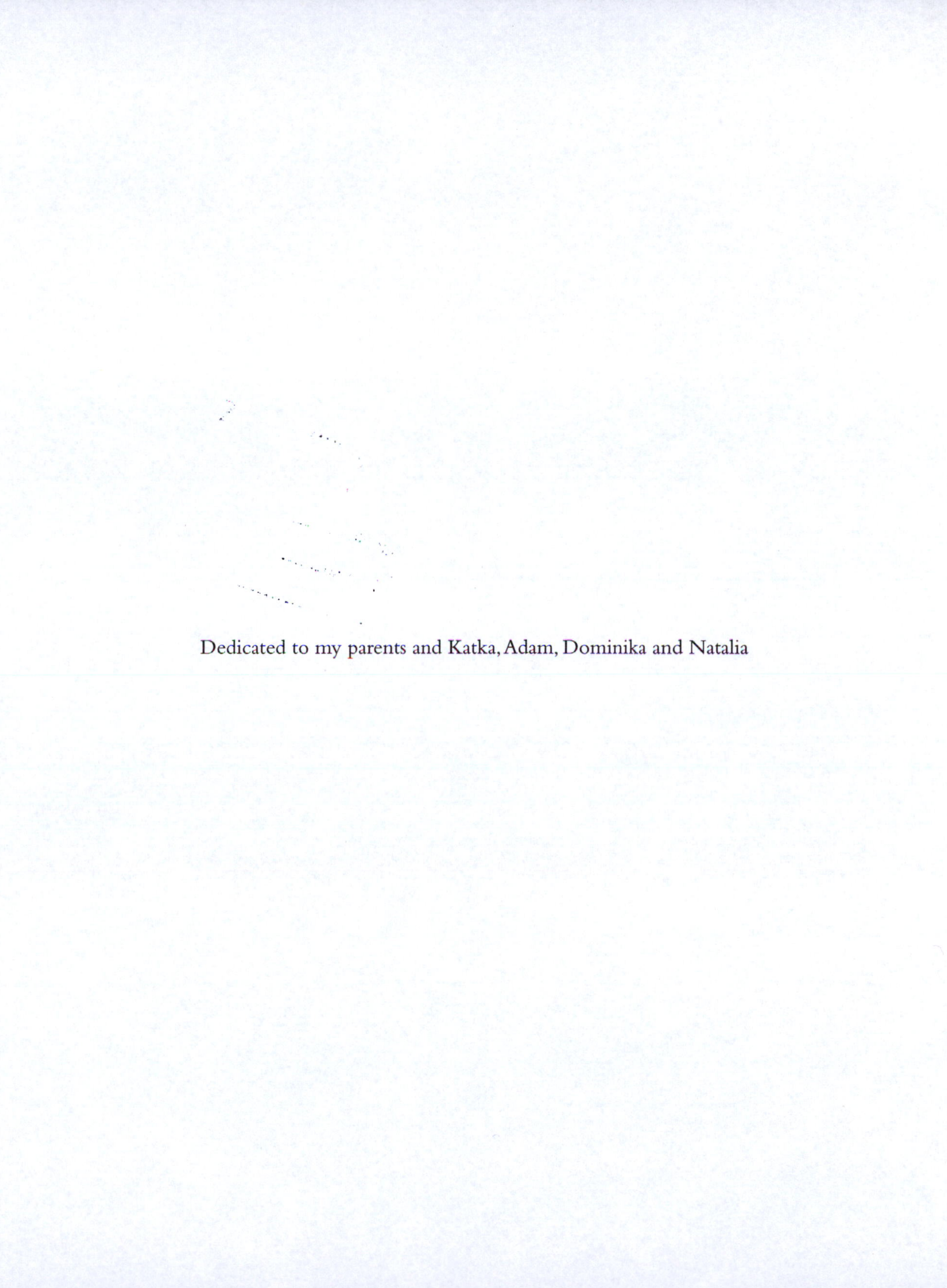

Dedicated to my parents and Katka, Adam, Dominika and Natalia

Contents

Acknowledgements

This book is partially based on its predecessor, published in Czech in 2006, *Základy vedení psychoterapeutického rozhovoru* (Timul'ák, 2006). I would like to thank the clients and the therapists of the original version of this book for allowing me to use their transcripts in this edition. I would like to extend my gratitude to the clients who gave consent for the use of their transcripts in this English version also. I would like to thank Katarína Karaszová and Soňa Urigová for translating parts of the Slovak version of the book that served as a base for some of the current chapters. My thanks also go to Kathleen and Neil Bristow for proofreading parts of the manuscript.

Thanks are also due to the team at Sage (Alice Oven, Emma Paterson and Rachel Burrows) for helpful editorial advice with the book as well as language editor and proofreader (Sarah Bury and Emily Ayers). I would also like to thank the reviewers of the manuscript. I would like to thank my wife Katka for all her support over the years and also my mum, who supported both of us on her many visits to Dublin. Special thanks go to all my friends and tutors in my homeland Slovakia, in Ireland and across the world for the learning opportunities they have given me over the years. I would particularly like to thank my first tutor Vlado Hlavenka, who sparked my interest in psychotherapy.

Introduction: The Goal and Organisation of the Text

This book is dedicated to counselling and psychotherapy[1] trainees as well as to trainee counselling and clinical psychologists and psychiatrists. The book has two goals: (1) to provide research-informed suggestions of how to conduct psychotherapy; and (2) to present them in a generic form so they can be used by trainees with different theoretical preferences. There are quite a number of introductory texts on psychotherapy and counselling, as well as many more advanced books on specific approaches to therapy. However, when books are focused on the basics, they usually cover just the rudimentary counselling skills (e.g. Egan, 2002; Hill, 2004, 2009; Nelson-Jones, 2009), without much context of overall therapy, and when books focus on a more advanced level, they are often written in the form of a manual that is intended for more established practitioners (e.g. Greenberg & Watson, 2006; Luborsky & Luborsky, 2006; Craske & Barlow, 2007). This book aspires to cover the middle ground. It is designed to be an introductory text that more closely resembles the actual practice of psychotherapy, for example focusing on case conceptualisation, the planning of treatment, multidisciplinary collaboration, and tailoring the therapeutic approach to the problem or disorder of the client, etc.

The book is, to a certain extent, similar to other books addressing this area (see Hill & O'Brien, 1999; Egan, 2002). It emphasises basic counselling and psychotherapy skills, as they were conceptualised and developed in the 1960s and 1970s by authors such as Truax, Carkhuff and Ivey, who were influenced by the tradition of client-centred therapy, problem-oriented therapies (Egan, 2002) and, more recently, integrative conceptualisation (see Hill & O'Brien, 1999; Hill, 2009). This text wants to build on this tradition and also to focus on other aspects of therapy, such as case formulation, working with specific situations in the therapeutic process, and working with specific types of client, etc. The text is designed in a way that allows trainees with different theoretical leanings to choose between the outlined conceptualisations, strategies, skills, and techniques. The text uses, in Part II on the basic skills of conducting psychotherapy and counselling, a specific logic, which is adopted more or less for didactic purposes rather than as a prescription that should be followed strictly by a therapist. This logic corresponds with the conceptualisation offered by American authors Hill and O'Brien (1999), who define helping skills as (1) facilitating exploration, (2) facilitating

[1]I use the terms 'counselling' and 'psychotherapy' interchangeably in this book.

insight, and (3) facilitating action. Their formulation assumes that exploration-facilitating skills stem mostly from the client-centred tradition, insight-promoting skills from the psychodynamic tradition, and action-promoting skills from the cognitive-behavioural tradition. The framework of this text will also include facilitating skills for making 'change' decisions, including an existential perspective, and it will focus on the use of specific cognitive, behavioural and experiential techniques. There will also be a short discussion on work with dreams. All of it will be put in the context of current empirically-based knowledge.

The book aims to go beyond describing the use of basic skills and to provide a brief guide to case conceptualisation in psychotherapy. There will also be discussion of ethical issues in psychotherapy and the overall process of therapy. The book includes specific situations that may occur in the psychotherapy process, such as conflict in the therapeutic relationship, discussions of the interpersonal relationships of the client, crying in the session, silences in the session, working with overwhelming emotions, problematic personality traits, etc. It will present the main features of working with the most common problems and disorders for which counselling and psychotherapy are indicated. The book also covers the use of psychotherapy combined with other interventions, such pharmacotherapy, social support, self-help interventions, etc.

The book is written in the tradition of research-informed, integrative psychotherapy (Grawe, 1997, 2004; Beutler, Clarkin, & Bongar, 2000). It presents counselling and psychotherapy as a unanimous, generic activity, while in reality there exist many competing therapeutic approaches. The emphasis is on empirically-informed principles of therapeutic change regardless of the theoretical origins of particular principles (Castonguay & Beutler, 2006). This, however, should not hinder the reader's use of the book within their own theoretical understanding and therapeutic preferences. This will be discussed throughout the book.

The research-informed perspective of this book contrasts somewhat with *evidence-based psychotherapy* (see Fisher & O'Donohue, 2007). This (evidence-based) understanding of current psychotherapy and counselling is mostly typical for the cognitive-behavioural perspective, which sees the importance of running randomised clinical trials (RCTs) in assessing the efficacy and effectiveness of psychological therapies. However, this trend is not without controversy as to what constitutes the 'evidence' (see Norcross, Beutler, & Levant, 2006). In line with those controversies, this book will use a 'research-informed' rather than 'evidence-based' perspective on psychological therapy (Grawe, 1997). The research-informed perspective means that therapeutic practice is very much influenced by research, but not solely by RCTs. All other research studies are taken into account – experimental as well as descriptive case studies, naturalistic outcome studies, preferential trials, consumer satisfaction studies, qualitative outcome studies, dose-effects studies, aptitude-treatment interaction studies, therapists and clients effects studies, process-outcome studies, descriptive-process studies, therapy events studies, theory-testing process studies, etc. (cf. Timulak, 2008).

The book is brief. Therefore many issues will be outlined only and references for further reading will be provided. Finally, this book focuses on individual (adult) therapy, so the reader will need to look elsewhere for books dealing with the skills used in group therapy, couple therapy and family therapy (e.g. Johnson, 2004; Yalom & Leczcz, 2005; Greenberg & Goldman, 2008).

The reader also has to remember that the reality of human suffering is complex. Psychotherapy often cannot address this complexity. It has to be carefully considered whether or not psychotherapy or counselling is the best intervention for a particular person. Psychotherapy can have an auxiliary or a primary role in addressing clients' problems. Alternative interventions may also be considered (e.g. medication, social intervention, social support, self-help work, information) and offered instead of psychotherapy, or alongside it. The therapist should therefore be able to assess the prospective client and not only decide on a therapeutic strategy, but also on whether therapy is indeed the best option.

Multidisciplinary approaches to the client's presenting issues are becoming a norm, and this book will also take this into account. The evidence-based medicine movement that stimulated empirical emphasis in psychological therapy emphasises the three pillars of health care approach: (1) the research evidence, (2) the clinical expertise of the provider, and (3) the client's choice of treatment (see for instance Norcross, Beutler & Levant, 2006). The last point, client's choice, is very much emphasised in current psychological therapy as well.

Part I

Introduction

One

Current Psychotherapy and Counselling

Abstract

This chapter presents the current field of psychotherapy and counselling in the context of their historical development. The emphasis is on research-informed developments within or across the distinct theoretical approaches (psychodynamic, cognitive-behavioural, humanistic and integrative). References for helpful resources are provided as well.

Psychotherapy is a healing activity that attempts to alleviate human suffering. It uses psychological means to influence psychopathological symptoms, problematic experiencing, behaviour, and personality characteristics as well as general functioning in life (see Kratochvíl, 2002). To start with, we will have a look at the current research-informed psychotherapy.

Theoretical approaches to psychotherapy and counselling

Counselling and psychotherapy were traditionally developed within several major and distinct paradigms, though most recently there is probably a growing trend towards psychotherapy integration and a more generic understanding of psychotherapy (see Grawe, 2004; Norcross & Goldfried, 2005). Often four main therapy paradigms are recognised: psychodynamic, cognitive-behavioural, humanistic, and integrative and eclectic therapies (see the four volumes of *Comprehensive Handbook of Psychotherapy* edited by F.W. Kaslow, 2004). *Systemic approaches* that developed in the tradition of family and couple therapy and its relatives, such as narrative therapy and constructivist therapies, can probably be considered as another distinct paradigm. Outside those major paradigms there are a significant number of other therapeutic approaches (see Corsini & Wedding, 2007). We will now focus on three broadly defined mainstream paradigms that have received most theoretical and research attention. A more complete overview is provided, for instance, in McLeod (2009).

Psychodynamic approaches represent the first theoretical block. These approaches stem from Freud's psychoanalysis and its long tradition (egopsychology, object relations, etc.). There is growing empirical evidence that supports these approaches (see Shedler, 2010). The developments of empirically studied interpersonal therapy can be loosely assigned to the psychodynamic paradigm as well (see Weissman, Markowitz, & Klerman, 2000).

Cognitive-behavioural approaches represent the second main theoretical paradigm. These approaches currently dominate the field of psychotherapy. This tradition emphasises empirical outcome research, which is well respected in the current era of accountability. Cognitive-behavioural approaches stem originally from two different traditions, cognitive and behavioural. Their combination is probably a pragmatic step as the two paradigms are closely aligned with scientific positivism and 'hard facts'.

Humanistic therapies represent a group of quite distinct approaches, such as person-centred therapy, Gestalt therapy, different existential conceptualisations and, more recently, emotion-focused therapy, all of which are focused on the person more holistically.

Eclectic and integrative therapies represent either a combination of therapies or therapeutic principles from different major paradigms that can be tailored to individual clients' problems (e.g. Beutler & Harwood, 2000), or an attempt to create a more comprehensive theoretical framework (e.g. Prochaska & Norcross, 2003) or a formulation of psychotherapy as a generic activity based on psychological, research-informed principles (Grawe, 2004). The traditional paradigms define the main focus and principles of psychotherapeutic practice. Their development is shaped by clinical experience, theoretical thinking and by research findings.

Psychodynamic approaches

Psychodynamic therapies build on Freud's psychoanalysis from the end of the nineteenth and the beginning of the twentieth century. Freud described several theoretical concepts relevant to psychopathology and psychoanalytic therapy. They covered, for instance, a motivation theory, where a central role was played by libido and pleasure-seeking behaviour. Freud also outlined a theory of human development, according to which psychopathology is created on the basis of unmastered developmental tasks of pleasure-seeking (libido-gratifying) behaviour. The psychopathological problems are then fixated in the different developmental stages, such as the oral stage, the anal stage, the phallic stage, the latent stage and the genital stage. Freud also developed a theory of psychological defences that reduce anxiety induced by the conflict between wishes and internal or external obstacles hindering their fulfilment. The defences were linked to individual developmental stages. Freud also described the so-called topographic model of the mind (consciousness, sub-consciousness and unconsciousness) and the structural model of mind (id, ego and superego) that represented a framework in which psychological processes are happening.

The basic element of psychopathology was, according to Freud, conflict of opposing motives, which he assumed to be in the unconsciousness. Neurotic symptoms were, according to him, a compromise between opposing unconscious motivational forces (the psychodynamics of latent wishes), which due to the fact that psychological energy stays the same, show in conversion symptoms (see Milton, Polmear, & Fabricius, 2004). The basic motives were then typically of a sexual or aggressive nature.

With regard to principles of treatment, Freud was emphasising that psychoanalytic work focuses on the uncovering of unconscious functioning. The tool of the therapist was the interpretation of unconscious conflicts which became visible through free associations, dreams and the transference of unconscious conflicts to the relationship with the therapist.

Freud's concepts were, over the generations, well received by a number of mental health professionals, and have subsequently been built on, developed and revised by other psychoanalysts. The most comprehensive concepts were:

- *ego-psychology* (dating from the 1950s onwards and associated with authors such as Hartman and Mahler), which stressed the cognitive functions of the ego and their use in treatment;
- *object relations theory* (associated with British authors Klein and Winnicott, and with Kernberg in America, originating in the 1940s and 1950s), which supposes that the object of wishes is the other person and that early interpersonal functioning in intimate relationships, and the cognitive and affective processes mediating this functioning, creates stable patterns of interpersonal relating (see Westen & Gabbard, 1999);
- *self-psychology* (originating in the 1970s and 1980s and particularly associated with Kohut), which emphasises motives connected to self-esteem and the experience of self-esteem, including identification with significant others in early childhood and empathy in treatment;
- in recent years, especially in North America, one can find *relational psychoanalysis*, which focuses on the reflection of interpersonal functioning between the analyst and the patient (cf. Mitchell, 1997).

Current empirical knowledge and psychoanalytic concepts

The richness of psychoanalytic theoretical conceptions was not always recognised in the mainstream of psychology. Despite this fact, many of the psychoanalytic conceptions, based on the analysts' clinical experience, correspond nicely with current psychological knowledge. This is illustrated by the American analysts Drew Westen and Glen Gabbard (1999; see also Westen, 1998) in their overview comparing psychoanalytic personality theories with current empirical psychological knowledge. For instance, Westen and Gabbard point to the proved importance of emotions as primary motivational mechanisms that have a potential to be adaptive. They cite evidence showing that people are motivated by parallel motivational systems which potentially lead to conflict. The presence of conflict is, according to them, also suggested by the existence of ambivalence in human experiencing, visible in the fact that positive and negative emotions correlate only moderately.

Westen and Gabbard (1999; cf. Westen, 1998) further emphasise the existence of an empirically-based agreement that a lot of mental life is unconscious; that stable structures of personality are formed in childhood; that needs and motives are influenced through the internalisation of the needs and motives of significant others. In addition, Westen and Gabbard document evidence that mental representations of self and others influence interpersonal functioning and psychological symptoms (for instance, differentiated, benign and interacting perceptions in projective tests correlate with psychological health). Similarly, people who do not report problems in self-rating scales, but whose childhood descriptions are incoherent or are describing a distressed childhood, have higher blood pressure and heart activity, both visible symptoms of anxiety that would suggest the presence of defences in self-reflection or self-presentation.

Westen and Gabbard's (1999; Westen, 1998) review also points to research studies showing the relationship between personality features in childhood and psychopathology in adulthood. They also refer to research studies that show how often cognitions are in the service of emotions and motivational processes. They stress the associative nature of human psychological functioning and parallel information processing, the awareness of which may be hindered by human wishes, fears and values.

Current psychodynamic scene

Psychodynamic approaches to psychotherapy are diverse and may differ according to traditions in different countries. They represent variations of the main paradigm, which assumes that psychopathology stems from unconscious motivational conflicts that are part of personality structures and of interpersonal functioning. These unconscious conflicts have their roots in personal history, especially in early experiences with significant others. The therapeutic work attempts to provide, with the help of the therapist and in the therapeutic relationship, insight and experiential working-through of the beliefs that are part of the conflicting motivation.

Traditional psychoanalytic training, with an emphasis on long-term personal analysis, still exists. Psychoanalytic associations (e.g. the International Psychoanalytic Association and the American Psychoanalytic Association) play a central role. Psychoanalytic and psychodynamic therapies are influenced by developments in mainstream psychotherapy, such as the emphasis on the brevity of therapy and the manualisation of the therapist's work. For example, time-limited therapy has influenced the development of focal psychoanalytic and psychodynamic treatment manuals (e.g. Luborsky, 1984; Strupp & Binder, 1984). More recently, handbooks were devoted to different psychoanalytic and psychodynamic approaches addressing different types of psychopathology (e.g. Barber & Crits-Christoph, 1995).

Empirical investigations of psychotherapy and psychodynamic constructs

Several psychodynamic constructs have been examined in empirical investigations. Probably the most studied construct is that of the therapeutic alliance (e.g. Bordin, 1979). There are different conceptions of this construct, the majority of which were elaborated by psychoanalytic theoreticians (see Horvath & Bedi, 2002). Several instruments exist that assess the quality of the alliance as perceived by therapists, clients and external raters. In general, the therapeutic alliance (especially as experienced by the client) appears to be a significant predictor of psychotherapy outcome (Martin, Garske, & Davies, 2000; Horvath & Bedi, 2002).

Interpretation as the main treatment tool of psychodynamic therapists is also well studied. Interpretations seem to be differentially effective depending on the client's quality of object relations (the lower the quality, the more counterproductive are interpretations of transference; see Crits-Christoph & Connolly-Gibbons, 2002), though this may be moderated by the quality of interpretation (Høglend et al., 2006). The empirical overview of Crits-Christoph and Connolly-Gibbons (2002) suggests that, especially in brief therapies, interpretations should focus on central interpersonal themes, but not necessarily as manifested in transference.

Significant attention in empirical research is also devoted to investigations of transference (the expression of the client's central interpersonal functioning in the relationship with the therapist) and psychodynamic case formulation (Luborsky et al., 1993). Good evidence shows that it is possible to capture empirically the client's problematic central interpersonal stance after only a few sessions in therapy (we will discuss this more closely in Chapter 3). It has also been shown that this stance is mirrored in the client's relationship with the therapist (Luborsky & Crits-Christoph, 1990). Furthermore, it has been proven that in successful psychodynamic therapies this stance changes into a more constructive form (Crits-Christoph & Luborsky, 1990).

Countertransference has also been empirically investigated. It has been shown that countertransference emanates from the therapist's unresolved conflicts, even though it is moderated by the client's behaviour and therapy-related factors (Gelso & Hayes, 2007). Once the countertransference is present, it may be difficult for the therapist to maintain appropriate therapeutic distance from the client, although it does not always have to affect the therapy negatively (Gelso & Hayes, 2007). The central feature that was studied with regard to countertransference is its therapeutic use. The factors that seem to contribute to its therapeutic use are:

(1) the ability of the therapist to be aware of problematic inner experience together with the ability to understand its roots;
(2) the therapist's healthy personality structure (self-integration);
(3) the therapist's efficient anxiety management;
(4) the therapist's empathy; and finally
(5) the therapist's ability to conceptualise interaction in the therapeutic relationship (Gelso & Hayes, 2002, 2007).

These are some of the psychodynamic constructs that have received the attention of psychotherapy researchers. Investigations of others (e.g. defences) can be found in the volumes dedicated to research on psychodynamic therapies (see Miller et al., 1993).

Attachment theory and its impact on current psychotherapy

Psychoanalysis is also the study of human development and the influence of childhood experiences on adult functioning (Bateman & Holmes, 1995). This part of psychoanalysis has influenced current psychotherapy as well (see, for example, work of developmental analysts such as Bowlby (1988) and Stern (1985)). A practical application not only in the theory of psychopathology, but also in therapy, is the construct of attachment of John Bowlby (1988). This construct tries to capture the quality of the affective bond between mother and child as well as the quality of the later adult's interpersonal relating. Originally, Ainsworth (1989) empirically showed that there are three forms of infant attachment, and each depends on the infant's experiences with the caregiver: (1) secure attachment, (2) avoidant attachment, and (3) resistant or ambivalent attachment. This conceptualisation was further complemented by the fourth category of disorganised/disoriented attachment (Main, 1995). There are several conceptualisations of adult-relating in close relationships that correspond with child-relational stances (see Hesse, 1999; Holmes, 2001). An example is the conceptualisation of Kim Bartholomew (1997), where she distinguishes four forms of attachment in adults:

(1) *secure attachment* – the person perceives others as trustworthy and has a positive sense of self;
(2) *preoccupied attachment* – the person seeks acceptance in others and internally does not have a positive sense of self;
(3) *fearful attachment* – the person does not perceive others positively and does not have a positive sense of self; and
(4) *dismissing attachment* – the person has a positive sense of self, but does not see others as trustworthy.

Attachment theory complements object relations theory, plus there is a wealth of empirical material to support it. Attachment is not only about interpersonal functioning in close interpersonal relationships, but it also characterises affect regulation in children and later in adults and it leads to the creation of working models of human relating for a child (and later adult). It has direct application to psychotherapy. The type of attachment is important not only for the case formulation, but also for the manner of relating that the therapist can offer to the client, so it can help to regulate the client's emotional experiencing as well as the client's coping outside the therapy. Another implication is in the area of work with people who have suffered trauma in childhood that has led to the formation of problematic attachment. The evidence suggests that reflective functioning may be impaired in people with such experiences (see review in Bateman & Fonagy, 2004) and therapy then needs to focus on its development.

Current empirically supported psychodynamic approaches

There are a number of psychodynamic approaches that have been researched and whose effectiveness has been assessed (see Box 1.1). One of the most studied approaches is *supportive-expressive psychoanalytic psychotherapy,* which has been described in the form of a therapist's manual by Lester Luborsky (1984; Luborsky & Luborsky, 2006; see also Book, 1997). The efficacy of this therapy was assessed in the treatment of methadone patients (see Woody et al., 1983; Luborsky, Woody et al., 1995). Studies have also verified its effectiveness in the treatment of cocaine dependence (Crits-Christoph et al., 1999), depression (Luborsky, Mark et al., 1995), or generalised anxiety disorder (Crits-Christoph et al., 1995). Supportive-expressive psychoanalytic therapy focuses on clients' understanding of psychopathological symptoms and their own core conflictual relationship themes that should lead to the overcoming of those symptoms and problems in interpersonal relating.

Box 1.1 Examples of empirically studied or developed psychodynamic therapies (as broadly defined)

- *Supportive-expressive psychoanalytic psychotherapy (studied in relation to addictions)* (Luborsky & Luborsky, 2006).
- *Psychodynamic-interpersonal therapy (depression)* (Hobson, 1985).
- *Mentalisation-based treatment of borderline personality disorder* (Bateman & Fonagy, 2004).
- *Interpersonal therapy for depression* (Weissmann, Markowitz, & Klerman, 2000).

Psychodynamic-interpersonal therapy (Hobson, 1985), which also incorporates experiential components, was successfully tested in the treatment of depression (e.g. Shapiro et al., 1994). This therapy was assessed with regard to its effectiveness in training therapists of different theoretical orientations (Guthrie et al., 2004). It is an interpretative form of therapy, looking at the relationship between the felt experience and interpersonal interactions.

Recently, another form of psychoanalytic treatment received attention thanks to its empirical testing and comprehensive theoretical outline. It is a mentalisation-based treatment of borderline personality disorder, which is marked by an intense emotional instability (Bateman & Fonagy, 2001, 2004). This approach requires partial or full hospitalisation and includes the services of broader medical personnel. Individual and group psychotherapy are key in this approach. Psychotherapy focuses on the identification of intentions in the client's functioning as well as on a reading of the intentions of the people with whom the client interacts (this process is called mentalisation). The ability of reflecting on one's own experiencing and intentions in the interaction is, according to mentalisation theory, missing in the people with borderline features.

Interpersonal therapy (Weissmann, Markowitz, & Klerman, 2000) may be broadly considered as a therapy akin to psychodynamic approaches. This therapy, after it was tested in a collaborative research trial sponsored by the American National Institute of Mental Health (Elkin et al., 1989), gained broad publicity. It conceptualised depression as an interpersonal problem concerning one of the following: bereavement, interpersonal disputes, change in the life role, or loneliness. The therapy is adjusted according to the type of interpersonal problem. This therapy was later tested for other problems, such as eating disorders (Wilfley et al., 2002).

Recommended reading

It is not possible to give a proper account of current (empirically informed) psychodynamic psychotherapy. More can be found in the following books:

Barber, J.P. & Crits-Christoph, P. (eds) (1995). *Dynamic Therapies for Psychiatric Disorders (Axis I).* New York: Basic Books.

Kaslow, F.W. & Magnavita, J.J. (2002). *Comprehensive Handbook of Psychotherapy: Vol. 1. Psychodynamic/Object Relations.* New York: John Wiley.

Cognitive-behavioural approaches

Cognitive-behavioural approaches follow the behavioural tradition in psychology (Pavlov, Watson, Skinner, Thornedike, Hull, Mowrer and others). The pioneers in its development were, for example, Eysenck, Lazarus, Wolpe (behavioural therapy in the 1950s), Ellis (rational-emotive therapy in the 1960s), Beck (cognitive therapy in the 1970s), etc. An explicit link between behavioural and cognitive therapy was introduced by Michael Mahoney, in his book *Cognition and Behavior Modification* (1974), and by Donald Meichenbaum, in his book *Cognitive Behavior Modification* (1977).

The cognitive-behavioural paradigm evolved through the merging of the behavioural and cognitive traditions in psychotherapy. However, not all of the proponents of these respective approaches approved this development (e.g. Eysenck). Behavioural approaches traditionally built on learning theory from general psychology. They adapted the principles of classical conditioning (Pavlov, 1927/1960), reciprocal inhibition (Wolpe, 1968 – anxiety can be suppressed by the activation of a counteracting physiological process such as relaxation), the two-factor theory of anxiety (Mowrer, 1960 – not only the anxious reaction itself, but also that avoidance contributes to anxiety), operant conditioning (Skinner, 1953 – voluntary behaviour can be conditioned through its consequences), social learning theory (Bandura, 1977 – learning through modelling behaviour), and so on.

The behaviour tradition closely linked any clinical developments with experimental research. Laboratory experimental research led directly to the development of clinical procedures from the very beginning (see the work of the authors mentioned above). The refinement of basic psychological knowledge then led to refinements in the therapeutic approach. This is still true. Nowadays, much attention is given to ongoing research, and treatments informed by this research are being developed (e.g. Barlow, 2002; Mineka & Zinbarg, 2006).

Cognitive approaches to therapy emphasised automatic thought processes. The basic premise of these approaches is the assumption that the meaning which is given to a stimulus influences emotional experiencing and behaviour. Psychotherapy therefore needs to focus on changing the faulty beliefs influencing the interpretation of stimulus. For example, Albert Ellis postulates that irrational beliefs influence the perception, interpretation and emotional experiencing of stimuli. Therefore, his goal for therapy is to use discussion to develop an effective philosophy without irrational beliefs (see Dryden & Ellis, 1988). Aaron Beck (Beck et al., 1979) emphasises the influence of problematic automatic thoughts and cognitive errors that influence emotional experiencing and these therefore need to be challenged and replaced in therapy. He postulates that these thoughts and errors stem from beliefs based on negatively or catastrophically interpreting previous experiences.

Although cognitive therapy developed from clinical experience relatively independently of parallel developments in cognitive science, its empiricist nature was always open to new findings from experimental cognitive psycholology (cf. Ingram & Siegle, 2010). Thus, appraisal studies, perception research, thinking and, more recently, emotion studies have found their place in the ever-evolving application of cognitive-behavioural therapies (cf. Barlow, 2008). Studies from cognitive neuroscience are also finding their way into informing the cognitive (as well as behavioural) strategies used in treatment (cf. Ingram & Siegle, 2010).

Craske (2010) provides a succinct account of the theoretical and empirically informed developments that are present and are combined in current cognitive-behavioural therapies. She points out how classical conditioning is currently being enriched by knowledge concerning relevant mediating factors, such as the predisposing characteristics of a person, a specific aversive event and the person's reactions to the event. She stresses current knowledge of the role of automatic as well as conscious cognitive processes in the development of conditioned reflexes. Similarly, she summarises how cognitive processes contribute to the development of contingency-shaping behaviour. Craske demonstrates how perceived or experienced self-efficacy is important for learning and successful therapy. She shows how cognitive appraisal is shaping emotions and behaviours, but also how these feed back to the development of beliefs and schemas.

Similarly, as learning theory can be complemented by cognitive theory, thus cognitive therapy theoreticians can complement their own predominantly cognitive approach by using behavioural techniques. Indeed, some cognitive-behavioural therapies put more emphasis on behavioural aspects (e.g. Craske & Barlow, 2007), whereas others place greater significance on cognitive aspects, such as Mahoney (1988, 2003) or Guidano and Liotti (1988). Currently, there are a variety of cognitive-behavioural therapies (cf. Dobson & Dozois, 2010), some of which also utilise concepts from other theoretical approaches (e.g. Castonguay et al., 2005). The emphasis on research and good evidence of their effectiveness, as well as an emphasis on specificity in the description of procedures, may be contributing to their speedy adoption and growing popularity.

Defining cognitive-behavioural approaches

As mentioned above, cognitive-behavioural therapies represent a broad range of approaches. Dobson and Block (1988; also Dobson & Dozois, 2010) see cognitive-behavioural therapies as those therapies that are built on the following assumptions:

(1) cognitive activity influences behaviour;
(2) cognitive activity can be monitored and changed; and
(3) desired behavioural change may be influenced by cognitive change.

Looking at these characteristics from the perspective of more behavioural approaches, one could add:

(4) behavioural change can influence cognitive change.

The theory of personality in the cognitive-behavioural paradigm takes into account the fact that human experience consists of four elements – physiology, cognition, behaviour, and emotion – and that a change in any of these elements brings change to all others (Scott & Dryden, 1996). Cognitive-behavioural therapies (CBT), then, are trying to change the negative interplay of those elements by promoting changes to cognitive processes and behaviour.

Cognitive processes that CBT targets include cognitive errors (e.g. dichotomous thinking, over-generalisation, mind reading, personalisation) and automatic cognitive schemes that stem from problematic core beliefs (e.g. DeRubeis & Beck, 1988). The main technique used to tackle the cognitive process contributing to client difficulties is cognitive restructuring (see Chapter 7). Problematic behaviour is also targeted. Behavioural interventions consist of self-monitoring, relaxation, behavioural activation, exposure, skills training, social modelling, etc., and may target either physiological symptoms or behaviour (see Leahy, 2004; many are presented in Chapter 7). The therapy is structured, based on a behavioural, cognitive and functional analysis of the client's problems (e.g. Craske & Barlow, 2007; see Chapter 3). The working style is collaborative, with the emphasis being placed on a high-quality alliance between the client and the therapist. Therapy aims to increase the client's self-efficacy through mastery of problematic behaviour, cognitive processes and emotions. This is achieved by engaging in a number of cognitive, physiological experiencing and behaviour-targeting tasks (see above). Furthermore, the in-session tasks are supported by homeworks that are used throughout the therapy.

Current empirically-supported cognitive-behavioural approaches

The term 'cognitive-behavioural therapy' is often understood as a synonym for empirically supported or evidence-based therapy. This 'misunderstanding' is well deserved as the majority of outcome studies in psychotherapy examine cognitive-behavioural therapies. The research not only focuses on the outcome of CBTs, but also on the relative effectiveness of its partial components (e.g. cognitive restructuring, exposure, relaxation). The different forms of research also examine the efficacy of CBTs. Indeed, when one examines a handbook compiling evidence-based interventions for specific disorders (e.g. Fisher & O'Donohue, 2007), one can see that it predominantly consists of CBTs.

The most researched and well known form of CBT for a specific disorder is *cognitive therapy for depression* (Beck et al., 1979). This therapy is probably the most researched psychotherapy as to its effectiveness (Hollon & Beck, 2004). The method of cognitive restructuring that comes from this therapy is present in almost every CBT approach. The efficacy of Beckian cognitive therapy is also studied for many other disorders (Hollon & Beck, 2004).

Cognitive-behavioural approaches dominate especially in the treatment of anxiety disorders. *Panic-control treatment*, a form of CBT applied to panic disorder (Craske & Barlow, 2007), is an example of one of the most efficacious psychological interventions that exist (Barlow et al., 2000). *Exposure and prevention of rituals* (Franklin & Foa, 2008) is one of the most researched and efficacious therapies for obsessive-compulsive disorder. Thomas Borkovec (Borkovec & Costello, 1993) leads a longstanding programme investigating the efficacy of CBT for generalised anxiety disorder. Similarly, Brown, O'Leary and Barlow (2001) are developing a form of CBT applicable to post-traumatic stress disorder (PTSD) (see also Foa, Hembree, & Rothbaum, 2007). Marsha Linehan (1993) developed and studied dialectical-behavioural therapy for borderline personality disorder. One can find an overview of research studies on CBTs, for instance, in the surveys provided by Hollon and Beck (2004), Emmelkamp (2004), or Kazdin (2004).

Box 1.2 Examples of empirically studied or developed cognitive-behavioural therapies

- *Cognitive therapy for depression* (Beck et al., 1979).
- *Panic-control treatment (panic disorder)* (Craske & Barlow, 2007).
- *Exposure and prevention of rituals (obsessive-compulsive disorder)* (Franklin & Foa, 2008).
- *Prolonged exposure therapy for post-traumatic stress disorder* (Foa, Hembree, & Rothbaum, 2007).
- *Dialectical-behavioural therapy for borderline personality disorder* (Linehan, 1993).

Recommended reading

There is a huge amount of literature on cognitive-behavioural approaches. The reader may choose among different books depending on his/her own preferences. Two informative, research-informed accounts can be found, for instance, in:

Barlow, D. (ed.) (2008). *Clinical Handbook of Psychological Disorders: A Step-by-step Treatment Manual* (4th edition). New York: Guilford Press.

Kaslow, F.W. & Patterson, T. (2002). *Comprehensive Handbook of Psychotherapy: Vol. 2. Cognitive-Behavioral Approaches*. New York: John Wiley.

Humanistic and existential approaches

Humanistic, experiential and existential approaches represent a great variety of different theoretical models. They are grouped together, especially in reviews or edited books (e.g. Rice & Greenberg, 1992; Cain & Seeman, 2002), but in reality they are quite distinct. According to Cain (2002), humanistic approaches, in the broader sense of the word, define: the *view of the person* (e.g. actualising, having free choice and responsibility, being unique, searching for meaning); *values* (respect for the right to self-determination and diversity); an *actualising tendency* (postulated as the underlying motivational tendency to maintain the self and to fulfil its potential); *relational emphasis* (the healing quality of relationships); *phenomenology* (knowing through one's own direct experience); *self* (sense and reflection of one's self); *emotions and meaning* (their centrality in behaviour).

Probably, the most practised of the humanistic approaches is person-centred therapy (the older term being client-centred therapy), which stems from the work of Carl Rogers. The roots of this therapy can be dated to 1942 when Rogers published the book *Counseling and Psychotherapy*. The theory of psychopathology of this approach, as formulated by Rogers (1959), assumes that the child is born with an innate actualising tendency that leads the child's development. The child actualises his or her self through assessing what is good for him or her on the basis of organismic valuing process. Developmentally, the child's self-experiences and self-perceptions form his or her self-concept, which is further actualised. As the child also has the need for the positive regard of significant others, the significant others' reactions (conditions of worth) may be more important than the child's own organismic valuing process. Thus, self-concept, based on the conditions of worth rather than on the basis of one's own organismic process, develops and is pursued. The conditions of worth then determine whether self-experiences are allowed to be brought into awareness (they may be distorted or denied) and so incongruence between the self and the totality of experiencing develops. This is then a source of problematic functioning.

The theory of therapy thus puts an emphasis on the healing power of the therapeutic relationship and the client's inherent potential for growth. It assumes that the client in a safe, authentic, unconditional and empathic relationship will be less defensive and gradually more accepting of his or her own experiencing self (Rogers, 1957, 1958, 1959). In practical terms, the emphasis is put on the quality of therapeutic interviewing, which conveys healing attitudes of acceptance and empathic understanding through responding empathically to the feelings and personal meanings in the client's explorations of his or her own experiences. Empathy also includes responses to aspects of the client's experiencing that are not fully in the client's awareness.

Gestalt therapy is another influential humanistic approach. Its originator, Frederick Perls (Perls, Hefferline, & Goodman, 1951), emphasised the healing power of awareness and dialogical relationship. The theory of personality (Yontef & Jacobs, 2005) assumed that people exist through differentiation and contact with others. The person grows through assimilating what leads to development and through rejecting what is not helpful. The boundary between one's self and environment (especially one's interpersonal environment) should be permeable (openness) but firm (autonomy), allowing for experiences of connection, but also of separate identity. The main problem, as seen by Perls, is in the inflexibility of organismic self-regulation in the interaction with one's environment, which is caused by a limited awareness of one's own experiencing and one's own needs. Awareness is hindered by defences such as confluence (fusion with the other), isolation (detachment), retroflection (self-self treatment instead of interaction), introjection (assimilating environment), projection (attributing aspects of the self to the environment), and deflection (avoidance of contact) (Yontef & Jacobs, 2005). The theory of therapy assumes that in a dialogical relationship the client will have a space to broaden awareness (contact) of his or her own experiencing, will accept responsibility for his or her own experiencing and will experiment with it. For that purpose, several experiential techniques, such as the use of chair dialogues, were designed. The techniques are used to put thoughts or feelings into action and to increase awareness.

Experiential approaches stemming from client-centred therapy (e.g. the focusing-oriented therapy of Gendlin) and emotion-focused therapy of Les Greenberg and his collaborators (Greenberg, Rice, & Elliott, 1993; Greenberg, 2002) also put emphasis on the exploration of experiencing and on broadening of the client's awareness. Emotion-focused therapy can especially be perceived as a further development of person-centred and Gestalt therapy (and effectively also their merger). This therapy was based on a programmatic research into experiential therapies. In its theory, it postulates that emotional experiencing has central informative power in human functioning. It sees human functioning as a dialectic between (1) sensory and visceral information, emotions and emotion schemes (including cognitive representations and meanings) and (2) conceptualisation of self. The emphasis is put on the healthy dialectical-constructive processing of experience. The therapy focuses on the unpacking of primary adaptive emotions and the transformation of primary maladaptive emotion schemes by accessing primary adaptive emotions. For that purpose, empathic relationship and active experiential interventions are used. We will look at them in Chapter 7.

Existential therapies consist of several independent approaches (Cooper, 2003, 2008b), for example *Daseinsanalysis* (Binswanger, Boss), *Logotherapy* (Frankl), American *Existential therapy* (Yalom, May), British *Existential analysis* (van Deurzen-Smith, Spinelli). The common feature of these approaches is the understanding of human suffering as the natural reality of life and not as psychopathology. Problems are seen to stem from encountering the givens of life (e.g. the inevitability of death, real anxiety encountered in life), and the meaning of life is an antidote to psychopathology.

Current empirically-supported humanistic and existential approaches

Humanistic and existential approaches, with the exception of person-centred therapy, were never dominating empirical research on psychotherapy. Even the research in person-centred psychotherapy is rather a historic reality of 1940 to 1970 (though, as we will see below, there is some resurgence in it). Traditionally, it was mostly process research that dominated in this paradigm, though outcome studies were also conducted. The process research focused on Rogers' postulated qualities of the therapeutic relationship, on the depth of experiencing, significant events in the therapeutic process, and other fruitful therapeutic processes (see Rennie, 2002; Sachse & Elliott, 2002). Many process research instruments were developed in this tradition (e.g. Barrett-Lennard's Relationship Inventory (Barrett-Lennard, 1986); Experiencing Scale (Klein et al., 1969); Client Vocal Quality Scale (Rice & Kerr, 1986)). Outcome research had already started in the 1950s (e.g. Rogers & Dymond, 1954). The studies fulfilling current standards show that person-centred therapy is promising in the treatment of depression (e.g. King et al., 2000) and, to a certain extent, in the treatment of panic disorder with agoraphobia (Teusch & Bohme, 1999). Elements of this therapy were shown to be useful in the treatment of adolescents with depression (Birmaher et al., 2000) and also in psychotherapy for schizophrenia (Tarrier et al., 2000).

The outcome of motivational interviewing, a derivative of person-centred therapy for working with addictions (Miller & Rollnick, 2002), but also with other problems (Arkowitz et al., 2008) is very well studied. The review of 26 randomised trials (Burke, Arkowitz, & Dunn, 2002) shows it to be an effective intervention (cf. also Babor & Del Boca, 2003).

Emotion-focused therapy (in its individual form it is also known as process-experiential therapy (see Greenberg, Rice, & Elliott, 1993); for its application with couples, see Greenberg & Johnson, 1988; Johnson, 2004; Greenberg & Goldman, 2008) is empirically well supported. Apart from the fact that it builds on the research tradition in person-centred therapy, this therapy was developed on the basis of process research and was tested as to its outcome (see the overview in Elliott, Greenberg, & Lietaer, 2004). In its individual form, it is the best established as a treatment for depression, though it has also been tested for other disorders such as PTSD. Its couples' application is one of the most studied couples therapies (Sexton, Alexander, & Mease, 2004).

Box 1.3 Examples of empirically studied or developed humanistic therapies (as broadly defined)

- *Motivational interviewing (addictions)* (Miller & Rollnick, 2002).
- *Emotion-focused therapy (couples, depression)* (Greenberg, 2002).

Recommended reading

Research-informed accounts of humanistic therapies can be found in:

Cain, D. & Seeman, J. (eds) (2002). *Humanistic Psychotherapies: Handbook of Research and Practice*. Washington, DC: American Psychological Association.

Kaslow, F.W., Massey, R.F., & Massey, S.D. (2002). *Comprehensive Handbook of Psychotherapy: Vol. 3. Interpersonal/Humanistic/Existential*. New York: John Wiley.

Eclectic and integrative approaches

Eclectic approaches are typical in the *ad hoc* use of techniques coming from different theoretical approaches (technical eclecticism). A typical criterion for the use of some techniques is the client's problem or personality (e.g. internalising or externalising clients). Integrative approaches, on the other hand, try to bridge and assimilate different existing therapeutic theories into meta-theories that are coherent but draw on originally independent theories. A form of eclectic or integrative work is very popular. For example, a survey among American therapists shows that between 30% and 50% of them identify themselves as eclectic-integrative practitioners (see Prochaska & Norcross, 2003; Norcross, 2005).

There are several approaches to psychotherapy integration (Norcross & Goldfried, 2005). Some look at the common factors present across the theoretical approaches, some look at the ways of combining techniques from different approaches, some try to formulate transtheoretical principles that bridge different theoretical approaches and, finally, some look at different approaches that can be assimilated into the primary orientation of a therapist. An example of the common factors model is the work of Jerome Frank (Frank & Frank, 1991), who suggested that the similar effectiveness of different therapeutic approaches (cf. Wampold, 2001) can be explained by the common factors they contain. He assumed that the effective components are:

- an emotionally charged relationship with the helping person;
- the healing context of psychotherapeutic care;
- the meaningful explanation of the patient's problems and required psychotherapeutic care; and
- the ritual – the therapeutic procedure.

Another approach to psychotherapy integration is that of technical eclecticism. A significant contribution from this perspective was made, for instance, by Larry Beutler and his colleagues (Beutler, Clarkin, & Bongar, 2000; Beutler & Harwood, 2000). Beutler, in his prescriptive therapy, collects empirically-supported therapeutic principles regardless of their theoretical origin. The idea is that the therapist will be able to use them regardless of his or her own original therapeutic orientation.

Some integrative approaches combine two or more traditional schools of therapy. An example of such a therapy developed in the UK is cognitive-analytic therapy (Ryle, 2005). This therapy primarily combines the psychoanalytic and cognitive-behavioural traditions. Many, originally psychoanalytic, concepts stemming from the object relation tradition are translated into cognitive and behavioural ways of working. The therapist assumes an active role in promoting change and insight.

Transtheoretical approaches to psychotherapy integration attempt to come up with an overarching theoretical structure that coherently integrates different theories.

An example is the work of Klaus Grawe (2004), who outlined his model of psychological therapy as targeting psychological symptoms (by using cognitive and behavioural techniques) and also the underlying conflicts that lead to them (by using psychodynamic and experiential techniques). Another example of a transtheoretical model is the work of Prochaska and Norcross (2003; see also Prochaska & DiClemente, 1983). Their model combines processes of change (e.g. consciousness-raising, relief, environment re-evaluation, self-re-evaluation) with the stages of change (precontemplation, contemplation, preparation, action and maintenance) and different levels of change (symptoms and problematic situations, cognitive processes, interpersonal, family and intrapersonal conflicts). According to these authors, integrative therapy should consist of the different application of processes of change in different stages of change at the appropriate level of change.

Another approach to psychotherapy integration is assimilative integration (Messer, 1992; Lampropoulos, 2001). This approach assumes that the therapists integrate the principles or techniques of other theoretical orientations with the orientation that the therapists prefer or in which they were trained. This integration can be based on research evidence of those principles and techniques. For some examples of how assimilative integration can be spelled out, see the assimilative psychodynamic therapy of Stricker and Gold (2005) or the assimilative cognitive-behavioural therapy of Castonguay et al. (2005).

Research-informed integrative and eclectic approaches

As mentioned above, some of the eclectic and integrative approaches are trying to use research evidence as the basis for their approach to therapy. An example is prescriptive therapy (Beutler & Harwood, 2000; the other name for this approach is Systematic Treatment Selection (Beutler, Clarkin, & Bongar, 2000)), an application of the idea of gathering principles of therapeutic change informed by research from different theoretical orientations. This approach is described in several books (e.g. Beutler, Clarkin, & Bongar, 2000; Beutler & Harwood, 2000) and an edited volume (Castonguay & Beutler, 2006). One of the first guidelines to its use is presented in the 'prescriptive' recommendations for the treatment of depression by Beutler, Clarkin, & Bongar (2000). They looked at the patients' characteristics, the treatment characteristics, and how they could be combined. They summarised the treatment of depression into basic and optimal principles of therapy for depression, which can be used by the therapist regardless of their therapeutic orientation.

Another research-informed approach to psychotherapy integration is the psychological therapy of Klaus Grawe (2004). Grawe identified two levels of intrapsychological processes leading to mental disorders. On the first level is the person's effort to reduce internal conflicts and on the second level is the development of a disorder that stems from these conflicts. The main implication for psychological therapy is the importance of addressing both levels of the problem. The whole model of psychopathology is informed by basic psychological science as well as by dynamic system theories. The theory of therapy is again backed up by empirical research. It consists of three components:

(1) the *activation of resources* of the patient (activation of what is functional in the patient as well as support provided by the therapeutic relationship);
(2) the *destabilisation of parameters of psychological disorders through specific interventions* (these interventions may focus on problematic experiencing, problematic cognitions, or problematic behaviour); and
(3) the *modification of motivational schemata* that led to the development of the disorder (this is achieved through their clarification and corrective experiences).

In its practical application Grawe's (2004) model combines strategies from several theoretical orientations. It offers a structured case conceptualisation that follows an articulated theory and also draws on a variety of tasks and techniques from experiential, psychodynamic and cognitive-behavioural therapies.

Recommended reading

Kaslow, F.W. & Lebow, J.L. (2002). *Comprehensive Handbook of Psychotherapy: Vol. 4. Integrative/Eclectic.* New York: John Wiley.

Norcross, J.C. & Goldfried, M.R. (eds) (2005). *Handbook of Psychotherapy Integration* (2nd edition). New York: Oxford University Press.

Variables that are important for the effect of psychotherapy

Apart from the developments within specific theoretical frameworks, current psychotherapy research that shapes therapeutic practice also cuts across theoretical orientations and covers variables relevant for any theoretical approach. For instance, there are several client variables that have been shown to be predictors of psychotherapy outcome. An example is the severity of psychological difficulties, which is a strong and consistent predictor (for reviews, see Garfield, 1994; Asay & Lambert, 1999; Clarkin & Levy, 2004). Other variables that are consistently reported in the reviews of empirical evidence on client variables (Asay & Lambert, 1999; Clarkin & Levy, 2004) are, for example, motivation to change, ego strength, psychological mindedness, capacity of relating, ability to identify a focal problem. Important factors are also the availability of social support and other forms of help (Asay & Lambert, 1999).

Another significant area of research is studying the rate and reasons for clients' premature termination of therapy. For instance, it is important to know that 30–60% of clients drop out from therapy prematurely (Reis & Brown, 1999). The studies of the process that leads to drop-out showed that therapist inflexibility and a failure to recognise a rupture in the therapeutic alliance may be strong factors influencing drop-out (Rhodes et al., 1994). Another concept that helps in the understanding of prematurely ended and unsuccessful therapy is the model of stages of change of Prochaska, Norcross, and DiClemente (Prochaska & DiClemente, 1983; more recently see Prochaska & Norcross, 2002; see also the section on integrative approaches above). This assumes that the clients may be at a different stage of the change process when they enter therapy. Empirical findings (Arnkoff, Glass, & Shapiro, 2002) demonstrate that one of the moderating variables with regard to psychotherapy drop-out and outcome may also be the clients' expectations about therapy. The expectations may relate to the outcome of therapy, the client role in therapy, the length of therapy, and so on. Expectations may also include preferences of certain forms of therapy, the specific length of therapy or the therapist's age or gender.

This is not an exhaustive list of significant variables (see for example Norcross, 2002). For instance, the next chapter will explore the role of a good therapeutic alliance and the importance of the therapeutic relationship for the successful outcome of therapy. Other chapters will also rely heavily on research-generated knowledge. Psychotherapy and counselling research is a live scientific area that covers all possible clinically and theoretically relevant questions (cf. Cooper, 2008a; Timulak, 2008). Therapists of any orientation may find in it a breadth of information that can inform the way they engage in therapy.

Recommended reading

Cooper, M. (2008). *Essential Findings in Counselling and Psychotherapy*. London: Sage.
Timulak, L. (2008). *Research in Psychotherapy and Counselling*. London: Sage.

Knowledge relevant for conducting psychological therapy

When talking about current psychotherapy and counselling, one must also be aware of knowledge from other areas relevant to the provision of therapy. These are usually covered on training courses in clinical and counselling psychology, psychotherapy and counselling. The courses incorporate a knowledge of healthy and pathological psychological functioning, lifespan development, multicultural issues and general psychology (e.g. cognitive psychology, psychology of emotions, psychology of personality). A knowledge of psychopathology and of the language used in the mental health setting

(DSM–IV – American Psychiatric Association, 2001; International Classification of Diseases, ICD–10 – WHO, 1992) for describing human suffering is vital for communicating and retrieving important information. The texts and studies on the phenomenological experience of different problems and disorders can also be helpful (e.g. Wertz, 1985). A knowledge of common medical conditions that can present themselves in the form of psychological symptoms is useful too (Morrisson, 1999) as is an awareness of the psychological needs of somatically ill people (Kolbasovsky, 2008). In addition, it is important for therapists to know about alternative treatments (see Chapter 10) such as psychopharmacology, social support, self-help programmes (Patterson et al., 2006). On the other hand, therapists can learn a lot about human experience through art, personal experience (also in personal therapy), peer discussions, supervision, etc.

Recommended reading

The main texts on psychopathology:

American Psychiatric Association (2001). *Diagnostic and Statistical Manual of Mental Disorders* (4th edition). Text revision. Washington, DC: APA.

World Health Organisation (1992). *The ICD–10 Classification of Mental and Behavioural Disorders: Clinical Description and Diagnostic Guidelines*. Geneva: WHO.

The therapist's guides to psychopharmacology:

Beitman, B., Blinder, B., Thase, M.E., Riba, M.B., & Safer, D.L. (eds) (2003). *Integrating Psychotherapy and Pharmacotherapy: Dissolving the Mind–Brain Barrier*. New York: W.W. Norton.

Patterson, J., Ari Albala, A., McCahill, M.E., & Edwards, T.M. (2006). *The Therapist's Guide to Psychopharmacology*. New York: Guilford Press.

Medical conditions and psychological problems:

Kolbasovsky, A. (2008). *A Therapist's Guide to Understanding Common Medical Conditions*. New York: W.W. Norton.

Morrisson, J. (1999). *When Psychological Problems Mask Medical Disorder: A Guide for Psychotherapists*. New York: Guilford Press.

Multicultural issues in counselling and psychotherapy:

Sue, D.W. & Sue, D. (2008). *Counselling the Culturally Different*. Hoboken, NJ: John Wiley.

Part II

Basic Skills of Conducting Psychotherapy and Counselling

This part of the book presents skills used by therapists of different orientations and information on many of them gathered by empirical investigations. The skills are presented in a coherent system, but the reader should bear in mind that it is done so for didactic purposes. They do not need to be used in the order in which they are presented in this book. Also, their use depends on a particular case conceptualisation and the therapeutic strategy stemming from that conceptualisation.

The focus is on the skills and attitudes of the therapist that contribute to the building of a good therapeutic relationship (Chapter 2) and the ethical aspects of therapeutic work (Chapter 4). This section of the book emphasises the skills facilitating the exploration of the main purpose of therapy and its better understanding by the client (Chapter 5), and also on the facilitation of the client's decision to change if such a decision is the objective of therapy. We will also look at the implementation of steps leading to change outside the therapist's office (Chapter 6). Specific cognitive, behavioural and experiential techniques will also be presented (Chapter 7).

A particular use of specific skills or techniques is embedded in a specific case conceptualisation and specific theoretical approach to therapy (Chapter 3). We will therefore examine empirically-informed psychodynamic, cognitive-behavioural, humanistic-experiential and integrative approaches to case conceptualisation. A rationale will be provided that typically leads the therapist's thinking in these respective approaches and examples of heuristic decision-making on the best approach for a client will also be presented. We will also briefly cover potential integrative frameworks that the therapist may be using.

Two

Building the Therapeutic Alliance

Abstract

This chapter presents the concept of the therapeutic alliance and its relevance for a successful therapy. Important attitudes, ways of being and the skills the therapists can employ in order to build an alliance with their clients are presented. These cover, for instance, authenticity, openness, empathy, ethical engagement, focused reflection, humility, etc. The discussion of skills focuses on the skills needed in contracting, resolving conflicts, handling disclosures, etc. The influence of the therapist's values is also discussed.

The basis of any psychological therapy is a good therapeutic relationship and alliance between the therapist and the client. A solid therapeutic relationship depends on the attitudinal qualities of the therapist, the therapist's way of being and the therapist's skills in forming the alliance. We will first examine the attitudes of the therapist and his or her way of being, which are prerequisite to forming any relationship/alliance, and then we will look at the more technical aspects of establishing the alliance.

Therapist's attitudes and ways of being

An influential conceptualisation that stimulated the development of psychotherapy and empirical research is Rogers' (1957) conceptualisation of the core conditions of therapeutic change. Three of the core conditions (unconditional positive regard, congruence and empathy) represented the attitudinal relational qualities of the therapist or his/her ways of being. They, even from a current perspective, capture important qualities that the therapist can bring to therapy. Other specific attitudes, discussed below, can be a good base for the therapist entering the therapeutic relationship.

Congruence/authenticity/genuineness

Several definitions of authenticity (I use the term 'authenticity' interchangeably with the terms 'congruence' and 'genuineness') exist (e.g. Rogers, 1957). Usually, it is described as:

(1) the therapist's accurate defenceless self-awareness of own experiencing; and
(2) the therapist's defenceless being in the relationship with the client in congruence with the therapist's inner processes (see Lietaer, 1993; Klein et al., 2002).

Although the review of research studies examining the relationship between the therapist's congruence and therapy outcome is quite inconclusive, it does not rule out the importance of this concept for therapy outcome (Klein et al., 2002). If internally congruent, the therapist is aware of his/her inner experiencing and his or her outward behaviour matches it. The therapist who has a substantial level of incongruence may be unaware of subtle inner processes that prevent him or her from being optimally therapeutic. This incongruence may be confusing for his/her clients as they may pick up on the processes that are not reflected by the therapist.

Therapists can work on their own congruence by monitoring their own experiencing. An internal openness and non-defensiveness can help therapists to detect various countertransferential experiences towards their clients that can potentially be used therapeutically (Gelso & Hayes, 2002). An interpersonal non-defensiveness of the therapist means that the therapist is able to stay relational with the client without a need for excessive defensiveness. The therapist's non-defensiveness may also mean that the therapist, respecting his or her own boundaries, is open to share his or her experience if it is important for the therapeutic relationship or therapy. This openness and transparency may be a model for the client's engagement in therapy.

Genuineness may also include an awareness of the therapist's own motivation when working with a specific client. The therapist's involvement in a specific therapy may be coloured by the therapist's own intellectual interest, internal doubts or ambitions, or the expectations of the employer, supervisor, etc. Although it is natural that the therapist's genuine interest in helping clients is also accompanied by many processes that are within him or her, it may be good to reflect on one's own motives. This way, the main purpose of therapy is not lost as some clients may be sensitive to the therapist's competing motivations (see Timulak & Lietaer, 2001).

Openness

The attitude of openness towards the client's experiencing corresponds with Rogers' (1957) concept of unconditional positive regard for the client. A review of empirical studies shows that this attitudinal quality may contribute to the quality of the therapeutic relationship and to the therapy outcome, though there may be other factors that moderate this influence (Farber & Lane, 2002). As person-centred author Barrett-Lennard (1998) puts it, unconditional positive regard refers to valuing and welcoming every aspect of the client's experience. If the therapist is open towards all aspects of the client's inner world, the client is more likely to bring them to therapy and they can be explored and worked with therapeutically. If the therapist feels apprehensive and afraid of some clients' experiences, it is unlikely that they can be worked on therapeutically.

Obviously, some therapists have limitations with regard to the different client issues they can work with. On the other hand, the therapist's training and personal and professional development typically broadens his or her capacity so that he or she can work with a range of issues and people's experiences. It is also important to be aware that limitations when working with some client experiences may stem from the therapist's own wounds, vulnerabilities, sensitive spots, fears, etc., and that these can become the focus of training, supervision and personal therapy. Still, it is only human that the therapist has limitations and recognises his or her own boundaries when working with clients with specific problematic experiences.

An important quality of the therapist may be his or her openness towards being personally enriched by the interaction with the client. Studies on therapists' development show that one of the sources of therapists' growth is their interaction with clients (cf. Skovholt & Ronnestad, 1992; Freeman & Hayes, 2002). The experience of witnessing the intimate struggles of fellow human beings may indeed be very personally enriching. However, openness towards change that comes out of the interaction with a client is not only a beneficial quality for the therapist; it also encourages equality between the client and the therapist, and that can become a cornerstone of the therapeutic relationship and alliance. The therapist's humility may be good for the resolution of ruptures in the therapeutic relationship (Rhodes et al., 1994; Safran & Muran, 1996).

Empathy

The therapist's empathy is another concept introduced by Rogers (1957). Empirical evidence shows that the therapist's empathy has a significant impact on psychotherapy outcome even in therapeutic approaches that do not emphasise empathy (Bohart et al., 2002). The therapist's empathy is conveyed through the therapist's sensitive tracking of the client's process of experiencing. The therapist is not only attuned to and acknowledging the client's changing felt experiences and personal meanings, but also sensitively responds to the aspects of experience that the client may not be fully aware of. The therapist's attunement is not only an attitudinal quality (a way of being; Rogers, 1980), but is also actively communicated to the client (the communicative aspect of empathy; Rogers, 1957).

The therapist's empathy has several functions (we will discus them further in Chapter 5). It contributes, for example, to the building of a good therapeutic alliance and a safe and healing therapeutic relationship. It helps to regulate the client's problematic emotions and promotes the deconstruction of personal meanings. It fosters cognitive-affective exploration and deepens the client's self-understanding and reflective function (see Bohart & Greenberg, 1997; Watson, Goldman, & Vanaerschot, 1998; Bohart et al., 2002; Watson, 2002). Empathy can also provide an opportunity for corrective emotional experience and it can empower the client.

Ethical engagement in the relationship with the client

The therapist's ethical stance should not only be limited to compliance with a professional code of ethics. The therapist's high ethical standards communicate respect and value to the client. However, by upholding value and respect, the therapist also models thoughtfulness and consideration in interpersonal relationships, a mature and healthy interpersonal quality. The therapist's integrity and ethical soundness also contributes to the client's trust in the therapist and the therapeutic relationship (see Gross, 2001).

The therapist's ethical engagement manifests itself in the therapist's involvement in the ethical dilemmas in which the client is engaged. On some occasions, it can involve dilemmas that are not apparent to the client, but become apparent to the therapist. Though for many years psychotherapy embraced a supposedly value-free attitude to the client's life, currently a broader awareness exists, which is that the therapist's action cannot but be value-laden (Bergin & Richards, 1997; Tjeltveit, 1999). This awareness, however, does not lead to clear-cut answers to many situations that may arise in the process of therapy. Thus, the therapist is often an ethicist (Tjeltveit, 1999). We will look at these issues in Chapter 4.

The therapist's value system and its impact on the therapy process

Although, for a long time, psychotherapy presented itself as value-neutral, empirical investigations are showing that certain therapists' values are influencing their clients (Beutler, Machado, & Allstetter-Neufeldt, 1994). The values relevant for mental health are incorporated by the clients, while other values, such as religious values, are not readily transferable (Beutler, Machado, & Allsteter-Neufeldt, 1994). Studies also show that the perceived values of therapists may be significant when clients choose their therapist. This is especially so for religious clients (Worthington & Sandage, 2002).

Therapists' values can surface through their interaction with clients (cf. Tjeltveit, 1999). It is not possible to remain neutral to different aspects of the client's world if the therapist has strong opinions about them. Since it is not possible to avoid one's own values, it may be very important for the therapist to reflect on the influence of their own values on the therapeutic process. Bergin and Richards (1997) recommend that the therapist maintains an explicitly minimalising approach to the place of their own values in therapy. This means that the therapist is open about his or her own values, but brings them to therapy only when they are relevant for the therapy process, while still supporting the client's right to hold his or her own values. Bergin and Richards (1997) consider approaches that try to avoid the problematic impact of the therapist's own values in therapy. They recognise four problematic styles when considering the therapist's own values (see Box 2.1).

Box 2.1 Four main problematic ways of dealing with the therapist's values (Bergin & Richards, 1997).

Denier – the therapist who does not recognise that he or she is bringing his or her own values to therapy and that his or her therapeutic approach also expresses certain values.

Implicit minimiser – the therapist who is aware that values are present in therapy, but who thinks that he or she can minimise these values by not expressing them, not realising that he or she is using them covertly.

Explicit imposer – the therapist who requires his or her clients to adopt the therapist's values; failure to do so results in the therapist rejecting their clients or emotionally punishing them.

Implicit imposer – the therapist who is attempting covertly to persuade his or her clients about the therapist's own values.

The therapist's values may not come to the fore in therapy at all or they may appear quite dramatically as an unexpected response to something in the client's presentation. The therapist cannot avoid being human and 'existential clashes' of values may sometimes be inevitable. It is important, however, that the therapist does not lose his or her professional responsibility towards the client and respects the client's autonomy. We will look at these issues in Chapter 4.

Humility of the therapist

Several studies have shown that the humility of the therapist can contribute to the quality of the therapeutic relationship and to the resolution of ruptures in therapeutic relationships (Agnew et al., 1994; Rhodes et al., 1994; see also Timulak, 1999).

Humility can be demonstrated by making the client aware of the therapist's own limitations, and by respecting that the client's perspective is important. Admitting to errors or misattunements in the work with the client can help in resolving potential conflicts (Safran & Muran, 1996, 2000).

Focused reflection

Psychotherapy is a very thoughtful and considerate activity. It requires a certain discipline on the therapist's part. The therapist's focused reflection on the therapeutic work is an expression of this discipline. The therapist's reflection is manifest in his/her conceptualisation of the case, in note-taking, in preparing for sessions, in the use of supervision, in the studying of literature pertinent to the case, in ethical considerations, in listening to recordings of therapy sessions if they are available, etc. Considering the progress of therapy is also part of this reflection. Monitoring the outcome of therapy and the therapeutic relationship has been assisted in more recent times with the use of empirical tools. Studies have demonstrated that this monitoring is improving outcomes (Lambert, Hansen, & Finch, 2001; Miller, Duncan, & Hubble, 2005; see also below).

Focused reflection is part of what is sometimes referred to as reflective practice (Schön, 1983; Stedmon & Dallos, 2009). This distinguishes between reflection on the therapy process while it is happening (e.g. in session) and reflection on one's own work outside the interaction (e.g. in supervision). Reflective practice is, however, also a broader term that refers to reflecting on one's professional practice in its entirety, and not just within a particular case.

Recommended reading

Theoretical and research reviews of the therapist's congruence:

Klein, M.H., Kolden, G.G., Michels, J.L., & Chisholm-Stockard, S. (2002). Congruence. In J.C. Norcross (ed.), *Psychotherapy Relationships that Work: Therapist Contributions and Responsiveness to Patients* (pp. 195–216). New York: Oxford University Press.

Lietaer, G. (1993). Authenticity, congruence, and transparency. In D. Brazier (ed.), *Beyond Carl Rogers* (pp. 17–46). London: Constable.

Rogers, C.R. (1957). The necessary and sufficient conditions of therapeutic personality change. *Journal of Consulting Psychology,* 21, 95–103.

Rogers, C.R. (1961). *On Becoming a Person: A Therapist's View of Psychotherapy.* Boston: Houghton Mifflin.

Theoretical and research reviews of countertransference:

Gelso, C.J., & Hayes, J.A. (2002). The management of countertransference. In J.C. Nocross (ed.), *Psychotherapy Relationships that Work: Therapist Contributions and Responsiveness to Patients* (pp. 267–283). New York: Oxford University Press.

Theoretical and research reviews of the therapist's unconditional positive regard:

Farber, B.A. & Lane, J.S. (2002). Positive regard. In J.C. Norcross (ed.), *Psychotherapy Relationships that Work: Therapist Contributions and Responsiveness to Patients* (pp. 175–194). New York: Oxford University Press.

Theoretical and research reviews of the therapist's empathy:

Bohart, A.C., Elliott, R., Greenberg, L.S., & Watson, J.C. (2002). Empathy. In J.C. Nocross (ed.), *Psychotherapy Relationships that Work: Therapist Contributions and Responsiveness to Patients* (pp. 89–108). New York: Oxford University Press.

Bohart, A.C., & Greenberg, L.S. (eds) (1997). *Empathy Reconsidered: New Directions in Psychotherapy*. Washington, DC: American Psychological Association.

Theoretical reviews of the ethical aspect of the therapist's work:

Doherty, W.J. (1995). *Soul Searching: Why Psychotherapy Must Promote Moral Responsibility*. New York: Basic Books.

Tjeltveit, A.C. (1999). *Ethics and Values in Psychotherapy*. London: Routledge.

Building of the therapeutic alliance

We will now focus on the more practical aspect of building a relationship. In practical terms, a good therapeutic relationship is reflected in the quality of collaboration between the therapist and the client. The construct that captures this collaboration and is widely used is 'therapeutic alliance' (e.g. Bordin, 1979). Different concepts of therapeutic alliance exist (see Horvath & Bedi, 2002). This construct comes from the psychoanalytic and psychodynamic tradition. It stresses the therapist's as well as the client's contribution to their collaboration in working to overcome the client's suffering (see Chapter 1). In the area of empirical research, Bordin's (1979) concept of working alliance proved to be especially helpful and stimulating. One of the most often used research questionnaires, the Working Alliance Inventory (Horvath & Greenberg, 1989), which assesses the therapeutic alliance, is based on Bordin's work. Bordin's concept sees the alliance as consisting of three elements:

(1) an agreement on the goals of therapy;
(2) an agreement on the tasks of therapy; and
(3) a non-specific emotional bond between the therapist and the client.

Agreement on the goals of therapy basically refers to agreement on the overall aim of therapy. Agreement on tasks focuses on the way client and therapist will work together in achieving these goals. Finally, the bond is a rather global, relational and non-specific quality that is somewhat independent of the more technical aspects of mutual collaboration. The therapeutic alliance has been shown to be an important, and early, predictor of successful psychotherapy (Horvath & Bedi, 2002).

There are several practicalities that the therapist needs to consider in achieving a good alliance with a client. These cover, for instance, establishing a contract with the client, the therapist's personal transparency, the therapist's client-centredness and working on difficulties in the relationship.

The therapeutic contract

The therapeutic contract consists of several aspects. It covers communication with the client about his or her expectations of and goals for therapy. It covers the therapist's presentation of therapy and what is expected from the client. It covers practicalities such as the length of therapy, the cost of therapy, the therapist's handling of cancellations, suggestions on what happens if the client wants to terminate therapy, information on note-taking, and so on. The contract is also part of the process as different aspects of it are being reviewed at regular intervals.

An important aspect of the therapist's contract is the awareness that while the therapist is doing the contracting regularly, the client is most likely new to it. The therapist thus has to pace the delivery of information and adjust information for a particular client and check the client's understanding. The client is entering unknown territory because he or she does not know how the therapist will work and what is expected from him or her. Even if the client has had previous therapy, he or she may not know what to expect from the new therapist. At the same time, the client is in the vulnerable state for which he or she is seeking help. The beginning of therapy is therefore naturally anxiety-provoking. The client may be afraid of the therapist's criticism that the client or the client's close significant others have contributed to the client's difficulties (which is an assumption of many theoretical models of psychotherapy). The client may also be wary that the therapeutic work will be emotionally painful and may even amplify the client's symptoms.

In bigger agencies, the contract for therapy may already have been started by a professional other than the therapist. The therapist then needs to be aware of how the client's perceptions have been shaped prior to their first encounter. Some authors (e.g. Luborsky, 1984) suggest a 'socialising interview', during which the therapy process is explained to prospective clients. Such interviews can be carried out by a professional other than the client's therapist. However, for practical reasons, these sorts of inductions are probably most often expected from the therapist. The clients may also read about therapy in advance, or brief information packs may be provided by an agency or the therapist prior to the first meeting, and can then be discussed in the session (see Box 2.2 for an example of a brief description of therapy). Clients are entitled to have information about the therapy and the therapist before they embark on therapy and before they consent to it. It is important that their consent to therapy is informed and that they have an opportunity to ask the therapist questions. One must, however, bear in mind that it is very tricky to establish when the client is really informed, as research shows that understanding information about therapy may be limited (Kitchener & Anderson, 2000). The client is especially entitled to know what the probability is that therapy will be beneficial for his or her problem and what the potential risks are with regards attending therapy.

Box 2.2 An example of brief introductions to different therapy approaches

The following is a brief description of non-directive counselling (counselling) and cognitive-behavioural therapy (psychology) from the preferential trial of King et al. (2000: 56). Clients could choose one of the therapies on the basis of its description.

Counselling:
Counsellors provide the patient with time and support. They help them explore and understand their problems. Counsellors listen and encourage people to work out their own ways of helping themselves using their own abilities and strengths.

Cognitive-behavioural therapy provided by psychologists:
Psychologists provide the patient with time and support. They examine the way people think and act, explore alternative ways of thinking and behaving, and together with the patient develop practical ways in which people can help themselves.

Although the therapist or agency may have written information on the therapist and the way he/she works (see Box 2.3 for an example), it is not possible to have written information that matches the client's presentation and the problems that have brought the client to therapy. Information about the therapy and the therapist must therefore be used in the context of the client's needs and problems. Initial session/s thus provide an opportunity for the therapist to assess the client's difficulties, the client's expectations and preferences about therapy, and the therapist's tailored offer of what they can provide with regard to the client's problems and expectations. These sorts of negotiations may take more than one session and can happen in the context of work that has already demonstrated a therapeutic potential. The client's induction to therapy then follows and it may take a few sessions for the client to gradually learn how the therapy works. It is important to be aware of the fact that despite the therapist explaining and providing information, clients may not gain a proper sense of therapy until they have experienced it personally (see Timulak & Lietaer, 2001). This can sometimes be overlooked by therapists as they, of course, are well used to therapy.

Box 2.3 An example of information about therapy

Information about psychological services

Education and experience

This should contain information about the therapist's training and professional experience so far. The therapist's credentials and the membership of a professional body (e.g. Registered Counselling Psychologist of the Psychological Society of Ireland).

Way of working

Here is an example: *My way of working is building on my training and interest in psychotherapy research. In my work, I try to apply principles based on scientific research and I also put emphasis on ethical reasoning. I work with clients on the basis of verbal agreement on the goals and tasks of our collaborative work. In that, I try to respect the client's view on how we should address his or her issues. I apply an approach that is based on the sensitive, empathic exploration of the client's concerns, their better understanding and implementation of changes into the client's life. I draw primarily on the techniques of emotion-focused therapy, but principles of other approaches may also be used if appropriate.*

Further information

Example: *The client's consent to complete standardised psychological methods at the beginning and end of our co-operation may be sought. I regularly use a consultant supervisor in my work. Part of this may require the use of the session tapes. If this was the case, consent to tape a session would be sought before such session(s). I take professional notes during the sessions. These are securely kept in a locked cabinet. Any identifying information is stored separately from the process notes. Psychological work is confidential, although its limits are set by the (appropriate) Code of Professional Ethics and by the law.*

Positives of psychotherapy and psychological counselling

Example: *Psychotherapy (psychological counselling) can be helpful in coping with psychological difficulties or burdening life events. It can be a useful tool in helping to achieve changes in the way of being and in understanding oneself better. It can also contribute to the remission of symptoms and general well-being.*

Negatives of psychotherapy and psychological counselling

Example: *Because of the fact that psychotherapy (psychological counselling) focuses on the problematic parts of one's life, it can sometimes be experienced as intruding and stirring up negative experiences which may not be agreeable to the client.*

Parameters of therapy

Example: *The length of collaboration will be agreed verbally and is flexible depending on the needs of a specific client. My judgement will also be used as to whether we are meeting the goals that we set and/or whether further work would be helpful. In a case where you do not experience therapy as helpful, it is good to bring it to the session. You can always end the therapy. If this is your intention, I would prefer it if you could tell me in advance, so we have time to conclude the collaboration.*

Statement of agreement

Example: *I have read and understand the information contained in this document and agree to participate in psychotherapy (counselling).*

Name and date

Note: The contract can also be adjusted in a written form for a specific client if both parties agree to include any amendments.

Contracting is important because the therapist needs to establish the preferences and expectations of the client and to see whether these can be negotiated in therapy. If they are overlooked, the client may not engage in therapy properly. What is also important is that the contract and how the client is doing in therapy are reviewed regularly during the therapy process. The therapist can use tools to monitor the outcomes of therapy and the quality of therapeutic relationship (Lambert, Hansen, & Finch, 2001; Miller, Duncan, & Hubble, 2005) and these can demonstrate improvements in the effectiveness of therapy. The regular review of therapy may lead to a re-evaluation of goals and ways of working in therapy. The therapist can request feedback from the client (e.g. *What is your feeling about our sessions? What do you like about them? What would you like to change?*), but the therapist must also be aware of the deference that clients often experience towards the therapist (cf. Rennie, 1994) and be prepared that it may be difficult for the client to express concerns. Use of the tools presented in Box 2.4 may therefore empower clients and give them a voice.

Box 2.4 Examples of tools that can be used for monitoring the progress of therapy and the therapeutic relationship

- The *Outcome Questionnaire-45* (OQ-45) contains 45 items that cover three specific domains: symptom distress, interpersonal relationships and social role performance.

(Continued)

(Continued)

The instrument comes with software enabling the therapist to benchmark the client's progress from session to session against successful as well as unsuccessful clients who filled out the questionnaire. Additionally, therapists can decide if they want to use clinical support tools that could help them address problems in therapy (i.e. measurement of alliance, measurement of the client readiness for change, and measurement of the social support of the client; see Whipple et al., 2003).

- The *Outcome Rating Scale (ORS)*, was recently developed by Miller and Duncan (see Miller, Duncan, & Hubble, 2005). The ORS is a visual scale consisting of four items covering three areas (personal well-being, relationships, social functioning) and the overall sense of well-being. The huge advantage of this tool is that it takes less than one minute to fill it in. A tracking system similar to the one being used with the OQ-45 is being developed. The instrument is also supplemented by the *Sessions Rating Scale* (see Duncan et al., 2003), a four-item visual analogue instrument measuring three aspects of the alliance (relationship, goals, approach) and overall alliance. Both instruments are recommended to be used every session to inform the progress of therapy and the therapeutic relationship.
- The *Target Complaints* (Battle et al., 1966) is an instrument that can be used as a general schedule for the interview about the client's most bothering problems rather than just simple self-report scale. The client and the therapist may work together on the formulation of the client's target complaints and the extent to which they are bothering.
- The Shapiro's *Personal Questionnaire* (Philips, 1986; Elliott, Mack, & Shapiro, 1999) is an instrument that allows not only the formulation of the client's presenting issues at the intake, but also the addition of the problems that occur in the course of psychotherapy. It also allows the evaluation of how long these problems existed before therapy started.

Reviewing therapy is also a natural part of ending therapy. Apart from reviewing the client's change through the use of outcome measures (for an overview, see Timulak, 2008), the therapist may facilitate the client to make sense of therapy and therapy gains. The therapist may facilitate discussions, for instance by asking: *What did the client like about therapy sessions? What would the client like to change, looking back? What did the client find helpful or not helpful?* (An example of stimulating questions can be found in Elliott's Client Change Interview, which is used for research purposes – see Box 2.5) The therapist and the client can thus work on the story of therapy (Grafanaki & McLeod, 1999), which can help the client integrate their own learning and changes.

Box 2.5 Examples of questions from the Client Change Interview that can be used when reflecting on therapy (adapted from Elliott, Slatick, & Urman, 2001)

What has therapy been like for you so far?
How has it felt to be in therapy?
How are you doing now in general?
What changes, if any, have you noticed in yourself since therapy started?
Has anything changed for the worse for you since therapy started?
Is there anything that you wanted to change that hasn't changed since therapy started?
In general, what do you think has caused these various changes? In other words, what do you think might have brought them about? (Including things both outside therapy and in therapy)
Can you sum up what has been helpful about your therapy so far?
What kinds of things about the therapy have been hindering, unhelpful, negative or disappointing for you?
Were there things in the therapy which were difficult or painful but still OK or perhaps helpful? What were they?
Has anything been missing from your therapy?

Used with permission of Robert Elliott

Therapist's disclosure

An important skill that contributes to a good therapeutic alliance is the therapist's handling of disclosure of his or her own experience or perspective. The clients are naturally interested in how the therapist sees them and what the therapist's thoughts are on the client's presented problems. In some cases, the client may be checking the therapist's stance prior to opening a particular issue (see Timulak & Lietaer, 2001). For example, the client may want to find out whether the therapist is religious as the client would like to explore some uncertainty in personal faith in God. Indeed, especially in the early stages of therapy, the clients can be pre-occupied by the therapist's perspective and may thoroughly scrutinise the therapist (Timulak & Lietaer, 2001).

It is therefore important that the therapist comes across as transparent and does not solely focus on the client's anxiety which led to the question and which is a very traditional response. Although it is important for therapy that the anxiety that leads to such questions is acknowledged and potentially explored, therapists who do not respond frankly, while holding their own boundaries, can be seen as defensive and avoiding engagement (Timulak & Lietaer, 2001). However, the therapist has to be mindful of how he or she communicates his or her own perspective. Bohart and

Tallman (1999), recommend focusing on process characteristics rather than statements about the client's overall functioning (e.g. *In these types of situations I noticed you tried this*). The therapist can then always clarify how his or her answer is experienced by the client and how it is linked to the origin of the question. An example of a helpful therapist disclosure is given in Box 2.6.

Box 2.6 Example of the therapist's self-disclosure and the impact it had on the client

The client, who is in her early twenties, was in therapy due to depression-related symptoms such as anhedonia and tiredness from overworking. During a post-session research interview following the fifth session of her therapy, this event was reported. The transcript and reflections of the therapist and the client come from a study examining significant events in person-centred psychotherapy (Timulak, Belicova, & Miler, 2009). The identified event is shortened and modified for educational purposes, and asterisks mark significantly helpful interventions by the therapist as judged by the client. The client is discussing her bad timekeeping and overall feeling of having too many duties and deadlines to meet.

C: *Nobody has the same problem. God, if it only was more real! Something that could be classified, this is the problem that so and so many people have and, and ... I feel out of my mind, totally unrealistic. (T: Hum) All normal people and all students are enjoying their life and having no problems, have fun and life, it is so natural for them. And I have difficulty to have fun. (T: Hum). This is mental.*

*T: *I don't think you are the only one with such a problem.*

C: *I guess there are people like me there, but I have never met any.*

T: *You have not met anyone like that.*

C: *I am sure that if I said this to anybody...*

......

C: *I feel that the concentrating on work is easier then, then ... it is like that that using a computer or reading books and thinking is easier than to be out there, in real life. I see it as an escape. Escape to work.*

T: *Is this what you see as different from other students? (Silence 4 sec.)*

C: *I don't know which students are escaping to work, that's fact. I am different, that's for sure. If I disclosed that this is my problem that I work too much and ... I don't know. If I have nothing to do, then I don't know what I should do, I would be totally bizarre.*

T: *They would not understand you, they would just say: 'Do nothing then'.*

C: *Yes. I was a bit worried that when I come here so you will say 'Do nothing'. (T: Hum) What is totally logical, it is clear 'Do nothing', but I...*

*T: *It is not that logical and definitely not an easy thing to do.*

C: *I was afraid I wouldn't be able to explain this to you. That this is so ridiculous, that, that I cannot 'do nothing'. But I ... just can't. It is not working. If you said to me 'do nothing' I would leave the therapy, but nothing would change. (Silence 6 sec.)*

*T: *So maybe what you are trying to say is not that I don't want to work, but this is how I feel, it is difficult and sometimes I am having problems with it.*

C: *Hum (silence 15 sec.)*

The client's reflection of the event:

(1) *When I talked I couldn't formulate my problem or my thoughts clearly, and as we talked more about it, it seemed to be more senseless, more stupid, and then the therapist said that there might be more people and I felt totally relieved in that moment. I mean if she did not say that so I had the tendency to repeat it over and over, without any meaning. I have a feeling that it helped me to get through the thought that it was stupid – so I could function after that.*
(2) *It was relief for me to hear that there can be more people that have this feeling of 'craziness' so I was not alone in this world.*
(3) *I have a feeling she was listening carefully and she cheered me up.*

The therapist's reflection of the event:

(1) *I've perceived her that she was concentrating on experiences, when she felt crazy – that she was the only one who had this kind of problem. So I'd like to communicate to her that I don't see her as if she was the only one with this problem, that she is not the only one with such a problem for me – she then said that she also thought that she was not the only one – it was as if she accepted the reality and looked at another experience that didn't agree with this feeling.*
(2) *I felt she thought that I must think the same about her and she also said that to me that I must think how stupid it was what she was saying.*

The therapist's disclosure of his or her view of the client or of a topic relevant to the client can reduce the client's feeling of vulnerability in the relationship. By being transparent, while keeping his or her own personal boundaries, the therapist is contributing to the building of therapeutic alliance. The therapist is also modelling how to be relational and risk-taking in the relationship, a quality that is good for therapeutic exploration. Hill and Knox (2002) provide an excellent review of the research on the therapist's self-disclosure.

Therapist's responsiveness

An important skill that can contribute to the quality of therapeutic alliance is the therapist's responsiveness to the client (Stiles, Hanas-Webb, & Surko, 1998). Research shows that the client's engagement in therapy is one of the most significant predictors of therapy outcome (Orlinsky, Grawe, & Parks, 1994). The therapist's consideration of the client's expressed or inferred needs can be a significant contributor to the client's involvement in therapy. The therapist's responsiveness, as well as the overall client-centredness of the psychotherapy services, can also have an empowering impact on the client as he/she communicates that the client has a say in the care that he or she is getting.

Working through the relationship ruptures

Psychotherapy process research shows that the client's vulnerability and the imbalance of the therapeutic relationship are represented in the client's deference towards the therapist (Rennie, 1990, 1994). This deference may sometimes mean that the client does not indicate a difficulty in the relationship even when there is one. On the other hand, the client's vulnerability can lead to ruptures in the therapeutic alliance, which can result in the client's withdrawal or by more or less direct confrontation with the therapist (Safran & Muran, 2000). Withdrawal can be presented in the client's denial of obvious feelings, intellectualisation, etc. As withdrawal normally indicates some dissatisfaction, it is important that the therapist acknowledges it and encourages the client to express any dissatisfaction (Safran & Muran, 2000). The dissatisfaction may be expressed through complaints about the therapist, the therapist's approach, insufficient progress in therapy, etc. Safran and Muran (2000) developed a model of therapeutic work with the ruptures in the alliance based on their long-term research. The model of working with the client's expressed criticism is presented in Box 2.7.

Box 2.7 The model of resolving ruptures in the alliance (adapted from Safran & Muran, 2000)

1 **Identification of confrontation marker.** Confrontation can be present in the client's complaints about the therapist as a person, complaints about the parameters of therapy (i.e. time schedule), or complaints about the absence of progress in therapy.
2 **Disembedding.** The therapist interrupts confrontation and may admit his or her own contribution to the problematic interaction. The therapist re-establishes the 'analytical'

space, provides feedback, facilitates greater explicitness in the client's demands, discusses (meta-communicates) their own interaction, discloses the impact of the client's confrontation, supports a direct expression of confrontation and critique, etc.

3 **Exploration of construal.** The therapist facilitates the expression of the client's needs, expectations, wishes, perceptions present in the conflict, etc.

4 **Avoidance of aggression.** The client avoids the direct expression of anger due to his or her own anxiety and guilt. It may make the aggression indirect. The therapist facilitates the client's awareness of this fact.

5 **Avoidance of vulnerability.** The therapist facilitates the client's awareness of the fact that the anger prevents an awareness of the client's own vulnerability triggered by the therapeutic interaction.

6 **Vulnerability.** If the therapist showed a willingness to take seriously reasons for the client's anger, admitted his or her own contribution to it, and was able to contain the client's aggression, it leads to the client's expression of vulnerable feelings and wishes, which are often connected to hopelessness. However, now it is not hopelessness communicated cynically and aggressively, but truly.

Stages 3 and 4 and 3 and 5 run parallel (they present the process of experiencing or the process of avoiding the experiencing). Stage 6 follows directly after either stage 3 or 5.

Working with ruptures is very challenging and requires a steady response from the therapist (Gelso & Hayes, 2002). Ruptures in the therapeutic alliance may often be expressions of the client's core conflictual relationship patterns (Luborsky & Crits-Christoph, 1990) or, even on a more general level, of the overall attachment style (e.g. Eames & Roth, 2000). It may therefore be useful to process them in therapy and learn from them. A successful resolution also enhances the strength of the alliance. Box 2.8 demonstrates an example of the building of therapeutic alliance at the beginning of therapy (the first session), together with an example of a minor conflict in the therapeutic relationship.

Box 2.8 An example of working with signs of a conflict in the therapeutic relationship

This example comes from the first session of therapy with a young client who has problems in interpersonal relationships and who participated in a significant events study (Timulak, 2001).

(Continued)

(Continued)

The two extracts from the therapeutic session are followed by commentaries of the client and the therapist after the session. The post–session interviews were conducted separately with the therapist and the client. The two presented events were identified as helpful by the client. The first event shows an example of a rupture in the alliance; the second example presents the therapist's reference to the first event.

The first event starts in the 40th minute of the first session:

(18 sec. silence) Therapist interrupts silence with a sentence:

T: We have 10 minutes left (6 seconds of silence)

C: That was stupid.

T: Stupid?

C: It wasn't necessary.

T: I mean, I mean that, mean that ...

C: I understand.

T: It is for my own guidance as well as for our mutual information. I do not want to say we should finish, it is just for our guidance.

C: I understand that what you said wasn't wrong, but I just wanted to say (T: hmm) that it wasn't necessary.

**T: I don't always get it right.* (The client rated this expression as the peak of the helpful event.)

C: I don't feel it ...

T: You didn't feel great when I said we had to finish.

C: Hmm. But I didn't feel that it was intentional, that you wanted to hurt me, that 'We have only 10 minutes left', just that it was said here.

T: What felt so wrong about it for you? What did not feel right? (T: Hmm). Have you been thinking about something and I (interrupted) it or...

C: You know, it is natural, that we are trying, I am trying to build a relationship, you know, to trust and so (T: in theory) and now it is as if a friend said, 'you know what, we have 10 more minutes and we have to go...'. That's why (T: Hmm). Or that a person is getting closer to...

T: I understand.

C: But I know, it is necessary. I might have a problem. Because, if I am beginning to get to something, or start to explore something, it takes for a long time. Yes.

The post-session commentary on this event by the client:

It is not that it surprised me, but it didn't make me feel good. But I am aware that the therapist was able to admit to that totally, totally and cope with that, as if he made a mistake. He didn't make a mistake, as he had to say it. It was not his fault.

... I am with a new person, I think he had some uncertainty himself as well, though he is more used to it than me, but there had to be some initial, unknown ... but he had to have been in similar relationships before, so it wasn't so strange for him as for me. He also did not know how it would go and maybe was curious about how it would work out. It may be important to build the relationship at the beginning. And this was a moment that could damage the relationship. As if you are doing something and you are on a nice road and you do something wrong and he was able to ..., so well he processed this very well. I think he realised that 'this could be helpful for this person ..., so we go on and we are going to deal with this, that I did it'. It was good that he was not afraid that he did something wrong.

The second event, a little later in the session:

T: *Are you OK with how we were doing today, I mean except for the '10 minutes' episode?*

C: *How we talk? (T: Hmm) Hmm. I mean, I am totally lost here, totally crazy. I don't know, for example, what I am going to say next time, what I will start with or ... simply what I am going to say. You know, that I started something and that it is horrible when I start ... And I thought or I imagined that it would develop somehow, that you would move it on some how, but it doesn't seem to be the case.*

T: *And it scares you that next time the session will be left to you? What you will do with it?*

C: *Yes, because...*

T: *I'd be glad to know what I can do so as not to leave you in this fear about what will happen next time, and I do not know what I could do about it. If I can help you with this, I'd be glad. And at the same time I don't see any problem with you having nothing prepared for the next time to start with. Though, you know... And I understand that not knowing is scaring you.*

C: *For example, I was talking to my mum about it. And she said: 'If I went to a psychologist I would be afraid what to talk about with him.' She didn't say exactly this, she said it like: 'What will I talk about there?' and I was saying: 'Mum, you are there because you are worried. You have a problem and it is the psychologist's role to get you through it. He will lead you, you don't need to be afraid that you don't know what to do,' This is how I saw it.*

T: *Hmm. It seems to be right to me that you are afraid of not knowing what will be next, because it goes with the territory. When we don't know what will happen next, we are afraid of that. (C: laugh) At the same time, I don't want to leave you in this, you know. (C: Hmm). It may not be pleasant.*

C: *I realise that when I drove my car, when I decided to come, I decided very quickly, I noticed the leaflet (therapy and research offer) and I said to myself immediately: 'Yes, I will go there'. And I thought that I would take it somewhat ...*

(Continued)

(Continued)

T: *Easier.*
C: *Easier.*
T: *That you will deal with it.*
C: *That it would be easier to talk, that it can go smoother. But now even those last, a while ago, I realised that 'It won't be for you so...' And I said to myself that I would like to do it because I want to do something for myself. And I said to myself that I don't want to be only an observer, because there is no meaning in it then, but still I thought it might be easier or so. (T: Hmm). It did not seem, when I am looking at it now, I see what kind of person I am, I know how I do it.*
T: *That, for example, your expectation is somewhat changed. About how easy for you it will be here?*
C: *No, I said to myself it is as if you are going to dentist. You should go in one month, no big deal, but if it is only one week, it becomes ... and when it is only one day, so...*
T: *When he drills your tooth it is again something else.*
C: *It is as if a person, I mean – I – I don't know what other people are doing, the person has to find a bigger courage.*
T: *It is more effort to come there.*
C: *Yes, but I don't feel it is bad.*
T: *It is difficult, but you don't see it as that bad.*
C: *I don't see it as hopeless or that I won't be able to make it easier, or that nothing will be resolved or that it will lead to nothing.*
*T: *Hmm, Hmm, that this is a part of the journey that you went through.*
C: *Hmm (T: Hmm) (silence 5 min). We are ready to go, aren't we? (T: laughs)*
T: *Well, I am not sure that I understood, whether you would like to come next time*

The post-session commentary on this event by the client:

I had a feeling that he accepts that one can be insecure and that it can be difficult. He accepted it, he accepts that it is difficult, but that it can lead to something. It is as if he felt what I feel, but he also offered me security.

The event is modified for educational purposes.

Recommended reading

Good recommendations for the building of the therapeutic alliance can be found in:

Luborsky, L. (1984). *Principles of Psychoanalytic Psychotherapy: A Manual for Supportive-expressive Treatment*. New York: Basic Books.

Luborsky, L. & Luborsky, E. (2006). *Research and Psychotherapy: The Vital link*. Lanham, MD: Jason Aronson.

Safran, J.D. & Muran, J.C. (2000). *Negotiating the Therapeutic Alliance*. New York: Guilford Press.

Research findings of the relationship between the alliance and therapy outcome, with recommendations for practice, are summarised in:

Gelso, C.J. & Hayes, J.A. (1998). *The Psychotherapy Relationship*. New York: Wiley.

Horvath, A.O. & Bedi, R.P. (2002). The alliance. In J.C. Nocross (ed.), *Psychotherapy Relationships that Work: Therapist Contributions and Responsiveness to Patients* (pp.37–69). New York: Oxford University Press.

Horvath, A.O. & Greenberg, L. (1994). *The Working Alliance: Theory, Research, and Practice*. New York: Wiley.

Three
Case Conceptualisation

Abstract

This chapter presents different research-informed approaches to case conceptualisation and subsequent therapeutic strategy. Research-informed examples from major approaches (psychodynamic, cognitive-behavioural, experiential and integrative) are provided, and an example of assimilative integrative approach to case conceptualisation is included.

The main scaffolding of therapeutic work is case conceptualisation or formulation.[1] Case conceptualisation informs the therapist's strategy for therapy. Each therapist encountering the client's presenting issue translates it into a theoretically informed understanding of what might be causing or perpetuating the problematic issue and what needs to happen in therapy in order to resolve that issue. Such case conceptualisation then informs the therapist's strategy for specific sessions and the overall therapy (see Figure 3.1).

Case conceptualisation is an area where there is a lot of disagreement among different therapeutic approaches. This is natural because although different approaches agree on many aspects of the skills that the therapist applies, and also on the description of psychopathology, they typically differ in their understanding of the causes of psychopathology. We will focus here on a few mainstream, research-informed approaches to case formulation and therapeutic strategy from different theoretical approaches (psychodynamic, cognitive-behavioural, humanistic and integrative), and then we will discuss the practicalities of case conceptualisation in everyday practice.

Before we focus on the different approaches to case conceptualisation and respective treatment strategies, it is important to stress that these are naturally flexible and responsive to the presentation of the client's problem in therapy (Stiles et al., 1998). The therapist's reflection plays a central role in adjusting therapeutic strategy and case conceptualisation (Stedmon & Dallos, 2009). It is especially so in exploratory therapies such as psychodynamic and humanistic therapies. These rely more on evolving conceptualisation and though they usually have a clear focus of therapy, it can be

[1] I use the terms 'conceptualisation' and 'formulation' interchangeably.

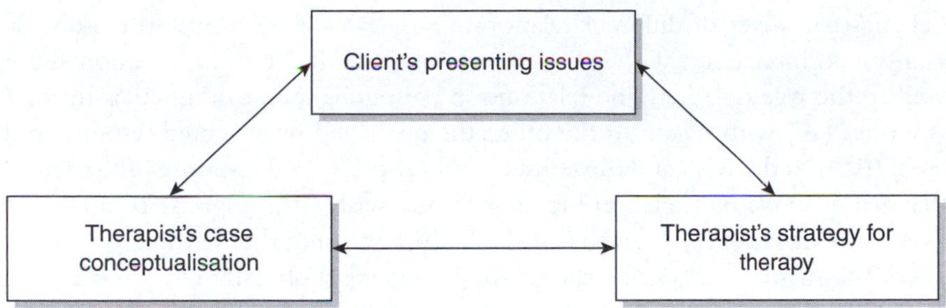

FIGURE 3.1 *The relationship between the client's presenting issues, case conceptualisation and therapeutic strategy*

quite flexible. On the other hand, CBT approaches rely more on an initial formulation that is closely adhered to throughout the therapy. However, CBT approaches can also target underlying difficulties, such as problematic beliefs that need to be elicited before they can be changed. These may be accessed later in therapy; only at this stage they inform the therapeutic strategy.

Research-informed psychodynamic case conceptualisation

Case formulation is traditionally a strong domain of psychodynamic therapies. In recent years, empirically-based methods of case conceptualisation were developed in this tradition and these followed on from more theoretically and clinically-based formulations. Empirically-based methods of case conceptualisation can be used for both research and clinical practice. Psychodynamic case formulation typically captures problematic interpersonal relating centred around the client's wishes and needs. This problematic interpersonal relating manifests itself in the transferential relationship towards the therapist. Luborsky et al. (1993) present 15 empirical methods of measuring transference. We will focus on two of the most studied psychodynamic methods of case formulation: (1) the Core Conflictual Relationship Themes method, and (2) the Plan Formulation method.

The Core Conflictual Relationship Themes method

The Core Conflictual Relationship Themes method (Luborsky, 1984; Luborsky & Crits-Christoph, 1990, 1998) is the conceptualisation tool of empirically-informed supportive-expressive psychoanalytic psychotherapy (Luborsky, 1984). The method can be used as a research method or clinical tool. The main idea is to examine the client's narratives of different relationship episodes. A relationship episode is an account of an interaction with other(s), including the therapist, or, occasionally, with the self in the role of other. The relationship episode is then examined as to the client's wishes (W) with regard to the other, the perceived or expected response of the other(s) (RO) to the wish and the consequently experienced response of the self (RS) to that. An example of a relationship episode and wish (W), response of other (RO), and response of self (RS) is given in Box 3.1. When using the method, one must be aware of the many nuances that the method contains (Luborsky & Crits-Christoph, 1990, 1998). For example, the wish may be explicit or inferred. Also, the emotional intensity of a response of self (RS) can be assessed.

Box 3.1 An example of wish, response of other and response of self (Book, 1997: 24–25)

This example comes from the first session of a 41-year-old client struggling with depression.

C: *So this idiot in a Porsche cuts in front of me. It really ticks me off. These jerks and their yuppie cars. We pull up side by side at the stoplight. I feel like rolling down my window and telling him what an idiot he is. But I didn't.*
T: *Why not?*
C: *I do not know.*
T: *What comes to mind?*
C: *He was driving this black Porsche with black tinted windows.*
T: *So who drives cars like that?*
C: *He had new Jersey plates, too. A lot of drug dealers come across Jersey. Who knows, he might have had a gun. Anyway, the light changed, he roared off, and that was that.*
T: *Well, how'd you feel when he roared off?*
C: *I am not sure. A bit let down. Irritated with myself, I guess. I felt deflated for the rest of the day. It just added to this feeling of glumness that I've been talking about. I don't know why this glumness has been going on for as long as it has. But I'm really getting tired of it.*

Book (1997) explains that the excerpt shows the client's *wish* to shout at somebody who is arrogant, *the expected response of the other* to be potentially violent, and *response of self* being deflated, silent, passive, irritated with oneself, etc. If the client reported a similar pattern in other interpersonal interactions, the therapist could formulate a Central Conflictual Relationship Theme.

The typical combinations of wish, response of the other to that wish and the consequent problematic response of self then represent the Core Conflictual Relationship Theme(s) that is involved in the client's difficulties. These Core Conflictual Relationship

Themes (CCRT) are then enacted in the relationship with the therapist. They will be repeated in the transferential relationship with the therapist. The therapist in therapy brings the CCRTs to the client's awareness, links them to psychopathological symptoms and works through them so that the client can change them (Luborsky & Luborsky, 2006).

Different studies that Luborsky and his colleagues conducted showed that the most typical wish was '*to be close and accepting*', the most typical responses of the other was '*rejecting*' and '*opposing*', and the most typical responses of self were '*disappointed*', '*depressed*' and '*angry*' (Luborsky & Barrett, 2007). The research also showed that the clients repeated their CCRTs in the relationship with the therapist (Fried, Crits-Christoph, & Luborsky, 1990) and that positive changes in psychopathological symptoms corresponded with changes in CCRTs (Crits-Christoph & Luborsky, 1990). In summarising their research on CCRT Luborsky and Barrett (2007) point out, for example, that differences in CCRTs for different diagnoses were found.

For research purposes, the method also uses 'standard' categories of wish, response of other and response of self, so that generalisations across clients can be gathered. The standard categories were devised empirically by examining a sample of a clinical population's wishes, responses of others and responses of self. Clinically, the method is used as a tailor-made approach, meaning that it is devised idiosyncratically for every client. The method can also be used as a diagnostic interview or a self-report questionnaire (see Luborsky & Barrett, 2007). As a means of conceptualisation, the method is used by the therapist for delineating core wishes that are met with perceived/experienced/expected core responses of others which then lead to self states. The therapist identifies these triads in the client's relationships with others and in the relationship with the therapist. The therapist points them out to the client and together with the client tries to work through the problematic responses of self that are seen as compromised reactions in the conflictual relationships. The therapist also urges the client to learn the skill of recognising CCRTs and to work through them independently on his or her own (for more details see Luborsky & Luborsky, 2006).

The Plan Formulation method

Another well-researched psychoanalytic/psychodynamic case conceptualisation method is the Plan Formulation method (Curtis, et al., 1994). The method is based on Joseph Weiss's theory of higher mental functioning (Weiss, Sampson, & Mount Zion Psychotherapy Research Group, 1986; Weiss, 1993). This theory assumes that at the centre of psychopathology there are pathogenic beliefs based on interpersonal experiences that were connected with the fulfilment of wishes. The theory assumes that the client in childhood either (a) had to suppress the satisfaction of some impulse due to the fear of losing a bond with significant others or (b) experienced guilt or unwanted responsibility due to the linking of the satisfaction of an impulse with a traumatic event concerning his or her significant others. These experiences then led to the formation of pathogenic beliefs around certain wishes. The pathogenic beliefs hinder the client's functioning as he or she fears that certain behaviours will endanger the other or the client.

The theory further assumes that the client feels safer in the relationship with the therapist through disproving his or her own pathogenic beliefs by testing them in the relationship with the therapist. From a longer-term perspective, the disproving of the beliefs is more gratifying than the satisfaction of a suppressed impulse that the belief obstructed. According to Weiss, Sampson & Mount Zion Psychotherapy Research Group (1986), the client tests the therapist through the transferential repeating of his/her own way of relating to significant others or through the turning of the passive into an active, meaning that the client treats the therapist in the way the client was treated by his or her significant others. The client therefore basically tests whether satisfying a wish is threatening either to the client or the therapist. According to Weiss, the therapist passes the tests by staying in his or her usual therapeutic mode. If the therapist does not pass the test, the client, according to Weiss, usually adapts the test, to make it easier for the therapist to pass it.

The Plan Formulation method focuses on five components relevant to case formulation (Curtis & Silberschatz, 2007: 201):

(1) The client's goals for therapy;
(2) The obstructions (pathogenic beliefs) that inhibit the client from pursuing these goals;
(3) The traumas that led to the development of the obstructions (beliefs);
(4) The insights that will help the client to achieve the goals;
(5) The tests in which the client will disprove his or her pathogenic beliefs.

These five components, which inform the therapist's case conceptualisation, are inferred from the client presentation in the first sessions of therapy (Curtis & Silberschatz, 2007). The client's goals for therapy are behaviours, attitudes and emotions that the client wants to achieve through therapy. They may not be fully clear to the client, so they may need to be unravelled and inferred in therapy. The obstructions are pathogenic beliefs that raise anxiety, preventing the client from obtaining his or her goals, and were developed as a response to traumatic experiences. A series of traumatic experiences may lead to the development of pathogenic beliefs, or several pathogenic beliefs may develop from a single trauma. Insights may pertain to pathogenic beliefs, goals for therapy, historic roots of the beliefs, etc. The tests are also inferred from the first challenging interactions directed towards the therapist at the beginning of therapy. The therapist develops his or her own understanding of the client's goals, obstructions, traumas, needed insights and potential tests. This understanding prepares the therapist for the client's tests and also informs the therapist's interpretations, which should promote the desired insights (for details on the Plan Formulation method, see Curtis & Silberschatz, 2007). The method can be used either clinically or as a research instrument (in that case several raters are involved). An example of case formulation using the Plan Formulation method is given in Box 3.2.

Box 3.2 An example of case formulation using the Plan Formulation method

The client, whose goal for therapy is to be assertive, independent and pursuing his own needs, who had controlling and dominating parents punishing him for 'selfish' behaviour, may have pathogenic beliefs that any independence, assertion and fulfilment of his own needs will bring harsh judgement, criticism and rejection. In therapy, the client will test the therapist by being assertive or by punishing the therapist for looking after the therapist's own needs (e.g. when arranging sessions). The insight will have to focus on linking traumas, beliefs, goals and tests. Furthermore, the therapist will not only have to pass the test and not punish the client for pursuing his own goals, but will also have to not be anxious about being criticised by the client for looking after the therapist's own needs.

Several other empirically-informed psychoanalytic and psychodynamic approaches to case conceptualisation exist (e.g. Horowitz & Eells, 2007; Levenson & Strupp, 2007). What they have in common is the recognition that conflicting motivation in interpersonal functioning or self-functioning has its roots in early experiences, either with primary caregivers or in a triad with both parents, and potentially with other significant others as well (e.g. siblings). This conflicting motivation is at the root of psychopathological symptoms. The formulation also focuses on the recognition of defences, reducing anxiety when this conflicting motivation comes to the fore. It focuses on the recognition of repeated interpersonal relating that stems from the conflicting motivation and its presentation in the relationship with the therapist. The formulation is based on the client's accounts at the beginning of therapy and is further refined in the course of therapy on the basis of the client's presentation. The main therapeutic strategy is to promote insight into the conflictual motivation and by doing so to work through the problematic motivation, perception of others, and typical interpersonal relating.

Cognitive-behavioural case conceptualisation

Cognitive-behavioural case conceptualisation typically corresponds with the mainstream DSM–IV or ICD–10 diagnostic assessment. For that purpose, structured interviews such as the *Structured Clinical Interview for DSM–IV* (SCID–IV – First et al., 1996) or the *Anxiety Disorders Interview Schedule for DSM–IV* (ADIS – Brown, Di Nardo, & Barlow, 1994) are conducted. These structured interviews improve reliability in assessing a particular disorder and contribute to the differential diagnosis. Medical check-ups are routinely recommended as many psychological symptoms may have potentially somatic roots (Morrisson, 1999).

CBT approaches see a great value in recognising discreet diagnostic categories that group clients according to their presenting symptoms. This does not mean that CBT theoreticians do not recognise a need for the refinement of diagnostic categories, so they not only describe symptoms, but also capture underlying dynamics triggering and maintaining difficulties. For that purpose, further information is typically used.

Standardised psychometric tests assessing psychopathological symptoms or constructs relevant to psychopathological functioning are used (e.g. the Beck Depression Inventory, Beck Anxiety Inventory, Penn-State Worry Questionnaire). The monitoring of symptoms (such as anxiety or low mood) is also a routine part of assessment as it helps to inform the treatment (it can also be a good intervention). The assessment then focuses on cognitive, emotional, behavioural and physiological symptoms, and the maintainers of these symptoms (Grant et al., 2008). The functional analysis (see Craske & Barlow, 2008), which assesses the role of symptoms in the client's overall functioning, is often performed as well. The assessment can also focus on the underlying schemas contributing to vulnerability for a particular disorder (Beck et al., 1979; Young et al., 2008).

The CBT case formulation and the treatment strategy then naturally flow from the assessment. Identified symptoms are targeted through the appropriate cognitive (e.g. cognitive restructuring) and behavioural/experiential interventions (e.g. behavioural activation, exposure, relaxation techniques). We will now focus on two examples of CBT assessment and case formulation.

Assessment and case conceptualisation in cognitive therapy for depression

Cognitive therapy for depression is probably the most studied therapy as to its efficacy (Young et al., 2008). The case formulation in this therapy starts with the careful assessment of depression (its symptoms and severity). It then focuses on the most pressing problems of the client, assessing links between the life situations, particular thoughts and particular emotional experience (Young et al., 2008). Behavioural and physiological aspects are also taken into consideration (see the interplay in Figure 3.2). Therapy first focuses on a relevant but amenable problem in the client's life. Problem-solving strategies may be used to address this. At the beginning of therapy, behavioural patterns contributing to depression are also elicited and targeted through observation and suggested changes. Cognitive symptoms such as maladaptive automatic thoughts

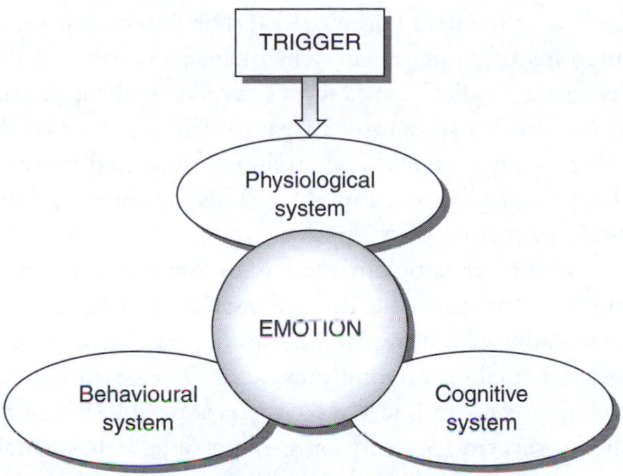

FIGURE 3.2 *The interplay of environmental, cognitive, emotional, physiological and behavioural factors in CBT case conceptualisation (Grant et al., 2008: 18)*

are also assessed early in therapy and then targeted through the gathering of evidence for and against them and through putting them to empirical tests. In chronic depression, underlying core beliefs (schemes) that feed into automatic thoughts are also detected and explored so they can be targeted through more focused work.

Case conceptualisation thus focuses on the main behaviours contributing to depression; the main automatic thoughts and ways of dysfunctional thinking contributing to depression; the main environmental factors contributing to depression; and also, potentially, on underlying core maladaptive schemes that contribute to depression. The formulation is individually devised for the client, explained to the client and agreed by the client. The formulation is at first outlined in terms of general functioning, but later in the process is brought to the specifics of particularly representative situations.

Assessment and case conceptualisation in panic control treatment

Panic control treatment is an empirically-informed therapy for panic disorder with and without agoraphobia. It was tested in a multisite randomised controlled trial (RCT) (Barlow et al., 2000) and showed one of the best outcomes ever achieved by a psychological treatment. The case formulation of this therapy focuses on the handling of symptoms of panic, anxiety and avoidance. It is based on a thorough assessment, which consists of several steps (see Craske & Barlow, 2008). It starts with the use of structured interviews such as the *Anxiety Disorders Interview Schedule*

(ADIS–IV – Di Nardo, Brown, & Barlow, 1994). The emphasis is on differential diagnosis, as the symptoms of panic are present in many emotional disorders. Part of the assessment is also a medical check-up as several medical conditions (e.g. thyroid conditions) can lead to symptoms of panic. Another part of the assessment is the self-monitoring of panic attacks and anxiety and related mood and worry. The agoraphobic behaviour may be monitored too. This monitoring should establish the realistic and contextual picture of symptoms.

The assessment is further supplemented with standardised inventories such as the Anxiety Sensitivity Index or the Body Sensation and Agoraphobia Cognitions Questionnaire (see Craske & Barlow, 2008). Another part of the assessment is behavioural tests. These may include walking outside or the assessment of anxiety caused by induced symptoms of panic (see Craske & Barlow, 2008). The behavioural tests help to establish the severity of symptoms. If possible, behavioural symptoms are supplemented by outcomes on physiological measures such as heart rate acceleration. Finally, Craske and Barlow (2008) propose a functional analysis, which attempts to establish typical symptoms, their situational antecedents, their internal antecedents, related misappraisals, related behavioural reactions, safety signals, and the consequences of the disorder for overall functioning.

The thorough assessment leads to the planning of the main tasks of the treatment, such as psycho-education, breathing training, planning of the exposure activities, and of the cognitive restructuring tasks. All of these are tailored specifically for the client, so the client can master the symptoms on his or her own.

As visible from both examples, CBT approaches focus on the thorough assessment of symptoms, so the tailored coping-enhancing activities can be prescribed, tried and further assessed. The postulated underlying mechanisms of the disorders (such as core beliefs or anxiety sensitivity/awareness or a history of illness and abuse) are targeted to a lesser extent, and if so, by using the same principles that target symptoms (e.g. cognitive restructuring, exposure, evidence-based reasoning, increased awareness of the underlying mechanism, their recognition, and learning to live with them) (see Craske & Barlow, 2008; Young et al., 2008). I will present some of the cognitive-behavioural techniques in Chapter 7.

Experiential case conceptualisation

Humanistic and existential approaches (also known as experiential approaches) traditionally did not focus on case conceptualisation. The reason for that can be seen in their exploratory nature and in their focus on ever-changing experiencing. The strategy was to be focused on the here-and-now and on the unfolding of the client's exploration of his or her problems. An example is the classical, client-centred therapy that focuses on the communication of authentic, acceptant, empathic understanding of the here-and-now. However, even client-centred therapy developed theoretical framework (Rogers, 1958; Klein et al., 1969) that could help the therapist to recognise whether the client's exploration (experiencing) is fruitful or not. This focusing on the evaluation of the quality of exploration (experiencing) is still important in current thinking about experiential case formulation. For example, certain forms of client-centred therapy (e.g. Sachse, 1998) appraise the client's expression of and reflection on his or her own experiencing and modulate the therapist's strategy accordingly.

We will now focus on the case conceptualisation as presented in emotion-focused therapy (Greenberg & Watson, 2006; Greenberg & Goldman, 2007), a relatively recently developed experiential therapy. This approach to therapy provides an explicit case formulation, which is not that typical for experiential approaches.

Case conceptualisation in emotion-focused therapy

Emotion-focused therapy is an approach that is currently being developed primarily as a treatment for depression (Greenberg & Watson, 2006), but its ambition is to be an approach that can be used for various conditions (mainly mood disorders, anxiety disorders and traumas, but also borderline personality disorder) (see Greenberg, Rice, & Elliott, 1993; Elliott, Greenberg, & Lietaer, 2004). The main focus of therapy is to access primary adaptive emotions and use them for informing or counteracting problematic emotion schemes containing maladaptive emotions. The therapy focuses on the exploration of relevant issues through evoking and accessing the emotion schemes involved in them. The case conceptualisation is held tentatively. It is explicitly shared with the client and agreement is achieved with regard to the goals of therapy.

Greenberg and colleagues (Greenberg & Watson, 2006; Greenberg & Goldman, 2007) report eight steps that are useful in case conceptualisation in emotion-focused therapy:

1 *Identifying the presenting problem.* This is established simply by focusing on what brought the client to therapy. The presenting problem is reframed later in therapy in terms of problematic emotion schemes.
2 *Exploring the client's narrative about the presenting problem.* This is achieved by the therapist providing empathic listening. It informs the formulation centred around the core problematic emotion schemes.
3 *Gathering information about past and current identity and attachment experiences.* The problematic emotion schemes are centred around important relational and personal identity histories that played a role in developing or maintaining of problematic emotion schemas (see Blatt, 2008; Greenberg & Goldman, 2008). Information is gathered and used in elaborating on the case formulation as well as informing the tasks suggested by the therapist in therapy.

4 *Observing and attending to the client's style of processing emotions*. Several aspects of experiencing are assessed here. The therapist observes whether the client is not over-regulating or under-regulating his or her emotions in general and in the here-and-now in the session. The level of emotional arousal is also assessed. To help with that, the therapist assesses the client's voice quality (Rice & Kerr, 1986) – whether it is externalised, emotional, limited or focused (the therapist tries to promote 'focused') – and the level of experiencing (Klein et al., 1969) – whether it is referring to current feelings and their bodily referents and fresh awareness. Narrative style is also taken into consideration, distinguishing between external, internal and reflective style and facilitating internal, following reflective, style. Finally, emotions are distinguished as primary (the most immediate direct responses to situations), secondary (usually emotional responses to primary emotions or thoughts) and instrumental (rehearsed emotions that are expressed in order to achieve particular goals, for example to appear threatening so that other people back off). The emotions are also assessed as to their productivity for resolving problematic emotion schemas (Greenberg, Auszra, & Herrmann, 2007). The therapist focuses on primary emotions. Primary maladaptive emotions are first helped to be bearable (productive) and then are transformed by accessing primary adaptive emotions (e.g. primary maladaptive shame is first tolerated and then changed by accessing protective anger against shaming and self-compassion towards vulnerability).

5 *Identifying the core pain.* While the therapist facilitates the client's exploration and presentation of their problematic experiences, the therapist focuses on the core, emotionally painful aspects of the client's presentation. Greenberg and his colleagues use the metaphor of a 'pain compass'. The most painful and poignant events and experiences that the client presents are at the core of the maladaptive emotion schemas that cause problems in the client's functioning. The core pain helps to create the focus of therapy. While the presenting issue is somehow connected to the core pain, identifying the core pain allows the therapist to formulate what is most problematic and what needs to be addressed. It is explicitly communicated to the client.

6 *Identifying the thematic interpersonal and intrapersonal processes*. The focus of therapy is centred around the core emotional pain of the client. The core emotional pain is presented in related interpersonal and/or intrapersonal themes. Intrapersonal themes typically focus on self-definition and self-esteem (shame-related themes or fear of shame-related themes) and interpersonal themes typically focus on attachment issues, such as fear of rejection or dependency (fear and sadness/loss-related themes) (see Greenberg & Goldman, 2008). The themes are interwoven with the core pain, presenting issues and the past and current experiences related to them. The core pain points to core maladaptive emotion schemas.

7 *Identifying markers informing the choice of therapeutic tasks*. Emotion-focused therapy, in its moment-to-moment process, utilises a number of therapeutic tasks that address the thematic and emotional aspect of the client's presenting problematic issue (see Elliott, Greenberg, & Lietaer, 2004). The tasks are initiated by the therapist on the basis of an appropriate marker (an in-session indicator of the

possibility of using a particular task). The tasks are, in general, research-informed experiential exercises that attempt to build relationships, access and allow emotional experiencing and re-process problematic emotional experiences, as well as transform intrapersonal or interpersonal problematic experiences that have been defined as the focus of therapy (e.g. two-chair dialogue for an identity-related, self-critical process, empty chair dialogue for an unresolved interpersonal injury). I will present some of those tasks in Chapter 7.

8 *Attending to the moment-to-moment process within the session and tasks.* Emotion-focused therapy (EFT) is an experiential therapy, which means that the therapist monitors and responds to the ever-changing experiencing of the client. When embarking on a specific task, the therapist also uses micromarkers that inform the therapist's attunement and adjustment of the task for the specific processing of the client. While some of the micromarkers are based on clinical experience, many are research-informed. Examples of the microprocesses present in the major tasks of EFT are presented in Chapter 7.

Emotion-focused therapy represents an elaborate, experiential approach to case conceptualisation. It contains a rigorous, planned, explicit setting of goals that is shared with the client, while maintaining a flexibility and freshness of experientially-focused therapy. The eight steps are attended to and inform the focus of therapy that the therapist uses flexibly. As the core emotional pain of the client is resolved, the therapy can lead to its natural end.

Though this case conceptualisation may look overwhelming and complicated, it is perfectly teachable with appropriate supervision. A good resource is a book presenting several cases of EFT for depression (Watson, Goldman, & Greenberg, 2007). Research into this therapy is still evolving and it also looks at refining the case conceptualisation (see Greenberg & Goldman, 2007).

Integrative case conceptualisation

When outlining case conceptualisation, research-informed eclectic and integrative approaches draw on empirical evidence across theoretical approaches (e.g. Beutler, Clarkin, & Bongar, 2000; Grawe, 2004). A good example of a research-informed integrative therapy case formulation is the work of Grawe (2004) on his *psychological therapy*.

Integrative case conceptualisation in Grawe's psychological therapy

Grawe's approach is embedded in his theory of therapeutic work (Grawe, 2004; see also Chapter 1). Grawe assumes that before we embark on the actual detailed treatment planning, we should consider an appropriate indication of psychotherapy. The indication should be optimally based on an interview with the client, an interview with the client's significant others, the results of standardised psychometric tools and diagnostic interview. The indication should then include diagnoses, current life situation, motivational conflicts, problematic interactional patterns, a required therapeutic approach (coping oriented or mastery oriented), optimal therapeutic modality (group, couple, individual), optimal therapist's characteristics (e.g. gender, age), expected therapeutic relationship behaviour, motivation for therapy and general treatment planning (see Box 3.3).

Box 3.3 Intake assessment and therapy indication in Grawe's psychological therapy (based on Grawe, 2004)

Problems to be treated:

- DSM-IV Axis I diagnosis
- DSM-IV Axis II diagnosis
- Problematic life situations
- Conflicting motivational schemata
- Problematic interaction patterns
- Additional problems

Therapeutic approach:

- Coping-oriented
- Clarification-oriented

Therapeutic modality:

- Individual therapy
- Group therapy
- Couples therapy
- Family therapy

Notes about the therapist characteristics:

- Gender
- Age

Notes on the therapeutic relationship:

- Complementary relationship
- Expected relationship tests

Primary motivations for therapy:

Treatment planning:

- What treatment combination appears most appropriate for this client.

After the initial intake, in the first few sessions, the therapist prepares a more detailed therapy plan (Grawe, 2004). The therapist focuses on the resources in the client's life that could help the client in overcoming problems. The therapist further focuses on the symptoms the therapy should target so the client can experience relief from an immediate suffering. The therapist also concentrates on the problematic interactional patterns and plans how these can be changed. Furthermore, the therapist looks at problematic motivational schemata (established patterns) that are at the root of the symptoms and problematic interpersonal patterns. The therapist examines the schemata that are in awareness as well as those that are not in awareness. The therapist distinguishes between avoidance schemata, in which needs are not being fulfilled out of the fear, intentional schemata, which focus on fulfilling needs, and conflicting schemata, which contain avoidant and intentional components. The schemata are also present in the client's relating to the therapist. They are led by the client's relational wish, the fear of how the therapist may react to it and the expected, desired behaviour of the therapist (see the Core Conflictual Relationship Themes method above). The therapist then concludes what kind of relational 'tests' he or she may be exposed to by the client (see the Plan Formulation method above). Following that, the therapist considers what should be his or her response to the wish so he or she can provide a corrective emotional experience with regard to the wishes of the client. Finally, the therapist considers what therapeutic goals the client is most motivated to address currently. All of this information then informs Grawe's sequential treatment planning (see the review in Box 3.4).

Box 3.4 Issues in therapy planning in Grawe's psychological therapy (based on Grawe, 2004)

Which resources can be activated and how?
What disorders are to be worked on and how?

(Continued)

(Continued)

What interaction patterns are to be worked on and how?
Which motivational schemata will be activated and how?
How should the therapeutic relationship be shaped?
Which therapeutic goals is the client motivated to tackle currently?
What should be the sequential order of therapy goals and how should they be addressed?

Grawe's approach represents an example of integrative therapy case conceptualisation. It draws on psychodynamic and humanistic theorising about important motivational and interpersonal problematic patterns and how best the therapist can relate to them, but it also focuses on managing symptoms (disorders) informed by cognitive and behavioural approaches. Although a lot of emphasis in this integrative approach is put on the initial assessment, the case formulation is re-evaluated periodically, so that it can be based on further information as it is revealed in the therapeutic process and can therefore be better tailored to the client's needs.

Case conceptualisation in everyday practice

We have looked at paradigmatically different approaches to case conceptualisation in psychotherapy. Their presentation is neat and in all cases plausible. However, how does the therapist in practice decide on the case conceptualisation? Can we assume that because most of the therapists claim that they are either integrative or eclectic (see Norcross, 2005) that they devise their theoretical case conceptualisation on the basis of the client's problems and the best evidence as to how they can be conceptualised and treated? Is it at all possible to establish on what principles the therapist should base his or her strategy for case conceptualisation when encountering a new client? Do we have enough knowledge about the differential usefulness of different theoretically-based case conceptualisations? Even if we had, would any therapist know all possible case conceptualisations and the relative evidence for their usefulness?

As most therapists are exposed to several approaches, but have in-depth training in only a few, it is very likely that they will typically approach their clients from one particular theoretical perspective, though this may be based on their idiosyncratic combination of several theoretical perspectives. It is also very likely that at the root of this perspective we can recognise primarily traces of one of the dominant paradigms (e.g. psychodynamic, cognitive-behavioural, humanistic, systemic). Therapists devise their own way of approaching clients over the years on the basis of their training and learning. This process is probably similar to assimilative integration, the construct presented by some theoreticians of psychotherapy integration (e.g. Messer, 1992; Lampropulous, 2001).

Assimilative integration originally assumed that one holds, as central, one theoretical approach to therapy and then assimilates aspects of other therapies (hopefully on the basis of research evidence) to this underlying theoretical framework. I like this conceptualisation, though I suppose this process may be idiosyncratic, especially later in one's career, and may be characterised by not being based on a central 'established' theory, but rather on a central 'idiosyncratically' developed theory that is further refined or altered on the basis of further training, clinical experience, reading, etc. Each therapist's idiosyncratic theory of the therapeutic strategy addressing psychopathological problems is then implicitly present when encountering a new client.

Since therapists' case conceptualisations differ on the basis of their theoretical preferences, training, knowledge and experience, and can also differ idiosyncratically, even among therapists who share their primary theoretical orientation, it is difficult to capture case conceptualisation as a uniformed activity. Therefore, I will rather provide one of several possible examples. I mainly focus on rules that may force the therapist to alter his or her primary and most typical approach to the client.

An example of assimilative case conceptualising strategy

Let us assume that the therapist's primary theoretical orientation is emotion-focused therapy. Listening to the client's problem presentation, the therapist is attentive to signs of the core vulnerability, the core unresolved emotional pain that has an intrapersonal and/or interpersonal connotation (i.e. identity, attachment). This core emotional pain (vulnerability) points to maladaptive emotion schemes that do not lead to an adaptive experience or action. The therapist is attentive to past and current unresolved relational (attachment) or intrapersonal (identity) narratives (issues) that contributed to the development of problematic emotion schemes and their current relevance. The therapist listens for the primary maladaptive emotions that need to be contained and regulated, and the primary adaptive emotions that need to be accessed in order to balance and transform painful maladaptive emotions. The therapist takes into consideration the general and content-specific style of emotional processing as it is important in transforming problematic emotion schemes, so he or she can facilitate a productive presence of emotions. The therapist plans for the specific, in-session tasks that could help the transformation of the problematic emotion schemes that are present in the session. The therapist focuses on the microprocesses within those tasks and on homework that can consolidate the benefits gained from the session.

This is what the therapist's typical style of meeting the client will look like. It will be a flexible approach and the therapist will responsively alter it though normally within the theoretical framework of emotion-focused therapy. So when does such a therapist depart from the EFT framework? When does he or she incorporate interventions from other theoretical approaches into the EFT framework? Here are some examples:

1 *The problem requires a different type of therapy or intervention (based on research-informed clinical judgement).* As part of the assessment, the therapist assesses whether the presenting problems require a referral as they may be symptoms of, for example, a medical condition (indeed, this is relevant for many psychopathological symptoms), or they may require a referral because of their severity and another intervention (e.g. medication) may be considered as an adjunct to psychotherapy or replacement for psychotherapy. The referral may also require the use of social services, advocacy services, etc. Furthermore, the therapist may determine that some other form of therapy is more appropriate (e.g. couple therapy), or that alternative, specialised, psychological therapy is required (e.g. when the problem is clearly not typical for EFT, such as substance abuse).
2 *The client's preferences do not fit the therapist's proposed therapeutic strategies.* Some emotion-focused techniques may be challenging for some clients due to their evocative nature. The option then is to tailor EFT for such clients (therapist responsiveness) through mutual agreement. Another option is to alter the therapy by employing techniques from other approaches that can be compatibly used within EFT (e.g. relaxation or compatible psycho-education), if it addresses the client's concerns. The therapist can also change the entire approach to therapy (e.g. using CBT techniques) even though I suspect that the therapy would still be EFT-informed CBT. Again, a referral would be another option.
3 *The setting/situation requires a different intervention (e.g. there are time constraints).* In some cases, the setting where therapy is conducted may require the adjustment of therapy. For example, the therapist may be asked to provide a brief (one-session) intervention as part of multidisciplinary team intervention (primary care psychology). In such a case, the therapist has to adjust the therapy so that it meets attainable goals in one session. It may require the use of psycho-education, for example.
4 *The original strategy does not work. By monitoring therapy and listening to the client's feedback a different approach is developed.* (We would hope that) many therapists typically monitor the outcome of the therapy they provide (e.g. by repeatedly using outcome measures – see Chapter 2 for examples of measures and empirical evidence supporting this approach). Thus, the therapist can see whether the therapy is progressing and is bringing alleviation of suffering for the client. If it is not, the therapist may discuss with the client why this is the case, assessing the problem, and may try to adjust his or her approach accordingly. The therapist can also consider changing the therapeutic strategy more dramatically and can introduce different techniques that should address the difficulties. Similarly, the therapist can change the entire therapy (if the therapist is competent in several approaches) or consider referral.

5 *New problems occur in therapy that were not disclosed in the beginning (e.g. an addiction comes to light).* The therapy may also be altered on the basis of a new presenting issue that may alter the therapist's original conceptualisation and require new techniques. In this case, new therapy or a referral may be considered.

I have presented here several approaches to case conceptualisation and a way of using several of them at once, while holding one of them (probably idiosyncratically adjusted) as central. I firmly believe that with our current knowledge it is beneficial if the therapist is trained and exposed to several approaches so that he or she can enrich his or her own case conceptualising and therapeutic strategy, and eventually also the moment-to-moment technique. As psychotherapy and our understanding of human psychological suffering still evolves, it is extremely important that the therapist is open to new learning and develops throughout his or her career, acquiring new skills, training experience and clinical experience, and keeping up to date with research findings. This should not mean that the therapist will not foster his or her own coherent approach to clients.

Recommended reading

This is an excellent advanced level book on case conceptualisation in therapy:

Eells, T. (ed.) (2007). *Handbook of Psychotherapy Case Formulation* (2nd edition). New York: Guilford Press.

Four

Ethical Aspects of Psychotherapy and Counselling

Abstract

This chapter examines the ethical dimension of counselling and psychotherapy. The underlying values of counselling and psychotherapy are outlined. Some principles of good professional practice are then described. Finally, the therapist's sensitivity to the ethical aspects of the client's presenting problems is discussed. Research-informed examples are used as appropriate.

Before we focus on the practical skills of conducting therapy, we will look at some of the principles of a safe and sound practice and the ethical dimension of therapeutic work. The ethics of therapeutic work is so central to therapeutic practice that it is impossible to look at the practical skills of therapy delivery without a clear awareness of its ethical context. The ethical awareness and sensitivity of the therapist is important from the perspective of the *safety of psychotherapy interventions*, as the clients of psychotherapy and counselling services are typically a vulnerable and suffering group. Ethical awareness is also important because psychotherapy and counselling deal with intimate issues of the client's life, in which psychological well-being may sometimes be linked to *ethical complexities*, of which the client may or sometimes may not be aware.

The ethical stance is already embedded in the type of relationship that the therapist offers. The characteristic therapeutic relationship that fosters collaboration and the client's autonomy is based on the values of respecting the individual's freedom of choice, which is an ethically-laden stance. Similarly, the manner in which the therapist conceptualises the client's difficulties and plans the therapeutic strategy (Chapter 3) is embedded in an ethical stance on what is good in human life and where the difficulties lie.

Conceptual issues

Before we look at the practicalities of ethics in psychotherapy and counselling, we may consider relevant conceptual issues. Important contributions in that regard have been provided by several authors (e.g. Doherty, 1995; Meare, Schmidt, & Day, 1996; Tjeltveit, 1999; Kitchener & Anderson, 2000; R. Miller, 2004; Pope & Vasquez, 2007). For example, Tjeltveit (1999) nicely illustrates (Box 4.1) the complexity of ethics in psychotherapy. He recognises several layers of ethical awareness that go beyond professional duty ethics (deontological ethics) of not causing any harm to clients and other relevant persons. He points to ethics in general (i.e. what is good and what is not), theoretical ethics (i.e. the reasons for ethical standards), clinical ethics (i.e. what is the best thing to do in a given case), virtue ethics (i.e. what qualities to promote in the client and the therapist), social ethics (i.e. societal ethical implications and context of a given therapy case, including the legal framework), and cultural ethics (i.e. the cultural shaping of ethical reasoning). All of these are present in the actual work with clients.

Box 4.1 Types of ethics relevant to psychotherapy (Tjeltveit, 1999)

General ethics – what is good and what is not, in life in general.

Theoretical ethics – what the theoretical reasons are for specific ethical standards.

Clinical ethics – what is the best thing to do in a given clinical case, taking into consideration all ethical aspects at hand.

Virtue ethics – what qualities to promote in the client and therapist in general.

Social ethics – societal ethical implications and the ethical context of a given therapy case, i.e. what will be the consequences of therapy for society and what society expects from therapy (this includes legal context).

Cultural ethics – the cultural shaping of ethical reasoning, i.e. how the cultural background of therapist and client shapes what they see as good or bad in therapy.

When we think of delivering a safe and helpful intervention, we have to be aware of its ethical roots (i.e. the values implicit in the therapeutic approach), the ethically sound way of delivering it (i.e. delivering it professionally for the benefit of the client) and the ethical implications of this intervention (i.e. how the intervention affects the client's life and the lives of the people with whom they interact). For example, if we are working primarily on relieving symptoms, such as depression and anxiety symptoms, and not on the existential dimension of the client's life, such as having those symptoms as a consequence of causing harm to others and having feelings of guilt because of that (e.g. causing death through not respecting the speed limit while driving a car), we may seemingly deliver a sound intervention maintaining all professional standards. The therapy may be quite successful and the client may have a more bearable life as they may be able to face those symptoms. However, the choice of therapy strategy precludes other potential contributions that therapy could offer. For example, the therapy could focus on the guilt as a generator for action that would bring meaning to the fact that what happened could not be undone. The therapist could then help the client to find such meaning. The client could, for example, decide what he or she wants to do with his or her life and devote energy to it, such as campaigning for safer driving. The form of therapy strategy thus can have direct ethical implications. The therapist is an ethicist whether he or she wants it or not (Tjeltveit, 1999).

Meeting ethical standards

In most of the countries where counselling and psychotherapy are established, codes of conduct exist for practitioners (psychologists, psychiatrists, counsellors and the like). These codes capture, in a written form, the standards of good therapeutic work, outline potential ethical problems and suggest ways of addressing ethical dilemmas as these are an unavoidable part of the psychotherapeutic practice. The codes of ethics thus raise an awareness of ethical issues pertinent to one's practice.

The codes of ethics are typically trying to capture basic principles that the profession agrees should be respected and conveyed in the therapeutic practice. The codes are also trying to specify the practicalities of these principles for everyday practice. While doing that, the codes are aiming to respect broader societal context, such as the legal framework. The codes may also focus on areas other than therapy, for example therapy-related activities such as training, supervision and research (e.g. the Irish Association for Counselling and Psychotherapy has different codes for these activities). The codes are regularly revised and updated, often on the basis of the issues raised in complaint procedures, which force an examination of how well the code is working in practice. For many years, there was a trend towards a higher specificity in the codes of ethics in order to prevent unexpected situations arising in practice. However, this approach is limited as the variety of issues that can arise is vast and unpredictable. Therefore, codes are increasingly focusing on principles and ethical reasoning (e.g. British Association for Counselling and Psychotherapy, 2010). Furthermore, the focus is more on the personal qualities of therapists (BACP, 2010; see Box 4.2) and the virtues they should embody in their contact with clients (Meara, Schmidt & Day, 1996; Kitchener & Anderson, 2000).

Box 4.2 Personal moral qualities stressed by the British Association for Counselling and Psychotherapy (BACP, 2010: 4). Reprinted with permission

Empathy – the ability to communicate understanding of another person's experience from that person's perspective.

Sincerity – a personal commitment to consistency between what is professed and what is done.

Integrity – commitment to being moral in dealings with others, personal straightforwardness, honesty and coherence.

Resilience – the capacity to work with the client's concerns without being personally diminished.

Respect – showing appropriate esteem to others and their understanding of themselves.

Humility – the ability to assess accurately and acknowledge one's own strengths and weaknesses.

Competence – the effective deployment of the skills and knowledge needed to do what is required.

Fairness – the consistent application of appropriate criteria to inform decisions and actions.

Wisdom – possession of sound judgement that informs practice.

Courage – the capacity to act in spite of known fears, risks and uncertainty.

In order to be coherent and succinct, the codes typically state principles based on the proclaimed values that they are trying to convey and respect (see Box 4.3 for an example of the underlying principles of the Code of Ethics of the British Association for Counselling and Psychotherapy). The basic principles underlying ethical codes may differ from country to country and in different professions (Bond, 1993, 2000). This is because the principles on which ethical codes are based represent the ethical stance of a specific profession in a specific national culture and in a complex historical societal context (including the legal framework). This ethical stance is fluid and evolving within the historical development of the profession (e.g. counselling psychology, counselling, psychotherapy). It then finds its expression in the specifics of the code. The specifics typically outline relevant areas where practitioners commonly need to be governed by the code's underlying principles. This should help to sensitise practitioners. Codes typically also outline steps to be taken in the case when an ethical dilemma is encountered (see Box 4.4).

Box 4.3 The underlying principles of the British Association for Counselling and Psychotherapy Code of Ethics (BACP, 2010: 3–4). Adapted with permission

Being trustworthy – honouring the trust placed in the practitioner (also referred to as fidelity).

Autonomy – respect for the client's right to be self-governing.

Beneficence – a commitment to promoting the client's well-being.

Non-maleficence – a commitment to avoiding harm to the client.

Justice – the fair and impartial treatment of all clients and the provision of adequate services.

Self-respect – fostering the practitioner's self-knowledge and care for self.

Box 4.4 Guidelines for ethical decision-making from *The Code of Professional Ethics of the Psychological Society of Ireland* (PSI, 2008)

1 Define carefully the issues and parties involved.
2 Scan the Code of Ethics and identify all relevant clauses. Also check other applicable professional guidelines (e.g. those of government departments or health boards) and any pertinent legislation. Consulting with colleagues is also often appropriate.
3 Evaluate the rights, responsibilities and welfare of all affected parties.
4 Generate as many alternative decisions as possible – the more the better.
5 Evaluate carefully the likely outcome of each decision.
6 Choose what, in your professional judgement, is the best decision, implement it, and inform relevant parties.
7 Finally, take responsibility for the consequences of the decision.

In the following section we will discuss some of the relevant aspects of conducting psychotherapy and counselling where these principles occur and lead the therapist approach.

Contracting and informed consent

A significant part of therapy that is often covered in codes of ethics is the informed consent to therapy and its procedures. This is a natural part of contracting between the therapist and the client. The therapist provides the client with information about him/herself, his/her way of working and the potential impact of therapy, including the likelihood that it will be helpful and also what the alternatives to therapy are (see Sperry, 2007). As part of the contracting, the therapist should also mention any difficulties therapy can bring 'the side-effects of therapy'; see the section on written information in Chapter 2). The contract also covers practicalities such as the length of therapy, the length and frequency of sessions, fees (if relevant), the policy on cancelled sessions, the limitations of confidentiality (see below), information about record-keeping or any supervision the therapist is undergoing, etc. Another part of the contracting process is providing information on any potential changes to the original agreement (e.g. if referral is needed or the therapist cannot provide the necessary therapy). The therapist may also explain the concept of duty of care and its different applications in therapy (e.g. the duty of care towards the client if the therapist cannot continue to provide therapy or the duty of care to minors mentioned in therapy; see Box 4.5). During the contracting stage the therapist also enquires about the client's expectations so these can also be taken into consideration (this is the principle of respect for the client's autonomy; see also Chapter 2).

Box 4.5 Duty of care – the concept description (Bond, 2000)

Duty of care – a requirement to exercise reasonable care and skill in rendering therapy services to clients.

It is important to bear in mind that regardless of whether the therapist uses written information, verbal information or a combination of both, the client's understanding of the contract conditions, and especially of therapy, may be limited (Kitchener & Anderson, 2000). Therefore, the therapist must be prudent and monitor the client's understanding. Also, it may be very difficult to explain how therapy works to lay people and therefore it may be useful to make it a part of psychoeducation during the process of therapy.

Every contract needs to be reviewed periodically. The therapy focus may evolve. Sometimes a new contract needs to be negotiated and a new informed consent may be necessary, even much later in therapy, for instance when the therapist introduces a technique that has not been used previously in therapy (e.g. a two-chair dialogue).

Another part of the contracting process is recognising that any given therapy is undertaken in a broader context. The therapist may be part of an institution, whose policy may impact on therapy (e.g. only a limited number of therapy sessions are available). Sometimes the therapist works as part of a multidisciplinary team (e.g. in a hospital or school) that may be involved in the complex treatment of the client and the therapy goals may be influenced by this (as well as confidentiality – see below). The broader context that impacts on the therapist's contracting and obtaining of informed consent is also his or her professional organisation, which may shape the conditions under which the therapy is conducted (e.g. by setting the limits of confidentiality).

A specific situation may also arise when working with children and adolescents. The parents or legal guardians of minors have legal and natural responsibility for children until a set age (often 16 or 18 years, depending on the country). Therefore, they typically have to consent to therapy. However, this may differ from country to country. In some countries, if a child or young person is considered to be 'sufficiently competent' and the consent from parents was sought but not granted, the young person may still be provided with therapy (Bond & Mitchels, 2008). In some cases, such as emergencies or if the treatment is necessary and a legal body supports it, the therapist may act on the basis of his or her own clinical judgement (see Bond & Mitchels, 2008).

In any case, informed consent and contracting should always include the children and adolescents (respecting their level of understanding) and not just their parents. A three-parties contract, child–therapist–parents, needs to be negotiated in such a case, and clear levels of communication between the parties about counselling should be established. It is not unusual for there to be tension during this contracting stage, as parents have legal and natural rights (with some exceptions; see above and Bond & Mitchels, 2008) and responsibilities with regard to their children, while respect for the child's privacy in therapy is central to the child's involvement in the therapy process (see below).

The therapist's competence

The quality of care the therapist provides obviously has an ethical connotation. Therefore, it is vital that the therapist reflects his or her own competence, so he or she can judge whether they can help a particular client. Sufficient information about the therapist's own credentials should also be communicated to the client, so the client can make an informed choice about the competence of the therapist as well.

With regard to his or her own competence, the therapist's ethical responsibility is to be committed to ongoing learning. The therapist's learning does not end with obtaining a qualification. Further continuous professional development is, normally, required by different professional bodies. It should probably also be a natural aspiration of the therapist to be as helpful to his or her clients as possible. Regular supervision is an important factor in recognising levels of competence and blind spots that need to be developed (e.g. see Orlinsky & Ronnestad, 2005).

Another important part of professional development is personal development and self-care (see the empirically-based work of Norcross & Guy, 2007). The therapist's healing capacity may potentially be enhanced by the richness of interests and hobbies in everyday life. Personal therapy may be an excellent opportunity to deal with vicarious trauma experienced when encountering their clients' traumas (Orlinsky, Norcross, et al., 2005; Orlinsky & Ronnestad, 2005).

The therapist's competence can also be boosted by involvement in academic and research work. This type of work brings a rigour to the therapist's critical thinking about psychotherapy (see Timulak, 2008), which can be a good quality in the therapist (see Beutler, Machado, & Allstetter-Neufeldt, 1994). Furthermore, each therapist, especially in current training programmes, is encouraged to consult research and professional literature when reflecting on specific cases, so the therapist's approach is as well informed as possible when encountering a client with specific problems.

Confidentiality in the therapeutic relationship

Confidentiality is a basic premise of psychotherapy (Bond, 1993, 2000). If there was not an intimate, confiding relationship between the therapist and the client, then the clients would not bring their private suffering into the open and it would not be possible for therapists to respond to it. Confidentiality, therefore, is the therapist's highest priority and should be carefully monitored when working with clients.

Confidentiality, however, has its limits. Some limitations are imposed directly in the standards of therapeutic work and are often presented in the codes of ethics. A typical situation when confidentiality in therapy is limited is when the client is at risk of harming him or herself or of being harmed by somebody or, indeed, in situations when the client can cause harm or has a knowledge about a potential harm. In each case, the client may be thinking of taking action him or herself, but the problem arises when the client disagrees with the therapist on acting in a way that would avoid the risk. Although the description of exceptions to confidentiality seems clear, it is much less clear in real-life situations. The therapists can easily find themselves in an ethical dilemma, observing a conflict between the different values that the professional code of ethics embraces.

Furthermore, therapy is conducted in a legal and broader societal framework that sanctions the requirement of breaching the confidentiality of different professions in specific circumstances. Typical examples are a court order to reveal notes from therapy sessions or a subpoena calling the therapist to talk about the therapy in court.

In any case, if the therapist is aware of any risk, the therapist should always try to work with the client collaboratively in the way that responds to the risk. If it is not possible and the therapist decides to breach confidentiality, the therapist must inform the client about it, attempting to do it in a way that diminishes the harm it could cause. All of it, however, needs to be preceded, at the beginning of therapy, by the therapist informing the client about the limitations of confidentiality.

When discussing the potential limits of confidentiality at the beginning of therapy, the therapist should explore with the client when such situations are likely to occur. As Bond (2000: 154) argues, 'predictability and reasonable certainty about how the information will be protected or disclosed' are essential. Typical problematic situations may be the risk of the client's suicidal behaviour, the client's violent behaviour towards others, such as a partner (see Box 4.6 for an example of an ethical dilemma), the client's reckless behaviour (e.g. driving drunk with children in the car), the client's reporting of being sexually abused as a child, and so on. More complex situations can arise in some contexts. For example, some countries (such as Ireland) encourage professionals to report past abuse, if the abuser is identifiable, even if this person is just mentioned in therapy by the now-adult client and the abuse was well in the past. The rule then is to establish whether this person is still a threat to children. The therapist then tries to encourage the client to report the abuse, but eventually may do so even without the client's consent (although the therapist would still inform the client). Such situations are very complex and it is important that the therapist uses supervision and wide consultation about how to handle such a process. Similar situations may be relevant in a case of terrorism in some countries.

Box 4.6 An example of an ethical dilemma concerning confidentiality

Imagine the following situation:

The therapist works with a couple in a long-term couple therapy in the context of drug rehabilitation. Both partners are recovering from drug addiction. The male client is known for his aggressive, violent, antisocial behaviour and potentially criminal activity (he has a history of being in prison). In the therapy process he reveals that he is very jealous and that he thinks he would be capable of beating up or killing his partner if she cheated on him. In the same session, he briefly leaves the room to make 'an urgent' call.

> *At that time the female partner reveals to the therapist that she cheated on her partner and that she is afraid that he could harm her. The partner then comes back into the therapy room to resume his involvement in the session.*
>
> As an exercise, try to come up with a plan of action of what the therapist should do.

Another important set of limitations comes with specific settings or client groups. Typical limits to confidentiality pertain to children (in many countries children under the age of 16, though in some countries up to age 18). Children's parents have a right to know that their child attends therapy and what the therapy entails (there is a lot of discussion about protecting the child's privacy in different age groups, but the therapeutic and legal perspectives often differ). A three-sided contract needs to be set around the rules of confidentiality and communication. Children should be respected and should know what the limitations of confidentiality are. The privacy of the child–therapist relationship is also respected, while its limitations are clearly outlined. The therapist may need to explain to the parents the importance of creating a private space for the child (this of course depends on the age). On the other hand, the therapist tries to involve the child in any disclosure to the parents (see Geldard & Geldard, 2008). The therapist also explains the importance of confidentiality and privacy for the therapy process to the parents. In general, the therapist is trying to be transparent and collaborative with the child and parents by respecting everybody's (sometimes competing) rights. Obviously, this can lead to potential tensions (see more in Geldard & Geldard, 2008).

Confidentiality also has its limits in multidisciplinary settings such as hospitals or schools (e.g. McMahon, 2008). For example, the therapist may have a contract with a school (the school principal), in which therapy is provided as part of school services. The clear understanding of confidentiality and its limits must then be established, for example, by also taking into account the principal's overall responsibility for the well-being of the child in school. A similar situation may occur in a hospital setting where, for instance, a consultant psychiatrist or other colleagues of the person in the primary role of the therapist may be co-responsible for the treatment. The contracting then has to be done within the institution in a way that allows the confidentiality of one-to-one therapy to be respected as much as possible as it is a prerequisite for any therapy to happen. At the same time, the rules of what is going to be done in the client's best interest by the entire institution (if it needs to be included) need to be outlined to the client and consented to by the client. In every instance, when the therapist thinks that it would be appropriate to advocate or consult with a wider team for the client's benefit, the client's explicit and informed consent must be sought by the therapist. Similar rules may be relevant for an individual practitioner, who may collaborate in some cases with GPs or other relevant bodies that provide care to the client.

The therapist should also be aware that therapy is conducted in a legal framework which may require the therapist to breach confidentiality. Typical examples are court dealings in which the therapist is subpoenaed. All evidence, including the notes of the sessions or the therapist's personal remarks about the client, may be requested by the court. The therapist, therefore, has to be aware of this when making notes. In such cases, the therapist should still be collaborating with the client, keeping the client informed (if possible) and should try to protect the privacy of the client, for example, by suggesting to the court how it could handle such information sensitively (by not making it public, etc.).

Respect for the client's choices – the client's autonomy

The client's autonomy is one of the main principles underlying most of the professional code of ethics in different countries and organisations (see Bond, 1993, 2000). The client's autonomy is captured in many aspects of ethical codes. It is one of the main principles behind contracting and obtaining informed consent. It is central to the confidentiality of the therapeutic work. Respect for the client's choices about therapy and the client's way of life is a profound ethical stance, present in current psychotherapy and counselling. The therapist is typically tailoring the therapy to a particular client and negotiates (see Chapter 2) the goals and tasks of therapy with the client. This may sometimes bring tensions, as the client's choices may contradict the judgement of the therapist. Authentic transparency, respecting the client's perspectives, is a stance that underlies any competent therapeutic endeavour (see also Chapter 2).

Dual relationships

One of the main potential problems for therapy is the nature of multiple or dual relationships. The therapist engages in a dual relationship with a client if, during therapy, before it or after it, their relationship has more than a therapeutic function. The problem of such a relationship is that it undermines the therapeutic work, which depends to a significant degree on the therapeutic relationship. There are also other problems in dual relationships. By their nature, due to the client's vulnerability, they are not equal relationships. This dynamic can be present even after therapy, if the therapist and the client engage in a further relationship.

The detrimental character of dual relationships is well documented in cases of romantic and sexual relationships between therapists and their clients. The empirical evidence suggests that about 80% of clients experienced such a relationship as harmful (Pope & Vetter, 1992), typically stating that the client's experience, for example, impaired their ability to trust, led to guilt and confused roles and boundaries (Pope & Vasquez, 2007). Interestingly, male therapists are significantly more likely to be involved in such relationships, and the therapist's prior boundary-surpassing, problematic behaviour is a much stronger predictor that such a contact will happen than the client's behaviour (Pope & Vasquez, 2007).

Given the nature and consequences of dual relationships, it is not surprising that many codes of ethics explicitly prohibit such relationships, either for some time after the therapy is concluded or completely (Bond, 1993). This has clear relevance as many therapists, during their career, occasionally experience countertransferential attraction to their clients (in fact, this experience relates to more than 80% of therapists though it is more common in male therapists – see Pope, Keith-Spiegel, & Tabachnik, 1986). The way of dealing with this attraction therapeutically, without harming the client, needs further research (see Ladany et al., 1997), though many recommendations exist (Pope & Vasquez, 2007).

Slightly less research attention has been devoted to studying dual relationships of a non-sexual nature. Pope and Vasquez (2007) summarise some interesting findings with regard to non-sexual dual relationships. For example:

- It seems that male therapists are more likely to engage in such relationships.
- There seems to be a relationship between non-sexual and sexual dual relationships, suggesting that sexual relationships are a culmination of other types of boundary transgression.
- A significant portion of therapists (up to 30%) had at least one client with whom they had other social contact.

Studying the occurrence and the nature of dual relationships is important as it is clearly recognised that it is not always possible to avoid a dual relationship of a non-sexual nature. In many instances, especially in more rural communities, local contact may make such relationships unavoidable. In other instances, dual relationships may occur after therapy, when the therapist and the client meet in unexpected circumstances (e.g. as colleagues in an institution such as a university). For example, the Code of Ethics of the American Psychological Association admits that some dual relationships between clients and psychologists can be unavoidable. However, the code admonishes psychologists for entering into such relationships in case the psychologist's objectivity is decreased or the relationship interferes with the psychologist's professional effectiveness, with a possibility of harming the client (Kitchener & Anderson, 2000). Kitchener and Anderson point to the study of Borys and Pope (1989), who found that four examples of dual relationships were assessed as non-ethical by American psychologists, psychiatrists and social workers. These are:

(1) Financial involvement, e.g. selling a product or giving a gift to the client.
(2) Dual professional roles, e.g. providing therapy to a current employee.

(3) Sexual intimacy, e.g. sexual intercourse with a client before, during or after therapy.
(4) Social involvement, e.g. inviting the client to a private party or other social event.

All these dual relationships have one common feature: there is a high risk of weakening the whole psychotherapy work by blurring the therapeutic contract and by partaking in a form of exploitation, as the client is in a vulnerable position that limits his or her choices. The main characteristic is that the therapist is following his or her own needs, and in doing so the therapist misuses his or her professional role.

There is also a problem with post-therapy relationships. Kitchener and Anderson (2000), considering the work of several authors, summarise eight reasons why post-therapy relationships should be avoided (as they are American authors, some of these reasons may be more relevant to the USA):

1 The former client may want to return to therapy, which would be affected by the post-therapy relationship.
2 The power differential may continue, which can make the client vulnerable.
3 The clients experience strong emotions towards the therapist, which can lead to a lower level of objectivity in the relationship.
4 The post-therapy relationships may not turn out well, which can decrease clients' confidence in psychology.
5 The public may perceive post-therapy relationships as unclear and unpredictable.
6 The therapist's objectivity in offering a potential future professional service may be compromised by the post-therapy relationship.
7 Clients may suppress information because they assume that some post-therapy relationship will exist after therapy.
8 In some states of the USA these relationships are illegal.

Anderson and Kitchener (1998), in their earlier work, presented a four-component guide that can be used in assessing the appropriateness of a post-therapy relationship (see Box 4.7). The model can serve as an example of how the therapist can reflect his or her own feelings when entering into such a relationship. Similar reasoning is also relevant for concurrent or pre-therapy relationships.

Box 4.7 A four-component model for assessing the appropriateness of a post-therapy relationship (Anderson & Kitchener, 1998: 93–96)

The therapist may assess:

1 The therapeutic contract and the parameters of the contracted relationship. Examples of questions to consider include:

- *Did we come to a formal or identifiable closure to our work together?*
- *Did the former client and I process the termination of our therapeutic relationship?*
- *Can I maintain the confidentiality of the therapeutic relationship in this post-therapy relationship if that is the client's wish?*
- *Does the former client understand that entering a post-therapy relationship may limit the opportunity for us to work together again in therapy?*

2 The dynamics of the therapeutic relationship – emotions towards the therapist, the differential power dynamics. Examples of questions to consider include:

- *What was the status of the power differential when termination occurred?*
- *In light of the power differential in the therapeutic relationship, to what extent is the former client's decision free of controlling influences?*

3 Social role issues. Examples of questions to consider include:

- *How similar or dissimilar are the role expectations and obligations of the new relationship from the role expectations and obligations of the therapeutic relationship?*
- *How might the knowledge gained in therapy influence my perceptions or judgements of the former client in the post-therapy relationship?*
- *How might the former client's perceptions of me gained in therapy influence the client's perceptions of me in the new role?*

4 The therapist's motivation. Examples of questions to consider include:

- *What are the personal and professional benefits for me if I enter into this relationship?*
- *Is this post-therapy relationship avoidable, and, if it is, why am I considering entering into it? One year from now, will I be satisfied with my decision?*

Dual relationships may also represent a specific problem in psychotherapy training. A relationship may involve the trainer and the trainee or the supervisor and the supervisee (including in research situations) or the personal therapist and the trainee. Especially in small countries, where practitioner communities are also small, the duality of relationships is a reality. Former trainees become colleagues whom you encounter in professional forums. The duality of relationships, or sometimes also the multiplicity of roles, has therefore to be reflected upon and monitored, so that the recipient, (i.e. the trainee) who is in a more vulnerable position, is not harmed.

Responsibility to the profession

Another ethical issue pertaining to everyday practice is the therapist's responsibility to his or her own profession. In interacting with clients and other professionals, either privately or publicly, each therapist represents his or her own professional body. Thus therapists build trust in psychotherapy and in their own profession (e.g. psychology). The therapist's responsibility also extends to witnessing how the profession is represented by other fellow professionals in public presentations or in the actual work with clients. The therapist should, therefore, respond to any mispresentation or misconduct of colleagues that the therapist is aware of. However, this must be done respectfully and with clients' welfare in mind. The therapist should also be willing to help colleagues, if they request help with regard to a clinical or ethical issue. Responsibility may also involve a willingness to participate in research because it further develops the discipline, or in a willingness to supervise trainees.

Supervision

An important part of an ethically safe and sound professional practice is the therapist's involvement in supervision. Firstly, studies exist that suggest that involvement in supervision enhances the therapist's effectiveness and the quality of the relationship that he or she provides (Bambling et al., 2006). Secondly, supervision is a significant part of the therapist's self-care (Orlinsky & Ronnenstad, 2005; Norcross & Guy, 2007). Thirdly, it may be an important resource for resolving ethical dilemmas that may occur in one's practice. Finally, the therapist's competence is monitored in supervision, so regular supervision can highlight gaps in the therapist's work, and indicate whether further training is required.

In order to fulfil its function, supervision must also observe the rules of ethically sound practice. This includes confidentiality and its limitations, clear contracting, reflecting on the duality or multiplicity of the roles of the supervisor and supervisee, etc. Safe and competent provision of supervision can enhance the supervisor's own professional development, not only in the area of psychotherapy, but also specifically in the area of conducting supervision. The supervisor may be involved in his or her own supervision (of supervision), training in supervision, or research into supervision. Codes of ethics often cover supervision as well and some organisations even have a specific code for the conduct of supervision (e.g. Irish Association for Counselling Psychotherapy).

Especially in the training context, supervision also has an evaluative character that has implications for trainees' further progression. The dual dynamics of the relationship, to teach/support and to evaluate, is therefore clearly present and inevitable. So is the supervisor's responsibility to the profession and to the trainees' future clients (the responsibility of the trainer in the training context is similar).

Note taking and note keeping

As mentioned in Chapter 2, it is the therapist's responsibility to reflect on his or her therapeutic work regularly. Part of this reflective approach is to take notes and maintain records in a professional manner. Keeping appropriate records is often recommended by professional bodies (e.g. the British Psychological Society) and required by employers. It can enhance the therapist's focus in therapy (see Chapter 2).

When keeping records of therapy sessions, there are several relevant issues. The informed consent that the client provides for therapy should cover record keeping, the function of records, access to records, the storage of records, etc. The client must always have access to the notes on his or her therapy sessions and has to be informed about what is recorded. The records should be succinct, intelligible, accurate, organised and kept up to date. These notes have to be protected, along with other sensitive personal data, including identifiable information. The data has to be securely stored in line with the appropriate legislation. In the case of most European countries, this would be the Data Protection Act. (See Box 4.8 for the basic principles of the Irish Data Protection Act. The British Act follows almost identical principles.)

Box 4.8 Principles of the Irish Data Protection Act 1988 and 2003

Data Protection Acts 1988 and 2003: A Guide for Data Controllers

There are eight rules of data protection:

1 Obtain and process information fairly.
2 Keep it only for one or more specified, explicit and lawful purposes.
3 Use and disclose it only in ways compatible with these purposes.
4 Keep it safe and secure.
5 Keep it accurate, complete and up to date.
6 Ensure that it is adequate, relevant and not excessive.
7 Retain it for no longer than is necessary for the purpose or purposes.
8 Give a copy of his/her personal data to an individual, on request.

Records have to be stored for a relevant period of time, which varies from country to country and depends on legislation regarding time constraints for initiating legal action or a complaint. Some professional organisations may advise their members on the timeframe for keeping records. In the case of minors, specific rules apply. Parents are entitled to have access to records. The timeframe for keeping records concerning minors in therapy is also different because child clients cannot start any legal action or complaint procedure involving their therapy until they are legally adults, that is until they reach the age of 18 (in most countries).

Other issues may arise in multidisciplinary contexts, when the client is in the care of other professionals. In this case, the client must be informed about who has access to the records and what is included in the notes. For more details, see an excellent discussion of this issue in Bond and Mitchels (2008).

Therapists need to be aware that notes can potentially be seen by other parties. For instance, as already mentioned, Courts of law may request the access to notes. Therefore, it is not advisable to keep separate personal reflections – so-called 'process' notes – as these would be treated like any other record of therapy (Bond & Mitchels, 2008).

Managing ethical dilemmas

Although codes of ethics provide valuable guidelines for the professional behaviour of therapists, they cannot foresee every situation that can arise in everyday practice (see Box 4.9 and also Box 4.6). Furthermore, the codes' articles can often be contradictory when used in a particular real-life situation. Many codes therefore provide guidelines for the *process* of solving a dilemma rather than attempting to solve the dilemma itself (Box 4.4 on p. 72 provides the guidelines for ethical problem-solving from the Psychological Society of Ireland's code of ethics).

Box 4.9 Examples of ethical dilemmas

1 The client offers a present (an expensive dessert) to the therapist after the 20th session (it is not the last session) as a thank you for the work so far.
2 A potential client, who is in a close relationship with the therapist's colleague, wants to attend therapy.
3 A client, who is in the process of getting divorced, asks the therapist for a report which the client wants to use in court. So far the client has attended three sessions and wants to use the report as proof that she or he has been preparing to raise children alone.
4 A depressed 16 year-old showing a moderate risk of suicide does not want the therapist to tell his parents that he has sought counselling.
5 A therapist discovers that a colleague who works with clients is severely clinically depressed.
6 A 15 year-old client tells the therapist that he is planning (with his friends) to assault a teacher who has evaluated him negatively in school.
7 A mother and her 17 year-old daughter describe for the therapist how they have assisted their father with a 'hysterical suicide attempt'. He was drunk and they were persuaded that he did not mean it, so they handed him a lot of pills once he started to threaten them with suicide.
8 A client tells the therapist that he is working illegally.

As an exercise, try to address these dilemmas.

Some codes of ethics (e.g. Canadian Counselling Association, 1999) recommend the weighing up of values embedded in different principles. For example, they may recommend waiting for some time before making a decision to see whether the therapist's perspective changes or not. Or they may recommend projecting the outcome of the therapist's decision or projecting how the therapist might view the issue at a later point in time. Virtually all codes recommend some sort of consultation, whether this is with a supervisor, peers, or even legal experts, if necessary.

Sensitivity to the ethical dimension of the client's problem

The therapist's role as an ethicist sometimes goes beyond adherence to a code of ethics. As Tjeltveit (1999) rightly notices, the therapist is always promoting a certain ethical stance (see also Chapter 2 about the therapist values). The ethical stance is already present in the therapist's concept of mental health and well-being. Tjeltveit (1999) also points to the values embraced by the therapist's profession as well as the therapist's individual values. Therapists, at least implicitly, want to promote good in their clients' actions. Each therapist hears the client's 'story' from the perspective of psychological knowledge as well as from his or her own ethical framework. Sperry (2007) acknowledges a significant shift in counselling and psychotherapy ethics in recent years, with a greater emphasis on integrating personal and professional ethics.

In spite of the rich tradition of psychotherapy, working with values and an ethical dimension have received little elaboration. The psychotherapy mainstream is now aware of the shortcomings of the 'value free' tradition in psychotherapy (see Beutler, Machado, & Allstetter-Neufeldt, 1994; Tjeltveit, 1999; Slife, 2004). However, the new conceptual frameworks for addressing 'the good' in therapy are not well developed. Little is formulated on the professional approach to dealing with ethical dilemmas (whether they are spoken or unspoken on the client's part). Nor is there much discussion on therapists' values influencing this process, although we empirically know that therapists' values do play a role in therapy (see Chapter 2; also Beutler, Machado, & Allstetter-Neufeldt, 1994).

Facilitating the client's ethical reasoning

The problematic issues explored by the client may sometimes contain ethical considerations. For example, the client considers taking revenge on a person whose decision influenced the client's life in a negative way. When the client expresses such a problem, he or she will also see any therapist's reaction through the perspective of whether the therapist approves or not of the client's plans. Even if the therapist does not respond, the client may in some ways interpret that as a response (e.g. the therapist does not see any ethical problem in it, or sees a problem but does not consider it as a major issue, or the therapist does not have the courage to express his or her own opinion). Therefore, it is important that the therapist reflects on the ethical dimension of the client's story and responds to it systematically and thoughtfully, while respecting the implications for the therapeutic relationship and the client's vulnerability since the therapist has significant power in being an expert in the relationship.

Here are a few steps and possibilities that the therapist may consider when encountering an ethical dilemma in the client's presentation:

1 *Identification of an ethical problem in the client's exploration.* The first step in working with an ethical dilemma in the client's presentation is its assessment. The therapist may ask him or herself whether the client's action can harm or neglect others or the client. Once the therapist has a clear sense that there is an ethical dilemma, the therapist may make it a centre of the discussion in the session. However, this step is key because the client is vulnerable and may perceive the initiation of such a discussion as judgemental. It may affect the therapeutic relationship and it can also cause psychological harm (by being negatively judged and potentially rejected). The therapist therefore has to balance the focus on the ethical issue at stake with a consideration of the client's vulnerability.

   Supervision may often be a very good place to reflect on the pertinent ethical issues in the client's presentation. An appropriate consultation with peers, while not breaching confidentiality rules, may also be helpful. The consultation may show that the therapist has noticed only a part of the ethical problem and it can illuminate other aspects and layers of the problem and potential optimal responses on the therapist's part.

   The identification of an ethical problem in the client's presentation serves several functions. On the one hand, the therapist is trying to promote good in the client's functioning; on the other, the therapist is also showing his or her own ethical sensitivity. The client can thus learn that the therapist is trying to be ethically sensitive and considerate in relation to the client too.

2 *Exploring the ethical dilemma from different perspectives.* After the ethical problem is raised, it may be reasonable to consider it from several perspectives. The client's personal values can also be explored and considered with regard to the intended action. In some cases, in a co-operative and sensitive way, the therapist may express his or her own opinion (e.g. see Tjeltveit, 1999; see also Chapter 2). However, this has to be done with a careful consideration of the therapeutic effect of such interventions and in the context of respecting the ethical requirements of supporting the client's autonomy. Exploring the motives and experiences behind the considered action, as well as gathering relevant situational information, can be useful too. The client's reflectivity is thus encouraged.

3 *Exploration of the consequences of the ethical issue for the client and others involved.* After the ethical concern is explicitly stated, the therapist may encourage the client to explore the possible consequences of any actions. Discussion of the consequences of individual actions in the safety of the therapeutic relationship

provides the client with a unique space to reflect without rushing into action. Furthermore, the client has a thoughtful partner, the therapist, who reflects on the situation collaboratively and attentively with the client.

4 *Reflection of personal learning in dealing with ethically charged issues.* Once the concern is resolved, it may be useful to reflect on what can be learned from it. The specific issue can be applied to similar issues that the client may become involved with in the future. The therapist can encourage such a reflection by asking reflection-stimulating questions such as: *What do you take from how you/we have dealt with this situation? What did you learn about yourself? What will you do in future when encountering similar situations?*

As mentioned at the beginning of this chapter, there is no established view on how to deal with ethical concerns seen in the client's presentation. Therapists differ significantly in their approach (see, for example, Box 4.10). Therefore, the ideas considered above should be seen as tentative suggestions. Further consideration can be given to thinking about these types of issues in psychotherapy and counselling.

Box 4.10 Suggestions for working with ethical issues raised in the client's presentation (adapted from Doherty, 1995: 42–45)

Doherty (1995) summarises eight types of response he uses in dealing with moral issues (he lists them in order of increasing impact on the client):

1 Validate the language of the moral problem when the client uses it spontaneously.
2 Introduce language that makes the moral horizon of the client's problem clearer.
3 Ask questions about the client's view of the consequences of his or her actions on others and explore the personal, family and cultural sources of these moral sensibilities.
4 Articulate the moral dilemma without presenting your own view.
5 Introduce research findings and your clinical view on the consequences of some of these actions, especially for vulnerable individuals (e.g. children).
6 Describe how you, in general, see the issue and how you are inclined to consider the moral options, emphasising that every situation is unique and that the client will make his or her own decision.
7 Say openly how concerned you are about the consequences of the client's action.
8 Say openly when you cannot support the client's decision or action, and explain your decision and its moral background and, if it is necessary, withdraw from the case.

Doherty (1995) emphasises that these examples are not prescriptive, but are only his characteristic responses. He appreciates that therapists may have their own styles (Doherty, 1995: s. 42).

Recommended reading

There is a lot of literature on ethics in counselling and psychotherapy. See, for instance:

Koocher, G.P. & Keith-Spiegel, P. (2008). *Ethics in Psychology and Mental Health Professions: Standards and Cases* (3rd edition). New York: Oxford University Press.

Pope, K.S. & Vasquez, M.J.T. (2007) *Ethics in Psychotherapy and Counselling: A Practical Guide.* (3rd edition). New York: John Wiley

Five
Interventions Facilitating Exploration and Understanding

Abstract

This chapter describes the basic skills promoting exploration and understanding utilised in counselling and psychotherapy. The skills are presented systematically, starting with the situations in which they may be used, the actual skills themselves and the reasons for their use in therapy. The exploration skills include attentive listening, responding to feelings and personal meanings, evocation of emotions, memories and associations, focusing on experiencing, the promotion of specificity, imagination of change, etc. The understanding promoting skills include the communication of empathic understanding, empathic conjecture, interpretation, promotion of the client's self-understanding, the provision of information, and focusing on interpersonal functioning in the here-and-now. Research findings are cited throughout to inform the use of the presented skills.

In this chapter we will focus on the therapist's skills in facilitating the client's experiential, exploratory, meaning-making and understanding-promoting processes. These processes are often central to exploratory, humanistic and psychodynamic psychotherapeutic approaches. They are, however, only significant when they are embedded in a meaningful case conceptualisation and therapeutic strategy (see Chapter 3). Cognitive-behavioural therapies may use these skills in different parts of therapy as well, but purposefully so they fit applied cognitive-behavioural strategy.

Interventions facilitating exploration

The main part of the therapeutic process in exploratory approaches is the client's exploration of his or her own experiences and their reflection. In psychodynamic therapy, it is often the exploration of associations, wishes, perceptions, expectations, etc., that go through the client's mind when the client is talking about concerning issues. Through such an exploration, the therapist gathers material that can be interpreted or responded to strategically by the therapist (by providing corrective experience). In experiential therapies (i.e. emotion-focused, client-centred), exploration typically focuses on the issue that is most vivid for the client, usually something that bothers the client (a problematic experience) in the here-and-now. The therapist may then respond empathically to the explored material and client's experiences by providing a healing presence, or can use the material strategically (e.g. in emotion-focused therapy) and shape the exploration in a way that can lead to a resolution of emotional injuries and distress. Exploration is also important in cognitive-behavioural approaches. It is typically seen there as a means for gathering more information which can be used in devising therapeutic interventions.

The client's exploration of his or her own problematic experiences is a natural part of the therapy process. Some approaches, such as the humanistic approach, see the exploration as having a therapeutic effect on its own. They argue (see Rogers, 1961) that the client's exploration in the presence of an authentic, empathic and non-judgemental therapist is less and less defensive, more open and thus more authentic, and this is accompanied by physically experienced relief (Timulak & Lietaer, 2001). Psychodynamic approaches see this less defensive type of exploration as a starting point for a more integrated self-understanding that brings healthier functioning (see Weiss, 1993).

The therapist's role in helping the client's exploration is central. The therapist offers relational qualities (see Chapter 2) characterised by authenticity, a genuine interest in helping, a non-judgemental approach and an attempt to understand the client's feelings and personal meanings. This provides a permissive environment that encourages non-defensive, authentic exploration. The therapist also encourages the client's exploration through specific skilful interventions, strategies and behaviour. We will now focus on them and on their role in therapy. We will also describe particular situations in therapy when they can be used. (This is inspired by Greenberg, Rice, & Elliott, 1993, who introduced the concept of particular in-session markers and corresponding therapeutic tasks in therapy.)

Encouraging the client's exploration

Therapy starts with the therapist encouraging the client to present the problem that has brought the client to therapy. In many humanistic and psychodynamic therapies the therapist encourages the client to focus on the current experiencing of a relevant problem. This is done repeatedly throughout the therapy and typically also at the beginning of every new session. In a cognitive-behavioural therapeutic strategy, such an encouragement may focus on the problem agreed between the therapist and the client as being important for resolving the client's difficulties, typically as a lead to an intervention that targets behaviour or cognitions and alters them.

The therapist encourages the client to focus attention inwardly. For example, at the beginning of a session the therapist may ask: *What would you like to focus on in today's session?* Alternatively, the therapist can provide possibilities: *What shall we focus on in today's session? Are we going to continue with the focus of the last session or would you like to address something else?* If the therapist wants to focus exploration on a specific issue during the session, the therapist can encourage the client to talk more about it (*Can you tell me more about what you mean by …?*) or can ask open-ended questions that stimulate exploration (*And how is this for you?*). It is good if the open-ended questions stimulate exploration holistically, focusing on perceptions, feelings, thoughts, bodily experiences, and so on (*What was the worst thing about that situation? How does it feel in your body? What went through your mind?*, etc...). Capturing different facets of the client's internal process is more productive than just staying with one aspect of the exploration. However, it needs to be based on the therapist's strategy. For example, when the client focuses more on thoughts, the therapist may want to draw attention to the body, or vice versa. Open-ended questions are one of the central forms of encouraging exploration, something which is also suggested by research evidence (Elliott, 1985; Hill, 2009). Encouraging exploration can be supplemented by an explanation to the client of why it may be good to focus on and discuss his or her problematic experiences. The therapist can explain to the client that in order to be addressed and resolved the problematic experiences need to be brought out into the open in the first place.

Attentive listening

The basic skill of every therapist is attentive listening. Attentive listening means not only listening to the content of the client's talk, but also to the meaning the expressed content has for the client. This includes the meaning of the interpersonal context of saying it to the therapist. Attentive listening is also listening to feelings experienced and expressed by the client. Attentive listening is the therapist's main mode of engagement in the whole course of therapy. A sign of the therapist's attentive listening is not only the fact that the therapist pays attention to what the client is saying and remembers it correctly, but that the therapist also tracks it in the context of the client's overall 'story'.

Attentive listening is, on the behavioural level, characterised by an attentive presence (e.g. appropriate eye-contact). It is also represented by an adjusted quality and intensity of the voice, which matches the client's expression. For example, when the client talks about something sad the therapist's voice may be quieter. Attentive listening can also be expressed by posture. For example, the client may be sensitive to whether the therapist's way of sitting communicates interest in the client (Timulak and Lietaer, 2001). Attentive listening can be expressed by the distance from the client. For example, intimate themes may be naturally followed by the therapist leaning forward. Attentive listening can be communicated by the proper use of silence, either leaving a space for the client or alleviating the anxiety that can sometimes be experienced during silence (e.g. at the beginning of the therapy; see Chapter 8).

Attentive listening has several functions in therapy. On the one hand, it can be healing on its own (see Rogers, 1961), in that the expression of attentive interest by the therapist provides a healing atmosphere, where the client is sharing and thus no longer isolated with the problem. On the other hand, attentive listening is also the background against which other therapeutic interventions are used. In general, it is an important part of any therapeutic intervention as the therapist is always attending to what the client is expressing, so the therapist can adjust the intervention or task that he or she is involved in (see the concept of responsiveness in Stiles, Hanas-Webb, & Surko, 1998).

Tracking perceptions, appraisals and emotional reactions

An important part of the client's exploration that the therapist can be focusing on is tracking the relationship between the client's perceptions in the situations the client is describing, their appraisal, and the impacts of these perceptions/this appraisal on emotional experiences. Every single situation the client is describing in the session consists of idiosyncratic perceptions and appraisals that have an idiosyncratic impact on the client. Before the therapist fully focuses on the experienced impact and unfolding of emotional experience and its meaning, it is also important to unpack what in the situation is triggering this impact. For instance, if the client gives an account of a row with his wife, the therapist can focus on the most poignant words, acts or expression that stay with the client (e.g. *She said that I disappointed her and her expression was showing contempt*) and trigger a specific emotional response (e.g. *I felt hurt, put down and rejected*).

Tracking the triggers (perceptions), their appraisal, and the following emotional response with its meaning is the constant structure that the therapist uses when listening to the client's story. This structure allows the therapist and the client to see any client's account through a useful matrix that focuses on perceptions/appraisal, emotional reaction and their meaning, as needed, on the basis of the therapist's strategy and the approach (for more, see Chapter 7).

Responding to and exploring the client's feelings (emotions)

One of the basic modes of encouraging exploration is the therapist's communicated acknowledgement and understanding of the client's feelings (Rogers, 1951). The acknowledgement and communication of understanding is typically complemented by the further exploration of feelings. Responding to feelings is visible in the therapist's capturing of the feelings present in the client's expression and the communication of 'hearing' them. Sometimes it may concern feelings (emotions) which the client has expressed. Sometimes the therapist responds to perceived feelings although they may not be verbalised (see empathic conjecture in Elliott et al., 2004). For example, the client may say '*...My problems haven't changed*' and the tone of the voice would convey sadness. The therapist's response could acknowledge such a feeling: '*I hear a lot of sadness in your voice*'. In responding to the client's feelings, the therapist tries to be sensitive and convey genuine caring, while also being aware that these feelings can be uncomfortable for the client (see also Hill & O'Brien, 1999).

Responding to the client's feelings is not limited to a particular, appropriate situation in the process of therapy. It is an activity that the therapist engages in constantly by observing the client's feelings and being ready to respond to them. At times, the therapist may use various specific interventions, which may be ways of responding to emotions. For example, if the client is overwhelmed by emotions, the therapist may suggest breathing to regulate the experience.

Responding to the client's feelings (emotional experience) serves several functions in therapy. Hill and O'Brien (1999), for example, name the following: it enables the client to enter his or her inner experiences; it affirms the client's feelings; it helps to model the expression of feelings; it helps to name feelings (which can help to modulate them) that would otherwise be undifferentiated and intangible. By naming feelings, the therapist also communicates that he or she is not afraid of the client's feelings and that they are appreciated and important. Naming the client's feelings that have been expressed can also be safer for clients than attempts to explore feelings which are not yet present in the client's expression. A sensitive, caring and tentative response to the perceived feelings of the client can also be done in a way that respects the client's vulnerability and the potential embarrassment of bringing personal material to the session.

Responding to and exploring the client's personal meanings

Similarly, just as the therapist actively listens and responds to the client's feelings, the therapist also responds to personal meanings in the client's story (see Rogers, 1951). Responding may be in the form of an exploration of these meanings or in the form of the communication of their understanding (I will discuss the communication of understanding further, below). Everything that the client says during therapy has some personal meaning for the client. The whole psychotherapeutic endeavour is focused on the unfolding and formulation of the client's personal meanings. In successful therapy, these meanings change from personal meanings, which are experienced as problematic, to healthier personal meanings (some research-based theories, such as the Assimilation of Problematic Experiences Theory (Stiles, 2002) capture this process – see Box 5.1).

Box 5.1 Assimilation of Problematic Experiences Scale (APES): the progressive evolution of problematic experiences into mastered ones (adapted and shortened from Stiles, 2002)

0 Warded off/dissociated. Client is unaware of the problem. Affect is minimal.
1 Unwanted thoughts/active avoidance. Client avoids experience. Affect is intensively negative (episodic).
2 Vague awareness/emergence. Client is aware of a problematic experience but cannot formulate the problem clearly. Affect includes acute psychological pain.
3 Problem statement/clarification. Client clearly states the problem. Affect is negative but manageable.
4 Understanding/insight. The problematic experience is formulated and understood. Affect may be mixed.
5 Application/working through. The understanding is used to work on a problem. Affect is positive, optimistic.
6 Resourcefulness/problem solution. The formerly problematic experience has become a resource, used for solving problems. Affect is positive, satisfied.
7 Integration/mastery. Client automatically generalises solutions. Affect is positive or neutral.

Adapted with permission from Oxford University Press

During the therapy session, the therapist is constantly aware of the client's meanings. Clients are always intentional in their expression and want to convey some meaning. This meaning may have several layers. For example, a male client's expression '*This friend of mine has always only been interested in what he is saying and not in what I would like to tell him*' can have several meanings. The client may be expressing his own anger and disappointment in his friend, or the client may want to use it as an illustration of his sense that people in general are not interested in him, or the client is expressing this because he has a sense that the therapist does not listen to him and is pointing to it indirectly. Clients are typically clear though not always forthright with their intentions. However, sometimes they may not be fully aware of the reasons of their communication. For example, confronting the therapist can be threatening for the client (see Safran and Muran, 2000), so the client may not be fully aware that what he says about the friend is said because the situation with the therapist resembles it ('the therapist also does not listen').

The therapist's response to personal meanings can also have several layers. Though a single utterance typically addresses only one layer ('*He has never been interested in hearing anything about you…*'), a sequence of the therapist's utterances usually tries to cover more possible meanings contained in the client's expression (e.g. '*Neither has he been interested in you*'), while balancing their exploration and understanding. In some specific instances the therapist can explore what meaning the client's communication has in the here-and-now of their interaction ('*I'm wondering whether something similar is happening in our relationship, too?*'). The decision as to what layer of meaning to respond to is embedded in the therapist's case conceptualisation and strategy.

Psychotherapy is an activity aimed at transforming the client's personal meanings (Power & Brewin, 1997). A significant part of healing in the psychotherapeutic process is through a deeper awareness of personal meanings, generated on the basis of the client's experience and reflection on it, as well as their new formulation. The therapist's facilitated exploration of the client's personal meanings, which is embedded in a meaningful and focused therapeutic strategy, is thus an important contribution to the therapeutic change. It leads to the therapist and the client collaborating on the construction of meaning based on the client's experience.

Active evoking of emotions

Another aspect of supporting the client's exploration is the active evoking of emotional experience. A lot of the clients' psychopathology centres around the avoidance of emotional experience (Allen, McHugh, & Barlow, 2008). Furthermore, emotions contain a lot of valuable information (e.g. if I really detest my working environment I can decide to change my job) (Greenberg, 2002). Finally, some emotions may be maladaptive (e.g. a maladaptive fear of spiders) and in order to help the client to learn how to overcome them, they first need to be accessed (Greenberg, 2002; Franklin & Foa, 2008).

The therapist decides to focus on the activation of emotions on theoretical grounds that are informed by the case conceptualisation and therapeutic strategy. Typically, it is done when an important emotion is referred to but not vividly experienced by the client. The evocation can then be achieved through a technique, such as the two-chair technique. I will present these types of techniques in Chapter 7. Alternatively, the therapist uses a particular way of responding (interviewing) that may elicit more emotional experience. For example, the therapist can ask: *What kind of feeling does this bring out in you?* Or the therapist may tentatively guess the client's emotion: *I can imagine that that had to be hurtful.* The therapist can also respond to the emotion which he or she perceives in the client's expression: *I hear that it annoys you.*

Greenberg and Safran (1989; also Greenberg, Rice, & Elliott, 1993; Greenberg & Paivio, 1997) distinguish three types of emotions (for more, see Chapter 8, Boxes 8.2 and 8.3):

1 Primary;
2 Secondary; and
3 Instrumental emotions.

The primary emotions are the freshest emotions experienced in a specific situation. The secondary emotions are emotions triggered by more primary emotions or thoughts. These secondary emotions, therefore, do not contain the most relevant information in the situation. They are often blurred and contain a mixture of different emotions. For example, the (male) client may express frustrating, hopeless anger, though in reality he may feel ashamed. Anger is then only a reaction to the unbearableness and painfulness of his shame (he cannot face and bear the shame). Instrumental emotions are played emotions that are centred around goals (interpersonal) that the client wants to achieve. For example, the client is whining in order to elicit support.

In all cases, it is important that the therapist responds to the emotional experience and meanings attached to it. Greenberg, Rice and Elliott (1993), however, strongly emphasise that, strategically, the focus should be on primary emotions as they are at the core of what needs to be attended to or changed. For example, clients with depression often experience secondary hopelessness and helplessness and can be in a generally unpleasant state. But this secondary emotional experience may be revealed in fresher experiences of primary sadness, hurt and anger, which are related to the specifics in their life situation (Pascual-Leone & Greenberg, 2007).

The active evoking of emotions in therapy revives the complexity of the client's experiencing of the problems. The relevant problematic experiences can thus be present vividly in the session and can then be transformed. The richness of information contained in primary emotions can be accessed. In the case of maladaptive emotions, they can be accessed so that they can be changed, typically through alternative emotional experiences (Greenberg, 2002).

Active evoking of memories and associations

During the therapy process there may be moments when the therapist wants to stimulate memories linked to the explored experience. This may be particularly useful when the client experiences strong maladaptive emotions (e.g. maladaptive shame) and the therapist may want to enact the situations in which the emotion was often experienced. The therapist may probe, for example: *When did you feel like this? What comes into your mind when you stay with that feeling?*

Similarly, it may be relevant to stimulate the client's associations in situations when the client experiences something that does not make sense. The therapist may probe here also, for example: *What comes into your mind when you stay with this?* The therapist may encourage the client to let his or her mind wander freely so that different possible associations can occur.

The creation of links between different memories, perceptions and experiences provides material for the client's focused work on unresolved issues, and it can be fruitful for the client's own reflection and the promotion of self-understanding. It makes separate experiences more coherent and comprehensible.

Promoting specificity in the description of problematic experiences

Counselling and psychotherapy are very personal activities. Some clients may find it difficult to articulate such personal experiences. We cannot do anything about problematic experiences that cause suffering if they are not expressed openly and specifically. If the client provides only general or vague formulations, such as *My relationship with my mother is not worth anything. Usually I react inadequately. My mother again said something awful to me*, the therapist's natural reaction is then to ask the client to be more specific: *Can you describe it a bit more, using a specific example? If you do not mind, can you tell me precisely what your mother said to you?*

The use of general descriptions may sometimes be due to the client's defensiveness or embarrassment. Often it is also an expression of a general style of emotional processing that may be impersonal and externalising (see Greenberg & Goldman, 2007). The therapist's probing for greater specificity in the client's description therefore needs to be sensitive and respectful, but at the same time coaching the client into being more concrete and personal (Greenberg, 2002).

Specificity brings vividness and emotional immediacy to the session. Painful and problematic experiences can thus be accessed without avoidance and addressed by an empathic therapist. They can also, if necessary, be actively changed by accessing alternative emotions (Greenberg, 2002). The clients can also learn that their own experiencing contains nuances that can be elaborated, attended to and reflected upon.

Focusing on experiencing

Exploration may also sometimes be helped by directly focusing on the client's bodily experiencing. Eugene Gendlin developed a specific technique of focusing on the client's bodily experiencing (Gendlin, 1981, 1996; see also Chapter 7). A suitable moment for focusing more directly on the client's experiencing is when exploration of the client's feelings and reflection upon those feelings loses its direct referent, that is its bodily 'felt sense' (Gendlin, 1964). Clients may then be invited to pay attention to how they feel the explored experience in their body. Similarly, Greenberg, Rice and Elliott (1993) suggest attending to the bodily sense not only when the bodily experience is not felt, but also when it is unclear. They use Gendlin's term, 'felt sense', and talk about 'an unclear felt sense' that needs to be attended to, named and explored (see Chapter 7).

Focusing on experiencing may be used as a more general interviewing style that can be employed when appropriate. For example, a client who describes her dissatisfaction in her relationship with her boyfriend, sighs and says '*It is very complicated and I myself do not understand it*' and then stays quiet. The therapist can focus the client's attention on her experiencing with the words: *What is the worst aspect or what are you most dissatisfied with in your relationship?* or *What is the thing that you are most dissatisfied with?*, and so on. There is a wide spectrum of interventions that the therapist can use (e.g. *What is it that you miss? What would you like? What do you long for?*). The common denominator of those interventions is that they force the client to focus inwardly and to pay attention to the core of her experience. This may sometimes be evoked by focusing on what is absent or what the client needs.

Focusing on experiencing makes clients aware of different aspects of their experience. Problematic experiences can thus be accessed and brought more fully to awareness. Paying attention to his or her own experiencing is an important skill that the client can learn in therapy.

Active clarification of experiencing

Focusing on the client's experiencing is normally followed by the therapist's active effort to clarify aspects of the client's experience. For example, the client may say '*It embarrasses me a lot when my boss criticises me in front of my colleagues*'. The therapist can clarify this further: *Does it embarrass you that it is done in front of your colleagues or is it the fact itself that the boss criticises you which is embarrassing? Or is it both?* Sometimes the client may make contradictory statements that need to be clarified. For example, the client may say '*I am with my boyfriend only because I do not want to hurt him by abandoning him*'. On the other hand, a few moments later she says '*I need him because I cannot stay alone*'. The therapist's clarification can then look something like this: *I hear that you are afraid of hurting your partner, but also that you fear being alone. Can you help me to clarify this?*

Ambiguity or contradictions in the client's statements are often the result of the sensitivity and painfulness of the explored theme. Therefore, the therapist's clarification needs to be embedded in an empathic and respectful presence. Logical contradiction should be respected and the emphasis should rather be on teasing out layers of the complex experience. Clarification may sometimes just capture a conflict in the client's experience that may be central in explaining why the experience is problematic.

The clarification of the client's experiencing allows the therapist to be closely attuned to the client's inner world. The process of empathy and clarification thus becomes a dance (Bohart & Rosenbaum, 1995). The exploration, through focusing on the client's experience, has its natural, collaborative pace. Clarification also contributes to the client's broader awareness. It brings problematic aspects of the client's experience to the fore, so they can be focused on and changed in therapy. Furthermore, clarification of experiencing and personal meanings is a good skill because it allows the therapist to convey empathy, unconditional positive regard and caring. It is an engaged attempt to clarify the experience, which stems from a profound caring that is conveyed to the client.

Imagination of possible change

Solution-focused therapy (e.g. Berg & Miller, 1992) introduced a 'miracle questions' technique, in which the therapist asks the client to imagine a possible change as a way of promoting both exploration and change (see Box 5.2). Sometimes, when the client's problematic experiencing brings a sense of hopelessnes and lack of clarity, imagining a possible change may uncover the client's need that is not met in the problematic experience. For example, in the above-mentioned relationship problem, the therapist may ask: *What would have to be different so that you would feel OK in the relationship with your boyfriend?*

Box 5.2 The miracle question from solution-focused therapy

Suppose that one night, while you are asleep, there is a miracle and the problem that brought you here is solved. However, because you are asleep you don't know that the miracle has already happened. When you wake up in the morning, what will be different that will tell you that the miracle has taken place? ... What else? (Berg & Miller, 1992: 13)

If the client is asked to imagine what the difficulty would look like if it was resolved, the client can then speak of a wish connected to an unmet need. The past and present unmet needs are often at the centre of the problems that bring clients to therapy. The active imagination of change not only stimulates an exploration of feelings, it may also evoke the state to which the client would like to get, which sometimes may promote hope as well.

Offer of the therapist's feelings

Occasionally the therapist may support the client's exploration by revealing his or her own feelings evoked by the client. This sort of intervention is relevant if the therapist considers the feeling important for the client's exploration. Examples of appropriate situations may be:

- a missing feeling in the client's expression;
- the client's direct discussion of the therapeutic relationship, which evokes an emotional response in the therapist (see Chapter 2); or
- the client's expressed need, which the therapist can respond to.

Usually, the feeling that the therapist wants to communicate to the client has to be important and persistent in the therapist and deeply considered, so that it is in line with the therapist's strategy. An example in which the therapist is expressing missing feelings may look like this: a female client says that her husband is physically abusive towards her, but she is not showing how it impacts on her. However, her description of the abuse may evoke compassion towards the fright and physical pain that the therapist can sense. The therapist's expression of feeling the fright and pain can support the client's experience and further exploration and sharing. The therapist may say something like: *I can sense the constant fear that this must be bringing, the fear of unpredictability and physical pain. I really sense that you need protection.* This example also shows an expression of feeling towards the client's need, though the need was not expressed directly by the client.

The therapist's expression of his or her own feeling is an intervention that should be used with caution, so that it does not stem from the therapist's own anxieties or unresolved issues. Again, it should be embedded in the overall strategy, though it may also be a more spontaneous response on the part of the therapist. The expression of the therapist's feelings may have a supporting effect on a client's further exploration of problematic experiences, as it may promote the type of dialogue that pays attention to and is open to emotional experiences (Knox et al., 1997).

The therapist's offer of observations and insights

Just as the therapist may offer his or her own emotional resonation with the client's presentation, so the therapist may also offer his or her own thoughts and observations. Normally, it is done in the form of sharing knowledge, case formulation, or providing psychoeducation. However, thoughts and observation may also be shared more immediately in order to stimulate exploration. The intention is to show responsiveness and attentiveness and maintain the dialogue that focuses on the client's story and current experience. It is important that the therapist's response is focused on the client's frame of reference (see Rogers, 1961) and not on the therapist's own issues. Often the therapist's response comes from conceptualising the client's story, but it may come to mind spontaneously. For instance, the client may be describing a specific part of a dream she had. This may spark an association in the therapist that the therapist may offer tentatively to the client: *When you talk about knowing that something bad will happen to you at this stage of the dream, it reminds me of a similar thing you mentioned when you described your feeling as you were driving home. Is there anything relevant in it?*

The rationale for sharing an association in order to enhance the client's process of exploration is that we are social, dialogical beings and what arises in both partners in the interaction (though focusing on one of them) may enrich the client's focus and reflection on his or her own experiencing. Furthermore, in this way the therapist also shows that he or she focuses on the client's inner world and that this focus is engaged and active.

Respecting the client's pace and intimacy

Another important characteristic that is present in the therapist's work is respect for the form and content of the client's exploration. Therapy is an intimate endeavour and the client undertaking therapy is in a vulnerable position. To feel safe and to be prepared to be open to look at personal painful experiences and share them with the therapist is possible only with an empathic and respectful therapist. An important part of that empathy and respect is a respect for the level of openness that suits the client.

Clients vary in how comfortable they are in sharing and examining their painful experiences. Though the therapist is aware that it is important to bring these painful and vulnerable experiences out into the open in therapy so that they can be addressed and resolved, the therapist has no other option than to respect the client's preparedness to be open or not. Though the therapist may explain the importance of openness in sharing the painful experiences, if they want to build trust and gain the confidence of the client, they have to also accept the client's pace of exploration.

Acknowledging the client's personally important language

An important manifestation of the therapist's empathy, which was already present in the classical, client-centred therapy, is the acknowledgement of the personally- and emotionally-charged language that the client uses. It is especially so if the client expresses significant personal experiences. The recognition of such language provides a special form of validation that can be healing in itself. It can also enhance the client's sense of safety and thus also the exploration of painful and problematic experiences. Often, this recognition captures idiosyncratic words which carry a highly specific meaning in a given context of the therapeutic process.

For instance, the client may say (stressing the words in bold): '*I simply* ***do not have any power to live*** *as nothing brings joy in my life.* ***Everything is so grey***.' The therapist's response may capture the stressed words by saying: ***You do not have any power to live as everything is so grey.*** In another example, a female client may say: '*When I meet a guy who is interested in me, it is important to me that I feel that* ***he*** *really* ***cares for me*** *and not that he is only interested in me because I am an attractive girl.*' The therapist may miss the importance of words by saying: *You have to know that he is not only interested in you because he is looking for an attractive girl.* The client may correct the therapist: '*No, I have to feel that* ***he*** *really* ***cares for me***.' The therapist then captures the meaning of the words: '*Um, the most important thing is whether* ***he cares for you***.'

The acknowledgement of the client's important words is so significant because they have their own emotional and cognitive connotation which captures the uniqueness of a particular experience. Such an acknowledgement may be central for the clients to feel that they are understood. This can lead to significant impacts within a therapy session. Some significant events studies suggest that such an acknowledgement can be very powerful and even linked to the outcome of the therapy (see Elliott & Shapiro, 1992).

Process observation

Another aspect of the therapist's activity that may meaningfully support the client's exploration is the therapist's sharing of his or her observations of the client in the session. This intervention comes primarily from Gestalt therapy and currently from its offspring, emotion-focused therapy. In this therapy, observation is typically focused on promoting the client's awareness by pointing out to the client important aspects of his or her non-verbal behaviour. In the context of emotion-focused therapy, the therapist shares observations of non-verbal behaviour that either stifles emotional expression or accompanies it. Focusing on it should then amplify this emotion or, in the case of suppression, should bring its avoidance to the client's awareness. For instance, the client expresses anger by the clenching of fists and the therapist shares this observation.

In the psychodynamic tradition, the therapist shares the observation of the client's interpersonal behaviour towards the therapist if it is relevant for the client's interpersonal behaviour in problematic relationships. Such an observation may serve to promote understanding and may be embedded in an overall therapeutic strategy (I will return to this subject in Chapter 8).

To share one's own observations in order to facilitate the client's exploration is usually only done with the intention of broadening the client's awareness and focusing the client on some of his or her non-verbal behaviour, which may be relevant for expressing and exploring experiences. For the client, it shows that the therapist is a skilful and engaged observer who can help him or her to focus on *their* problematic experiences in a way that would otherwise be inaccessible for them as it would be outside their awareness.

The therapist's offering of observations can be facilitative only when its intention is to deepen exploration and understanding. An offer of observation for the purpose of broadening the client's awareness is not the same as when the therapist's response is intended to 'catch' the client by pointing out behaviour that contradicts the client's verbal expression. Though at times the therapist may point out contradictions, the intention should be one of expanding awareness and not criticism. Therefore, this type of observation has to be done in the context of a good, collaborative therapeutic relationship and as an expression of it. For example, a female client was blushing while she was talking about her meeting with a new man. According to her statement, it was one of many ordinary encounters she had been experiencing recently. The therapist may respond: *You are saying it was just an ordinary encounter but you are blushing. Is that somehow connected with that encounter or with something else and it only seems like that to me?* In another example, when the therapist shares her observation of the client's anxious, non-verbal expression, which corresponds with the client's talking about his fear, she may say: *I can see that fear in your facial expression.*

Expanding the client's awareness can be helpful in directing the client's attention to important aspects of his or her experience which could otherwise go unnoticed. By offering his or her own observations, the therapist offers feedback which is not so common in everyday interactions. The disadvantage may be in giving clients the impression that they are being observed and evaluated by the therapist, which may strain the therapeutic alliance. Therefore, intervention focused on expanding the client's awareness should be used only rarely and in the later stages of the therapeutic process within a well-established therapeutic relationship.

So far, we have presented a number of strategies that can be used to facilitate exploration. Many of them are mutually overlapping. They are normally used coherently and strategically. They should fit not only the client's presentation in the here-and-now, but also a case conceptualisation and overall therapeutic strategy based on the overall and ongoing assessment of the client's difficulty.

Interventions facilitating understanding

The promotion of understanding is, just like the exploration of the client's problematic experiencing, an important part of therapeutic work. The therapeutic approaches differ in their emphasis on the benefits of increased self-understanding. Psychodynamic approaches consider it a major task of therapy. Cognitive-behavioural approaches see understanding as important for the client's engagement in the cognitive, emotional and behavioural tasks of therapy. Finally, experiential approaches see the role of understanding as consolidating experiential change, which is accomplished through healing experiences in the therapeutic relationship and through the processing of difficult emotions.

Thus, although differently treated in different forms of therapy, in all of them understanding is seen as important for the client's ability to resolve problematic experiences. Understanding helps to foster the client's mastery of problematic issues as it turns puzzling and unarticulated experiences into comprehensible and clear ones. Improved understanding may stimulate further cognitive processes, new ideas, decisions, etc. Although understanding, usually in the form of awareness and insight, often comes spontaneously in therapy (Timulak & McElvaney, 2009), it also comes after the therapist's strategic interventions. We will now look at some specific ways in which the therapist promotes the client's understanding.

Communicating an empathic understanding of the client's feelings

In the section above describing the facilitation of exploration, I mentioned that the therapist's responses to the client's feelings and personal meanings represent the therapist's basic 'exploration task'. The therapist is continuously focusing his or her own attention on the client's feelings and personal meanings. A form of this focusing is also an empathic communication of the therapist's understanding of them. Therapists explore the clients' feelings and personal meanings and communicate their understanding of them. Therapists do it naturally, complementing exploration with understanding, and vice versa.

The way the therapist communicates an understanding of the client's feelings often includes *the reasons for the client's feelings* (e.g. *Living with such problems for such a long time makes you feel desperate*). Sometimes it may also mean communicating *an understanding of the feelings expressed indirectly*. It means that even if the client did not express his or her own feelings directly, the therapist could tentatively respond to the feeling as well as to its reasons. In the example mentioned above, the therapist could provide an understanding by saying, for example: *Living with such problems for such a long time, trying so hard to change but without success, brings about a feeling of despair in you.*

All the therapist's responses demonstrating an understanding of the client's feelings need to be expressed sensitively, delivering a compassionate, caring presence. It is not the same as a cognitive understanding of the feeling. Rogers (1980) talks of an 'intimate being in the world of the other'.

The communication of understanding of the client's feelings contributes to the client's making sense of their experience. However, it can also help the client to modulate and contain their painful experiences as they are shared with and recognised by another person. The therapist's presence can thus have a soothing and regulating quality (see Watson, Goldman, & Vanaerschot, 1998). In addition, it can help the client to tolerate the difficult feelings. Furthermore, it can help to evoke the emotions that need to be accessed in therapy, so that they can be used productively. The communication of understanding may also promote an awareness of important aspects of problematic experiences. It can support insights into significant aspects of the client's self-experience. The empathic communication of the understanding of feelings gives the client an experience of being understood by another person. The client may also perceive the therapist as being interested in his or her inner world and thus experience the therapist's caring presence. It can enhance the therapeutic alliance and increase the client's feeling of safety in therapy and trust in the therapist. The empathic understanding can then lead to a specific and very nurturing kind of personal relationship.

Communicating of an empathic understanding of the client's personal meanings

Therapists respond to and communicate their empathic understanding of *both* feelings and personal meanings. The slight difference between the communication of understanding of personal meanings and the exploration of personal meanings lies in the fact that the communication of understanding contains and expresses this understanding. The communication of understanding means that the therapist verbally grasps the meaning expressed by the client and puts it into words. For example:

T: My reaction might have hurt you because it seemed as if I did not trust you.
C: Not **as if**, but you have really expressed that you actually did not trust me.
T: I really hurt you by what I said.

Obviously, the first response to the client was already an attempt to communicate the therapist's understanding. However, the communication of a more exact understanding came finally with the second response. In actual practice, an attempt to communicate understanding and the actual communication of understanding both have the same value. It is as if it was a continual process of dancing around the client's personal meanings (Bohart & Rosenbaum, 1995). The meanings are continuously realised by the client and re-created in the course of the therapy again and again. Understanding is thus also a continual process with no finality in it. The therapist is constantly tuned to seek and to communicate this understanding. The communication of understanding can be more definitive when the client reaches a new insight or a new formulation of some problem and the therapist intends to mark this progress. In general, however, just as with exploration, the communication of understanding also has to be tentative, so it invites the client to refine the therapist's intervention (see the example above).

By communicating understanding of the client's feelings and personal meanings the therapist contributes to the articulation of the client's experiences. It is also an expression of a specific form of relationship that provides the client with an experience of being understood and cared for. However, the communication of the understanding of the client's feelings and personal meanings not only contributes to the good quality of the healing relationship, but also has a therapeutic function in gaining a new understanding. Furthermore, it contributes to the client's emotion-regulation function, as empathic understanding helps to contain experience (see Bohart & Greenberg, 1997; Watson, Goldman, & Vanaerschot, 1998; Watson, 2002).

Facilitating the client's focus on understanding self and others

The therapist may also lead the client to make an active effort in understanding his or her experiencing or behaviour. For instance, this is typical for the mentalisation-based treatment (Bateman & Fonagy, 2004), a psychoanalytic treatment for borderline personality disorder. The marker for this type of intervention may be the client's confusion about his or her own behaviour or symptoms. The therapist may stimulate the client's self-interpretation by questions such as: *What sort of possible explanations come to your mind? If we go slowly through the context of the situation when the symptom (behaviour) occurred, what was happening in your environment and what was happening inside you?* etc.

A marker for the stimulation of the client's understanding can also be the inexplicability of some other person's action. For example, a male client says that he does not understand the motives behind the behaviour of his partner. The therapist can stimulate his understanding by questions such as: *What possible motives of her behaviour come to your mind? If you thought about why she had done it now, what would come to mind?* etc.

Clients sometimes respond to the therapist's effort to focus them on deepening their understanding with disapproval, because they feel that they will not be able to understand something which they haven't understood so far. The point is to encourage the client to think outside the box and to try out different possibilities associated with the incomprehensible experience. The therapist can support it with interventions such as: *What possible explanations occur to you? Try to let your thoughts, ideas and options cross your mind without thinking hard, no matter how unlikely or strange they are.*

In some cases, understanding oneself and others might be interconnected in an interesting way. Sometimes, when the client is not able to accept parts of his or her self, he or she is not able to accept them in others either. We will look more closely at some links between problematic aspects of the client's self and the client's interpersonal relationships and therapeutic work with them in Chapter 8.

The stimulation of self-understanding is relatively rare in the psychotherapeutic process, as therapists prefer to focus on the actual experiencing rather than superficial intellectualisation. It is especially futile with clients who have a tendency to intellectualise. That is why the focus on self-understanding usually occurs only after more direct experience-targeting interventions. Sometimes it is possible to promote understanding through the use of specific techniques (such as systematic evocative unfolding, which will be introduced in Chapter 7). One also has to remember that in the actual practice, the focus on understanding goes hand in hand with the focus on experiencing presented earlier in this chapter. The two are interwoven and complement each other.

Empathic conjecture of the client's experience

The term 'empathic conjecture' is used by Greenberg and Elliott (1997) to capture the therapist's communication of the understanding of the client's feelings and meanings which are not directly expressed by the client. The empathically attuned therapist may capture the client's experiencing at 'the edge of the client's awareness'. This type of response was also described by Carl Rogers (1980) in his description of empathic communication. The therapist uses empathic conjecture rarely, only when he or she experiences a strong sense of attunement to the client's inner world. Therapists can communicate what they assume is happening for the client. It has to be done in a non-authoritative and non-dogmatic manner, allowing the client to disagree if necessary (Greenberg & Elliott, 1997). The therapist's formulation should be presented as an offer that should be checked against the client's experiencing. For example, a male client says that he is afraid that his colleagues at work will reject him when they find out how insecure he feels. If the therapist feels (based on the previous discussion) that the client's fear might be connected with his fear that colleagues will judge him as a failure, the therapist may react tentatively: *May that fear also be about them judging you as unable to cope with your life? Or is it not like that?* The therapist thus makes conjectures about aspects of the client's experience.

Sometimes the client might be aware of an aspect of his or her own experiencing which he or she is embarrassed to express in front of the therapist. In such a case, the therapist's effort to tentatively conjecture an understanding might be experienced by the client as intrusive. The therapist therefore has to be careful when using conjectures, so that they are not experienced as intrusive.

When appropriately used, empathic conjecture can bring important aspects of the client's experience to the client's awareness. The conjecture can name aspects of the experience that are difficult for the client to express or differentiate. The experience can thus be more fully articulated and expressed, and potentially can also be accessed more fully. Thus, empathic conjecture facilitates the process of exploration and understanding of the client's problematic experiences. Furthermore, the client may experience the therapist's conjecture as an expression of a deep interpersonal understanding. This may increase the client's trust in the therapist and in the helpfulness of the whole therapeutic endeavour.

Checking the fit between understanding and experiencing

While encouraging the client's self-understanding, it is important to check whether this understanding 'fits' the client experientially. The therapist may check it directly by saying, for example: *Does this make sense to you? Does this feel right to you? Do you feel that it fits the feeling you have?* etc. This checking is even more essential when it applies to conceptualisations expressed by the therapist. While checking any conceptual understanding experientially, the therapist should offer the client a space for focusing on inner experiencing (Gendlin, 1964) and wait until 'the experiential response' comes (Gendlin, 1968). While we cannot be sure of the truth of any conceptualisation just on the basis of a felt response it evokes, it is a productive process that can sometimes lead to an experience of relief (see Hendricks, 2002). It also leads to a productive inner focus (Greenberg, 2002) that is typical of a good self-exploration. This process is the exact opposite of experiential focusing mentioned earlier, which looks instead at different aspects of experience (direction: experience – cognition, whereas here cognition – experience). A purely 'rational' understanding without an adequate experiential (motivational-emotional) component is unlikely to be relevant for bringing about changes in the client.

Interpretation

During the course of therapy, the therapist also formulates his or her own understanding of the interpersonal and intrapersonal processes that contribute (contributed) to or maintain the client's problematic experiences. Sharing this understanding and interpretation may be an important way of developing the focus of the therapy, or it may be an important tool, embedded in the case formulation and therapeutic strategy, that helps to achieve the goals of therapy. This is especially so in psychodynamic therapies.

A significant element of developing an understanding that the therapist considers appropriate to share with the client is not only the therapist's theoretical knowledge, but also the therapist's experience of the client. This is why the therapist's understanding usually takes some time to develop. The therapist also has to be mindful of his or her own 'countertransferential' experience, which may inform, but also bias, the therapist's understanding (Gelso & Hayes, 2007).

Interpretation is often embedded in a general empathic stance so that it is not experienced as labelling or criticism (Timulak & McElvaney, 2009). It is offered to the client as a specific form of understanding of the client's experiencing in order to stimulate the client's processing of problematic emotional experiences and foster the client's understanding of his or her own behaviour. It is an expression of tentative explanation offered in a caring manner, that should help the client to group problematic experiences, resolve them, and stimulate thinking about new ways of behaving.

Interpretation is not the same as simply sharing a feeling or association emerging in the therapist's experiencing, while listening to the client's narrative. The basic structure of interpretation always stems from a particular case formulation (see Chapter 3 for examples) focused on the central problematic aspects of the client's life. In psychodynamic therapies, it can focus on interpersonal patterns, the client's handling of his or her own experiences and behaviour, significant experiences (such as important dreams) or symptoms, especially in the context of the client's goals and wishes. In cognitive-behaviour therapies, it generally focuses on the links between thinking, feelings and behaviour, with a special emphasis on explaining cognitive functioning and the appraisal of situations. In experiential therapies (e.g. emotion-focused therapy), interpretations are typically used to provide a rationale for therapeutic tasks conforming to the centrality of emotional experience in resolving problems in life.

As interpretations target the core problems that brought the client to therapy, they are typically present as a sequence of related interventions (interpretations). Often, the therapist communicates certain understanding gradually and in a complex, multi-part way (Elliott, 1984; Elliott et al., 1994). Sometimes the therapist includes the client's behaviour in the therapeutic relationship in an interpretation. In such a case, in psychodynamic terminology this is called *transference interpretation*. Some interpretations can be called *historical* as they offer a view of the client's experiencing or behaviour in the context of the client's personal history.

A good therapist's interpretation is similar to empathic conjecture in that it should be touching the edge of the client's awareness. The therapist formulates an interpretation as an offer and is ready to put it aside if it is not beneficial to the client. The therapist's interpretation may often be presented in the form of empathic response. It may be an expression of the therapist's engagement in the understanding of the client. The client may experience it as an expression of the therapist's care. An example may be a situation when the therapist caringly puts into words the reasons why a client is experiencing pain: *You want him to take more care of you. That is something you haven't had enough of in your life so far.* Or the therapist responds to a client who has experienced rejection and bullying and is now sensitive to others' evaluation: *It was such a trauma that any situation even slightly similar brings a lot of fear and apprehension.* Or the therapist responds to a present experience in the context of an important aspect of the client's self: *It irritates you when I praise you for something, because it feels like I am patronising you.*

The therapist needs to be aware that interpretation may sometimes be experienced by some clients as intrusive. Therefore, the use of interpretation needs to be carefully considered. It should primarily be used when the therapeutic relationship is well established. The therapist needs to assess whether interpretation would be beneficial to the client. It should not be a communication of some insight just for the sake of it. Repeated conclusions from empirical studies of psychodynamic therapies show that transference interpretations, in particular, may be demanding (Crits-Christoph & Connolly Gibbons, 2002; Connolly Gibbons et al., 2007). Crits-Christoph and Connolly Gibbons (2002), in their overview of studies concerning relational interpretations (transference interpretations), reached the conclusion that relational interpretations should not be frequently used in therapy, especially not with clients with a low quality of object relations (e.g. with clients who have problems in close and significant relationships). This may be overcome if the interpretation is good and well planned (Connolly Gibbons et al., 2007).

The therapist's collaborative sharing of feelings, associations, conjectures or interpretations is a unique contribution that the therapist, as 'an expert', makes to the therapeutic process. The client's wisdom naturally has its value here as well, and it is met with the therapist's knowledge in the collaborative relationship. The process of collaboration then ensues. Many interpretations are creatively used by clients (Timulak & McElvaney, 2009).

Interpretations are interventions that reinforce the client's self-conceptualisation and coherence. The coherence of self represents one of the attributes of mental well-being (Greenberg & Van Balen, 1998). Hill and O'Brien (1999) propose that interpretations offer a conceptual frame for clients and explain their problems, and thus provide the grounds for further solving them. They stress that interpretations overcome the 'incomprehensibility' of many problematic experiences and thus weaken their power (see Frank & Frank, 1991). Interpretations also reinforce the client's ability to both self-reflect and reflect on the psychological attributes of other people's behaviour. Bateman and Fonagy (2004) provide a convincing argument that the reflective function contributes to mental health, not only by enhancing self-understanding and the understanding of others, but also by promoting emotion regulation.

Stimulating therapy reflection

An important point for the consolidation of progress in therapy is to reflect on changes that have happened during therapy (provided that changes have occurred). In that reflection, it may be especially important to put the changes in the context of the client's overall life history. The therapist can not only invite the client to reflect on therapy in the context of various difficulties and life experience, but may also offer his or her own reflection as well. Reflection is often natural in the closing phases of therapy, but may also be done earlier when the course of therapy is assessed and discussed by the client and the therapist. Stimulating reflection about the eventual progress the client has made in therapy, in the context of the client's overall life history, consolidates this progress. It also helps the client to summarise the gains achieved in therapy so that he or she is able to tell 'the story of their therapy' to the outside world (Grafanaki & McLeod, 1999).

Providing information to the client

The therapist's provision of information also contributes to the client's better understanding of the self and others. During the introductory psychotherapeutic sessions, the client's uncertainty about his or her own problematic experiences and symptoms can sometimes be responded to by the provision of information. A simple example is to explain the symptoms of a panic attack (see Craske & Barlow, 2008). Providing an explanation of psychopathological symptoms is one of the basic techniques of cognitive-behavioural therapy. Within this approach, the explanation of psychopathological symptoms is used as a routine intervention at the beginning of therapy. For example, in obsessive-compulsive disorder or other anxiety disorders (and also in a number of other problems), it is very appropriate to offer the client explanations based on the latest psychological and medical knowledge.

Providing information should not be considered merely as a one-off or one-way intervention. The therapist should leave space for discussion and check how the provided information affects the client. Providing the client with information is a part of cognitive learning in therapy. The client's capacity to benefit from the new information should not be underestimated. Also, it does not mean that the whole therapy has to turn into an educational experience. It is up to the therapist to use the provision of information within the therapeutic strategy and to make sure that it does not become a rationalisation process, whereby the therapist and the client avoid the actual problem.

Focusing on the present interpersonal behaviour and experiencing of the therapeutic interaction

In the course of therapy, there may come moments when the client's and the therapist's attention focuses on their mutual interaction in order to provide an understanding of the client's interpersonal patterns. Hill and O'Brien (1999) use the term 'immediacy' to capture the therapist's expression of immediate feelings in the relationship with the client (Hill & O'Brien, 1999: 236). The therapist's intervention here focuses on the effort to understand the interpersonal behaviour of the client as it is presented in the therapeutic interaction. The goal is a deepening of the understanding of the client's central interpersonal behaviour patterns.

The appropriate situation for this therapeutic intervention is when a client's behaviour, which either the client describes in relation to other people or which the therapist notices in relation to other people in the client's story, is present in the session. Sometimes such an observation is related to conflict in the therapeutic relationship (see Chapter 2). An example of the therapist's intervention focusing on present interpersonal behaviour is given in Box 5.3.

Box 5.3 An example of focusing on the present interpersonal behaviour and experiencing of the therapeutic interaction

A female client is talking about her partner in a very disregarding way and in a similarly disregarding way she is talking about the rest of her relatives and about her previous experience with psychologists. With regard to the current therapy, she is indirectly expressing some dissatisfaction as well, despite the fact that she looks relaxed and has worked through several sensitive issues with the therapist. The therapist opens this topic by sharing his observation:

T: *The way you talk about your partner and about other people (parents, sister, friends) seems strange to me. As if there was something that does not deserve respect. Sometimes you speak in a similar way about me too. At the beginning of today's session I felt that way too. You said how I made a professional effort to appear interested but nevertheless I was not able to hide how I really felt inside – not interested. I wonder how it is for you and what you are actually trying to tell me.*

C: *I have been doing it like this because some things are very sensitive and I am afraid that others might hurt me. So I pretend that they do not matter so much and that I do not have a very good opinion about them and they are not so important to me.*

T: *You feel insecure in the relationship with your partner, you are sensitive about many things and sometimes it seems to be similar in our relationship, too. You are worried that I would hurt you, disregard you or judge you.*

C: *Yes, for example with my partner – sometimes I'm not sure whether I really matter to him.*

Focusing on the present interpersonal behaviour is a very demanding therapeutic intervention and when badly timed it may lead to non-therapeutic consequences.

It is a version of relational (transference) interpretations and research suggests that it should be done in a sensitive way, taking into consideration the client's functioning (see Crits-Christoph & Connoly-Gibbons, 2002). On the other hand, focusing on present interpersonal behaviour can be an excellent option for a fruitful exploration of the relationship, which may help to resolve discontent and uncertainty that has accumulated in the therapeutic relationship, and may also become a prototype for problem-solving in other interpersonal relationships. We will look again at work with interpersonal patterns in Chapter 8.

Skills that promote exploration and understanding are central to exploratory approaches to therapy (such as psychodynamic and humanistic therapies) and they are also important for more prescriptive approaches (cognitive-behavioural therapy). I have presented here several interventions that contribute to exploration and understanding. Many of them overlap, even though they have been described separately in this chapter. In the real therapy process, the therapist naturally uses the full repertoire of skills, switching fluently from one to another. One must bear in mind that while doing this, the therapist uses some skills more than others, depending on the type of therapy, the case conceptualisation and the specific presentation of the client.

Recommended reading

A comprehensive, research-informed account of the basic skills used in therapy is provided by Clara Hill in her best-selling book:

Hill, C.E. (2009). *Helping Skills: Facilitating Exploration, Insight, and Action.* (3rd edition). Washington, DC: American Psychological Association.

Six

Promoting Change and its Application Outside the Therapy Session

Abstract

This chapter describes some of the interventions that can be used to promote in-session changes and their application, outside the session, to the real-life context of the client. Strategies cover those that validate client change within the session as well as those that focus on planning, implementing and reviewing changes outside the session. The focus is on emotional and cognitive as well as behavioural changes. Examples are used to describe these interventions and strategies.

In this chapter we will focus on the promotion of change and its application in the client's life outside the therapy session. Both of these activities are embedded in case conceptualisation and the overall therapeutic strategy. They are also embedded in the exploration and improved understanding of the client's problems and other in-session work. Different theoretical approaches put different emphasis on work outside therapy sessions, with cognitive-behavioural approaches seeing it as a central part of the therapy process, while psychodynamic and experiential approaches place less importance on it.

Promoting change

Exploration and elaborated understanding of the client's problems naturally lead to changes, the decisions to change and implementations of changes to the client's life. The clients in successful therapy experience new ways of being that lead to conscious decisions about changing aspects of their lives. The therapist can help not only in generating these new ways of being, but also in consolidating them by focusing on their implementation in the client's life outside the session.

Acknowledging and promoting client's 'talk of change'

It is important that the therapist recognises when the client speaks about themselves differently. Motivational interviewing theory uses the term 'change talk' for capturing the client's expressions that reveal an internal motivation to change, especially with regard to problematic behaviour (Miller & Rollnick, 2002). Usually these are expressions of a genuine intention to change, a willingness to attempt to change, thinking about change, etc. (Miller & Rollnick, 2002). It is, however, important to distinguish between an authentic consideration of attempting to change and a coaching that pushes through 'shoulds' that are rather an expression of inner criticism and a harsh attitude towards the self. The problem can also lie in an authentic, but still unrealistic, expression of the attempt to change.

The client's change talk occurs quite spontaneously in empathic exploratory therapies. If it happens, it is important that the therapist captures its personal value for the client and verbally acknowledges it and validates the client's determination to change. In such instances, validation and affirmation were found to be crucial for significant, helpful impacts in session (cf. Timulak & Lietaer, 2001; Timulak & Elliott, 2003). For example, if the client explores an inner conflict about whether to pursue a career or spend more time with their family and is leaning towards staying more with the family, it is important that the therapist does not miss it, but rather acknowledges it and affirms it.

Exploring the circumstances that enable the change

Another important factor that can help the change is to consider the circumstances that affect it. The therapist can make it a focus of the exploration. Practical considerations can be what the client wants to change, why, what can help the change, what the potential obstacle are, etc. The Change Plan Worksheet from motivation enhancement therapy (Miller, 1995), which is presented in Box 6.1, represents an example of a guide to this process.

Box 6.1 The Change Plan Worksheet in motivational enhancement therapy (Miller, 1995)

CHANGE PLAN WORKSHEET

The changes I want to make are:

The most important reasons why I want to make these changes are:

The steps I plan to take in changing are:

The ways other people can help me are:

Person	Possible ways to help

I will know that my plan is working if:

Some things that could interfere with my plan are:

Exploring the circumstances that enable the change is relevant only when an authentic decision about making a behavioural change has been made by the client. (It may not be relevant for more subtle experiential/emotional changes that can have their resolution directly in therapy sessions). The therapist has to assess how viable the client's determination to change is before exploring the circumstances that will help it. The successful outcomes of brief motivation enhancement therapy (Babor & Del Boca, 2003) suggest that such changes are possible quite quickly in therapy, even in such a complicated area as alcohol addiction.

Validating the client's potential for change

Each client has his or her own resources that can be used in therapy to promote change (Grawe, 2004). It is important that the therapist gathers information on what is functional in the client's life and how it can be used in bringing about the change. For example, an anxious client may be very good academically, so the plan of exposure exercises may also involve areas such as academic performance, where it is likely that the client will succeed. Another example is a client with obsessive-compulsive disorder (OCD) whose OCD symptoms are linked to an experience of being bullied by colleagues. The client's assertive anger towards bullying can serve as a motivational source for engagement in exposure and in the prevention of rituals treatment used in combating OCD (Franklin & Foa, 2008).

Interpersonal validation of the client

Sometimes situations occur in the therapy process where the client's vulnerability needs the therapist's validation. For instance, in the case of abuse, clients, when trying to make sense of the situation, sometimes blame themselves. It is then important that the therapist recognises abusive behaviour and makes clear that the client was a victim.

Interpersonal validation may sometimes be appropriate when the client expresses vulnerability, which is typically linked with unfulfilled, deserved need. For instance, if the client was constantly invalidated by significant others and freshly experiences the hurt that it brought during the therapy process, then the therapist, recognising the validity of such a need, may verbalise it and validate it for the client. This is sometimes done in emotion-focused therapy (Greenberg, 2002). When the client freshly expresses personal hurt (e.g. not being loved), the therapist may respond to it with his or her own authentic experience and express that he or she strongly feels that the need ('to be loved') is deserved and deserves to be responded to. However, it is important that it is not done prematurely, but in the situation when the client is bringing the fragile vulnerable experience of hurt into the open. The therapist needs to make sure that he or she does not respond from his or her own inability to bear the client's hurt.

Acknowledging need and hope-promoting experience

Some significant events studies that look at the client-nominated helpful events in therapy found that clients reported as very helpful those events in which the therapist acknowledged and empathically responded to hope, which was often connected to a need that was part of the client's experience (Timulak & Lietaer, 2001; Timulak & Elliott, 2003). These were typically events in which the client was in the midst of a vulnerable experience which also contained a hope-evoking facet that the therapist sensed and responded to affirmatively. These events were usually very idiosyncratic and central to the client in therapy. An example of such an event from a research study is presented in Box 6.2.

Box 6.2 An example of the therapist's acknowledgement of the client's need

This excerpt comes from a therapy case that was part of research on significant helpful events in brief person-centred therapy (Timulak & Lietaer, 2001). The therapist was a male psychologist in his mid-twenties and the client a young female. The excerpt starts in the twentieth minute of the second session. The client was querying whether the therapist experiences similar problems to those she does. After the session, a researcher interviewed the client and then, separately, the therapist. Part of the interview was a reflection on this excerpt. The client saw the therapist's intervention, marked by the asterisk, as significantly helpful.

C: *It is somehow deeper ... and even I do not know what it is (pause). It is as if I want to know a lot about you [the therapist] and that may mean that I am somehow bad ... as if a feeling of guilt has started to develop ... that I want to ask you something (pause). It is as if in order to trust you, I need to take something from you, or so ... (pause, 7 seconds).*

T: *By answering you, you take something off me.*

C: *Hum ... yes. Your space. Something. I can be intrusive you know (T: Aha, aha). As if I had a feeling that I am insecure, because I am insecure, that I want to know that the other has some weaknesses, and this is what I see as being bad. Bad is a strong word, but something like that ...*

T: *You can be bad to me.*

C: *Yes on you, to you, yes, yes. Such a feeling that I am not ... in myself ... and then well, yes ... (silence, 26 seconds).*

C: *It is interesting, I cannot continue in it. It is stuck, I cannot get further what is behind that ... It is strange for me (silence 8 seconds), because it somehow touches that barrier with people ... now I just touched on ... I just sense it, but I do not know it. I just feel it that it is connected. Something like, I think, I don't know, that I am somehow intrusive. Do you know what I mean? And that I should not. (T: Uhm) And that I do not have the courage to be intrusive and therefore I do not say many things, because I think I could make people uncomfortable or so (pause). But because I need it and I do not do it, thus I am taking away something from me (silence, 5 seconds).*

**T:* *It goes together for me (C: Yes). If I was myself and I am direct, then I can hurt them (C: yeah), and then I'm afraid that I'm bad (C: Yeah) in essence (C: Exactly). But if I do not do it, I feel bound (C: yeah) and the relationship is also not as you would like it (C: Exactly). (Pause).* *(The last part of the therapist's utterance acknowledges the client's need to be direct and maybe intrusive. The therapist is attuned, and by naming it is basically suggesting that their relationship is different, because it can be talked about here.)

(Continued)

(Continued)

C: Yeah... I am not fully in such a relationship ... I am afraid to say something about myself because I do not know the person ... I can't get through it ... because I'm afraid to open up, and as I do not ask them anything they are strangers for me. And ... (pause, 4 seconds) and it's strange ... I feel that it is helping me, but I do not want to rush it.... What I am saying ... something is resolving in me ... but I am cautious as if it could change quickly (T: yeah.) that I could have a different feeling.

In the interview after the session the client said about this moment:

I felt safe, I felt inner strength, felt relieved in the middle of my body, it was very liberating. These were things that I felt guilty about and I had a feeling that the therapist is accepting these feelings and these feelings disappeared. I felt that the therapist is very attentive, that he perceives the things that I am saying, that he understands and feels.

The therapist typically acknowledges an important hope-promoting aspect of the client's experience spontaneously as part of the empathic engagement in the client's process. The therapist thus provides an existential experience that the client's experience is recognised by the other and empathically understood. This may be encouraging for the client. The client may build on hope thus experienced and resonated with. For instance, when a female client who lost her partner in a car accident says that she has since remained alone, the therapist's acknowledgement of that experience, together with an acknowledgement of what the partner meant to the client, may bring this appreciation to the fore. This appreciation may activate the part of the experience that also appreciates the value of the fact that there was such a relationship.

Generating alternative emotional experience (self-organisation)

Emotion-focused therapy (Greenberg, 2002) puts an emphasis on transforming problematic emotions (emotion schemas) through the generation of alternative emotional states and emotionally-laden self-organisation. Thus problematic emotions, such as fear or shame of being harshly evaluated by the self or others, are undone by generating self-compassion and protective anger (see Greenberg, 2002). Once the painful emotions are accessed in therapy, the need for counteracting emotions can be attended to and those emotions can be brought up, experienced and enacted in therapy. For instance, shrinking shame, which is experienced by a client when he remembers being bullied when he was small, may be associated with the need for protective anger and self-compassion, which expresses caring for and protecting the bullied self (see Box 6.3). In a similar way to emotion-focused therapy, cognitive therapy (another empirically informed therapy) uses strategies to counteract anxiety and depression triggered by a cognitive appraisal with more empowering emotions which help to build a determination to face anxiety-promoting stimuli and create one's own sense of value.

Box 6.3 An example of generating protective anger and self-compassion which counteracts the fear and shame of being bullied. The therapist uses an empty chair exercise (for more detail see Chapter 7)

This transcript comes from the therapy of a client (Mark – a pseudonym) in his late twenties. The focus here is on feelings of fear of being judged negatively and how it relates to a past experience, when he felt the same when he was being bullied. The transcript starts when the client is attempting to remember a specific incident of being judged negatively in the past. The transcript is abbreviated at different points.

C: *That feeling that sticks out well is the boys when I was in first class. I told you about that before* (the client refers to bullying that he mentioned before).

T: *Yeah, you were four or five at the time, oh first class 6 yeah.*

C: *About 6 yeah. Definitely, yeah that comes in straight away. Even though it's so long ago that definitely does stick with me.*

T: *So who was the bully?*

C: *There was a few but there was a main guy called Dave.*

T: *OK. Could you picture him here? Yes.* (This is an empty chair technique – see Greenberg, Rice, and Elliott, 1993; see also Chapter 7.)

C: *Yeah.*

T: *Can you tell him kind of about how his behaviour makes you feel or made you feel or affects you?* (It would be better first to ask Mark how he feels when he imagines Dave, to get the emotional experience.)

C: *When you were you know, bullying me and stuff like that, like you completely ostracised me from the whole of the class. Em, you made me feel unnormal. It made me feel an outsider it just ... it completely made me feel insignificant and different and for no apparent reason you just, you know, you picked on me, completely ostracised me from the class and it just ... I didn't want to come in to school because, you know, I had no friends because of you. You made everyone look at me and, ye know, and not hang around with me and stuff like that, so it was quite belittling.*

T: *Can you switch and be him for a second? How do you make Mark insignificant, make him feel insignificant? How is he doing it? What makes him insignificant?* (This is done to highlight and bring to awareness what in the perceived behaviour of the alleged bully was most painful for the client.) (*Silence, 6 seconds*)

(Continued)

(Continued)

C: *Em, don't talk to me. I don't want to talk to you. Em, it's weird, I have this vivid memory of one time.*

T: *What would he do?*

C: *Em, he was ... another person shaking my hand and he came and said, look, how did he shake his hand and because ... like that ... don't talk to him sort of thing* (unclear). *That's a big memory I have, it's probably one of the only ones that sticks out.*

T: *Tell it to the other guy. Yes, don't shake the hand of Mark, yes* (still enacting the painful perception).

C: *Don't shake his hand, like, because why do you want to talk to him. I don't want to talk to him. I don't want to talk to him, like.*

T: *What's in it, what's the message in it, yes?*

C: *It's just he's insignificant. There's no point talking to him. I don't like him.*

T: *I don't like him, he's insignificant, yes* (amplifying emotionally painful perception).

C: *Yes.*

T: *He's nothing yeah, OK.*

C: *Yeah.*

T: *You did a little more with that than you did here why you should care* (more amplifying and pointing to the non-verbal behaviour)....

C: *Yeah I think when someone does that while they are giving out to you it's a belittling gesture. You know, it's like you're* (unclear) *kinda thing, You know.*

T: *Can you switch? Can you just check what happens inside when you get this* (unclear)? (The therapist elicits the emotional impact of the perceived behaviour of the other.) *What happens for you?*

C: *Sorry I'd.. anxious and tightness inside here.*

T: *OK. Could you tell him what's happening for you. What would you respond to it. How does it make you feel.* (The therapist facilitates enactment of difficult emotion.)

C: *It makes me feel belittled, it makes me feel different, abnormal, I mean there's no innate reason why you should think that or why you should not speak to me or get other people to speak to me and so what you are doing is just belittling me, reducing my self-confidence, ye know, making me feel insignificant.*

T: *So you do not deserve it.* (probing for a resilient and protective anger that would counteract feelings of shame and inadequacy).

C: *Yeah.*

T: *You have no right to talk to me* (coaching the client to express protective anger).

C: *No. You have no right to say even if you feel that way, don't be rude about it and don't also drag everybody else into it and that.*

T: *It's none of your business. Tell him more about it.*

C: *I mean it.. it's completely an unprecedented attack. There's no, ye know, there is no reason why you should do it. I've done nothing wrong to you so I ... I can't understand why you're doing this. It makes me feel even worse because I don't know the reason. I feel more self-conscious in case I'm doing something wrong, em, you just, you have no right to do it and even if I've done something wrong explain to me what I've done instead of just, ye know, being rude and giving out and bringing everyone along with you.*

T: *I have no sense why you're picking on me why you slagged me. It's just so unfair and I can't kind of protect myself.*

C: *Yeah, cos I feel so self-conscious now because I ... I don't understand why.*

T: *This was really hurtful, yes. This was really hurtful, what you were doing.*

C: *Yeah, this was really hurtful, really hurtful.*

T: *and I was a small boy who couldn't do anything about it* (empathic conjecture, probing for the experience of vulnerability that could elicit self-compassion).

C: *Yeah. I and it was for no reason as well, so something which just baffles me. Em, I just don't understand why?*

T: *It's really, kind of, I don't have any power to protect myself because its just so...*

C: *But I've no defence, because I have no idea why you are doing it. So I can't protect myself, ye know, at least if it was for a reason, for something I did or how I acted or something, I could either apologise or change that, but because there is no reason I've no way to defend myself, ye know. It's, it's just painful because you know I don't know the reasons, so I just keep playing it over and over.*

T: *Can you switch here and be adult Mark now? What would you tell the 6 year-old Mark, yourself? Tell him now.* (This aims at the enactment of self-soothing, self-compassion and self-protection from an adult part in the client.)

C: *Dave is just a kid. He may be a troubled kid, you don't know that and for some reason he's picking on you and there's no reason for it. He's just chosen you to pick on so, ye know you have to take it in your stride. You're* (unclear) *whatever, but don't let it get in on you because he actually is doing it for no reason. He's got problems of his own which is why he is doing it. Obviously he just he needs to feel powerful, whatever, but it's not because you're weird or you're different or whatever. I know that it makes you feel that, but it's actually not. It's his problem and not yours, so I know that it's hard but take it in your stride and just, ye know, if he's bullying you a lot tell the teachers or, ye know, if you can ignore him and hopefully it will pass. But just know that it's not because you're weird or insignificant or anything like that. It's purely his basis of whatever is troubling him or is calling him to bully you.*

T: *So it has nothing to do with you.*

C: *Yeah.*

(Continued)

(Continued)

...

T: *OK. Can you change? How is it to hear this? To hear this as the small Mark, small Mark in you?* (Checking whether self-soothing brought calming and reassuring impact.)

C: *Yeah, Yeah. I guess it's relieving. It's sort of, ye know, accept the confidence booster, because you kind of, I kind of feel well maybe it's not me, it's just him, ye know. I did nothing wrong, so I've nothing to understand.*

T: *Now tell Dave here yes it's not me, it's your problems. ... Tell him.*

C: *I done nothing wrong to you. I've never been rude to you. I haven't, ye know, done anything to annoy you, so all I can think of is the reason you're picking on me is because either you're troubled at home – you like power – or you just have a nasty streak in you because there is no good reason why you pick on me so ... Although I don't understand, I know it's not me, so I think there is something innately wrong with you or going wrong in your life that's causing you to bully, but I know it's not me so I'm just going to ignore you.*

T: *So it's kind of stop, yes? And I'm probably just too nice to you or I was probably too nice to allow you or something. You have no right to say to somebody don't shake hands with him or that you're somehow not ok.*

....

C: *So just leave me be and allow other people to do what they want, because if you don't like me, don't talk to me. That's fine, but just don't be getting other people to gang up on me as well.*

T: *OK. How is it telling it to him?* (The therapist is checking for impact.)

C: *It feels good. It feels kind of, ye know, trying to put him back. It's not, I suppose, put him back in his place, ye know just.*

T: *OK. If this was him (pointing to a pillow), where would you put him in his place. Just put him somewhere* (encouraging enactment of the emotional experience).

C: *Somewhere.*

T: *Yeah. Wherever where would you put him in his place, you are saying. Physically get him and get him somewhere.*

C: *I could always throw him out the door (laugh).*

T: *(laugh) Yeah, maybe you can.*

C: *I'd like to put him there (points to corner).*

T: *How does it feel?*

C: *It feels good just get him out of here, ye know. Yeah, it feels good.*

T: *It's also important that you know how to get this resolved for yourself, ye know, that you kind of build it so that you can get the sense of it, that it kind of empowers you as well, that it's more tangible or something.*

The excerpt shows how feelings of shame and fear of being exposed to similar experiences can be gradually resolved (if this was repeated across sessions) by accessing a protective anger and self-compassion.

When responding to problematic emotions by generating a healthy emotional response, painful emotions cannot be by-passed. Rather, they need to be attended to, differentiated, experienced, and only then the need for counteracting emotions can be distilled (Pascual-Leone & Greenberg, 2007). I will present some of the experiential and cognitive techniques that can be used for this process in Chapter 7.

Generating an alternative cognitive perspective (self-organisation)

Cognitive restructuring used in cognitive therapy focuses on challenging rigid anxiety- and depression-triggering appraisals of situations and developing more benign and flexible appraisal skills in their place (Beck et al., 1979; Westbrook, Kennerley, & Kirk, 2007; Barlow, 2008). Cognitive restructuring is used to target the crucial appraisals contributing to the client's difficulties. The client is taught to be able to generate alternative, healthier appraisals and to be able to use them. I will present this technique in Chapter 7.

Generating alternative behaviour

In the same way that cognitive restructuring is used to generate healthier cognitive appraisals of situations, so behavioural therapy uses the prescription of behaviours that counteract depressive moods. This technique, called behaviour activation, is a very powerful tool in building up resilience towards depression. Similarly, behavioural therapy uses exposure to stimuli which trigger anxiety and avoidance as a means of overcoming problematic anxiety symptoms. Exposure builds the client's resilience in the face of anxiety-provoking situations and eventually the client overcomes them by learning that they are sustainable. I will present both of these techniques in Chapter 7.

The application of changes outside the therapy sessions

Once changes are experienced within the therapy sessions, it is important to implement them in the client's life. Only then does therapy lead to real-life outcomes. The therapist may support this process by specific interventions, examples of which I will review here.

Stimulating the application of changes outside the therapy sessions

Once the client experiences a partial or full emotional resolution in the session, or enacts new behaviour or thinking that is accompanied by emotional resolution, it is important to build on such experiences and take them outside the therapy session. Sometimes this process happens spontaneously and the client comes up with his or her own determination to change things in his or her life. At other times, the therapist promotes the planning of steps that will aid change outside the session.

In cognitive-behavioural therapy, the behaviour that may change a problematic mood or may lead to learning that anxiety does not need to be avoided in certain situations that provoke it, but rather faced, experienced and contained, is the central feature of therapy. In some cases, such as behavioural activation for low mood technique, the rehearsal of a new behaviour outside the session does not even need to be preceded by new emotional experiences or insights in the therapy session. In other cases, such as exposure-based techniques for combating anxiety, the *in vivo* exposure is sometimes preceded by exposure in the imagination, which is done in the therapy session (Franklin & Foa, 2008). Despite the fact that concentrating on the application of a new behaviour is the focus specifically of CBT therapies, many other therapists probably use interventions stimulating it in their practice. That it is beneficial is clearly supported by research (see Grawe, 1996; Wonell & Hill, 2000).

Exploratory therapies, such as experiential and psychodynamic approaches, typically do not explicitly focus on changes outside the therapy session. At the same time, some newer approaches, such as emotion-focused therapy, use homework that explicitly consolidates gains attained in therapy. For example, if the client forgives a significant other for a behaviour that caused hurt, the therapist invites the client to think about how this forgiveness can be marked outside the therapy session in the client's life.

Some practical steps, such as planning new behaviour in small stages, rewarding oneself after accomplishing the new behaviour, monitoring progress, etc., may be useful in promoting a new behaviour (see Hill, 2009). It may not always be relevant for the client to change outside the therapy session. Experienced relief, emotional resolution and insight may sometimes be sufficient result for the client (see Timulak, 2007). On the other hand, it may sometimes be difficult to implement changes if the client's social environment does not allow it. For example, if the client is a victim of ongoing abuse and lives with the abuser, it may be difficult to expect that they try to actively overcome limitations stemming from PTSD symptoms. Social intervention may then be more appropriate (see Chapter 9).

Rehearsing new behaviour

Applying changes outside the therapy session may sometimes be preceded by trying them out in the therapy session. For example, the client has difficulty in looking after his or her own needs and being appropriately and protectively self-assertive in relationships at work. The client can rehearse appropriate assertive behaviour with the therapist, for instance by imagining that the therapist is a colleague at work. More authentic rehearsal may be attempted if the client tries to be assertive in the relationship with the therapist. The client can enact assertive behaviour, stating his or her needs and expectations from the therapist. The client may try to say to the therapist what he or she was reluctant to say out of fear or courtesy to the therapist previously, for instance, that he or she is annoyed with the therapist yawning in the sessions. Such rehearsal would also represent a good opportunity for a successful interpersonal experience as one would expect the therapist to be receptive to such self-assertion and to support it.

Rehearsal of the new behaviour is typical for behavioural approaches, less so for more exploratory approaches. However, in its authentic form, when enacted in the relationship with the therapist, it can be used in a variety of approaches provided that it fits the therapist's strategy, as informed by the case conceptualisation. The authentic encounter with the therapist may be a powerful therapeutic experience (see the value of personal contact in Timulak, 2007). The in-session experience of a new behaviour, rehearsed and enacted in the relationship with the therapist, may then be readily followed by similar outside-session behaviour.

Monitoring the application of changes

The therapist not only supports the client's focus on applying changes to his or her behaviour outside therapy sessions, but also actively monitors how these attempts go for the client. The therapist naturally reviews how the client handled any behaviour that was agreed in the therapy session. The therapist may focus on how the client experienced the new behaviour, what was difficult, what went particularly well and what can be learned from that experience. Cognitive-behavioural approaches sometimes even use the therapist's presence when the client enacts a new behaviour, especially in the case of exposure technique.

Monitoring the application of changes allows both parties to pick up any difficulties that the client may experience. It may lead to the readjustment of strategy if it did not work out as planned. It also contributes to the compatibility of sessions and outside-session activities.

Reviewing the application of new behaviour and changes in therapy

Just as the therapist encourages ongoing monitoring of how the client applies new behaviour in his or her life, so the therapist may also encourage a more broad and general evaluation and review of it. This may involve an element of evaluating the outcome of therapy with regard to the client's original presentation, and also with regard to the stated goals of the therapy. Formal instruments, using idiosyncratic accounts of the current client state such as *Target Complaints* (Battle et al., 1966) or

Personal Questionnaire (Elliott, Mack, & Shapiro, 1999), or standardised methods such as *Outcome Questionnaire-45* (Lambert, Morton, & Hatfield, 2004) or *CORE-OM* (Barkham et al., 2001) may be used for that purpose too.

Such a review naturally occurs in the final phases of therapy. The therapist may seek feedback not only about how the client experienced therapy – what was helpful or what was difficult – but may stimulate the client to look at how the client changed while in therapy. The therapist may ask, for instance: *What did therapy give you? How did you change? What else would you like to change?* The therapist may also focus on the anticipated difficulties that the client may encounter in the future. This type of review can be done repeatedly at different significant stages of therapy, such as in the tenth session, or the twentieth session.

The role of the review of changes acquired in therapy and of the implementation of new behaviour outside the therapy session serves as further consolidation of gains achieved in therapy. Grafanaki and McLeod (1999) refer to the 'story of therapy' that the client and the therapist co-construct together, and that can be presented to the outside world as a coherent whole. The review is important for obtaining a sense of closure and a clear conceptualisation about what has happened in therapy and what further work awaits the client in his or her life.

In this chapter we reviewed skills that may promote emotional, cognitive and behavioural change inside the therapy session and consolidate it further outside the therapy session. The skills presented here often follow exploration- and understanding-promoting skills and activities. The use of particular skills is embedded in the therapist's strategy, which is informed by the therapist's case conceptualisation and the client's in-session presentation. The skills that have been presented in the last two chapters are sometimes complemented by a sequence of steps – therapeutic techniques – that are the subject of Chapter 7.

Recommended reading

Useful promotion of change strategies and interventions are also reviewed in the following books:

Egan, G. (2006). *Essentials of Skilled Helping*. Pacific Grove, CA: Thomson/Wadsworth.

Hill, C.E. (2009). *Helping Skills: Facilitating Exploration, Insight, and Action* (3rd edition). Washington, DC: American Psychological Association.

Seven
Specific Therapeutic Techniques

Abstract

This chapter describes sequences of interventions that are called techniques or tasks. It presents a number of cognitive, behavioural and experiential techniques that are used in different approaches to therapy to target problematic experiences strategically in order to bring about their resolution. The selected techniques have one thing in common, they are all research-informed and can be learned as more or less stand-alone strategies. However, they should only be used in conjunction with an appropriate case conceptualisation.

All of the skills presented so far are typically used in a basic therapeutic interview. Sometimes, however, skills focused on the promotion of exploration, understanding and especially the promotion of change can be linked together in a series of steps that can be labelled a technique. Some authors also describe them as therapy tasks (e.g. Greenberg, Rice, & Elliott, 1993). Techniques or tasks are especially typical for cognitive-behavioural therapies, but some experiential approaches, such as emotion-focused therapy or Gestalt therapy, use their own experiential techniques. The use of specific therapeutic techniques is embedded in case conceptualisation and is used strategically in accordance with it. Many of the techniques were developed empirically, or they were at least studied extensively. We will look at examples of techniques that focus on cognitive processes, behaviour and (emotional) experiencing. At the end of the chapter we will also look at an empirically-informed way of working with dreams.

Cognitive techniques

Cognitive techniques are an important feature of cognitive-behavioural therapies. They have their roots in Beck's cognitive therapy and Ellis's rational-emotive therapy. The main use of these techniques is in identifying cognitions or images that stir problematic emotions (low mood and anxiety) and in changing them (Beck et al., 1979; Westbrook, Kennerley, & Kirk, 2007). There exist several distinct cognitive techniques, such as identifying cognitions and their impact, identifying cognitive errors, appraising cognitions, gathering evidence supporting and contradicting cognitions (see Beck et al., 1979; Westbrook, Kennerley, & Kirk, 2007). What they have in common is that they feed into overall cognitive restructuring.

Cognitive restructuring

Originally, cognitive restructuring was used in Beck's cognitive therapy of depression (Beck et al., 1979) for combating rapid, automatic, depressogenic thoughts, evoking low mood. Over the years, this technique has undergone many adaptations in different forms of cognitive-behavioural therapy. It is used to combat automatic negative thoughts, negative core beliefs, anxiety-provoking thoughts (worries), obsessions, and so on (see Barlow, 2008). Cognitive restructuring is firmly based on cognitive case formulation (see Chapter 3, Figure 3.2) and assumes that an underlying automatic thought or belief generates problematic emotional states and/or behaviour and therefore needs to be restructured to become more benign. Although some CBT theorists (e.g. Barlow, 2002) point out that the relationship between cognitions and emotions is not simply a case of thoughts preceding emotions or behaviour, restructuring of cognitions may nevertheless positively influence both emotions and behaviour.

Beck et al. (1979) originally referred to cognitions or images as being the key focus of cognitive restructuring. They referred to emotionally significant cognitions (hot thoughts). Other authors (e.g. Barlow, 2002; Allen, McHugh, & Barlow, 2008) refer to negative appraisals, stressing that it is the evaluative aspect of the cognitive processing that is problematic. Classical cognitive restructuring (see Beck et al., 1979; Westbrook, Kennerley, & Kirk, 2007) focuses on two aspects of cognitions: process and content. With regard to the *process* component of working with cognitions, it is important to be able to:

- *Identify cognitions.* This can sometimes be difficult as thoughts may be quick or the client may have a stream of thought processes, making it difficult to pick the most emotionally-charged cognition. Diaries can be used to monitor the client's emotional state and the thought processes linked to it. Sometimes the client needs to re-enact the situation or go to the problematic situation so that he or she can identify the problematic thought. The focus is on so-called 'hot cognitions', that is cognitions linked to the most significant emotions (Westbrook, Kennerley, & Kirk, 2007).
- *Identify problematic thought processes.* Clients are often engaged in a number of 'thinking errors' (see Box 7.1). These need to be identified, explained to the client, and the client has to learn strategies to overcome them. For example, if the client has 'dichotomous, all-or-nothing thinking', he or she can learn to use a wider range of ways of evaluating the problem (e.g. see Westbrook, Kennerley, & Kirk, 2007: 122).

Box 7.1 Common thinking 'errors' (Westbrook, Kennerley, & Kirk, 2007: 115)

Extreme thinking – e.g. dichotomous, all-or-nothing thinking, catastrophisation.
Selective attention – e.g. over-generalisation, magnification and minimalisation.
Relying on intuition – e.g. jumping to conclusions, emotional reasoning.
Self-reproach – e.g. self-blame, taking things personally.

The main aspect of work with cognitions from the *process perspective* is learning to identify them, to see how they are linked with emotions, to notice cognitive errors and to be able to develop more flexible and differentiated cognitive reasoning. Some authors see this flexibility as especially central (Allen, McHugh, & Barlow, 2008).

With regard to the *content* of problematic cognitions, we focus on the most pervasive, emotionally significant and recurrent themes that contain specific core beliefs and assumptions. We monitor problematic automatic thoughts (see Beck et al., 1979) and work on the restructuring of them directly. Over time we may also focus on the underlying assumptions (beliefs) from which the problematic automatic thoughts stem. For instance, in a specific situation of giving a lecture, I may have a thought that '*the audience will perceive me as not particularly clever*', which may stem from the underlying belief that '*something is fundamentally wrong with me*'. The therapeutic work would then focus on restructuring the problematic automatic thoughts as well as the underlying beliefs.

The work on cognitive restructuring consists of several steps (e.g. Westbrook, Kennerley, & Kirk, 2007; see also Table 7.1):

TABLE 7.1 *Steps of the cognitive restructuring according to Westbrook et al. (2007)*

1. Situation	2. Feeling	3.Thoughts	4. Why I draw this conclusion	5. What conflicts with my conclusion	6. New Conclusion	7. Researching it

(1) The automatic thoughts or beliefs, as well as the emotional reaction that they trigger or accompany, are identified.
(2) The level of how believable they are is assessed.
(3) Evidence supporting them is gathered exhaustively.
(4) Alternative evidence that challenges them is gathered.
(5) The level of how believable the original thoughts are is assessed again. Alternatively, the believability of the evidence counteracting the evidence behind the problematic automatic thought is assessed.

Normally, if done properly, a reduction in how believable the problematic automatic thoughts are, as well as a reduction in problematic emotional experience, is observed. Furthermore, new conclusions are drawn based on the evidence challenging the original problematic thought. These may be further supported by behavioural experiments that can consolidate them. For example, my thought that *'the audience will perceive me as not particularly clever'* may be based on (evidence) memories of having disengaged audiences, overhearing criticism of one of my lectures, etc. The opposite evidence or explanation may be: some of my lectures went well and the audience was very responsive; there is no direct link between liking the lecture and judging how clever I am. For example, even if they did not like the lecture, they may attribute it to them being not prepared, etc. The original believability is much lower and I am starting to build a new conclusion, such as *'the quality of the lecture has more to do with the audience and the content and form of the presentation than with how clever I am'*. Then I can further test this new conclusion in a behavioural experiment. For example, I can survey anonymously the audience's views of the lecture and the lecturer to see whether perspectives vary and whether they assess how clever I am.

There are different ways of conducting cognitive restructuring (e.g. McHugh, & Barlow, Allen, 2008; Young et al., 2008). All of them are focused and collaborative, trying to obtain evidence that makes the problematic automatic thought more benign. Cognitive restructuring is always embedded in a particular, usually cognitive, case formulation. It is often used in the cognitive-behavioural treatment of depression and anxiety disorders, but also with other disorders. Some authors (Allen, McHugh, & Barlow, 2008) emphasise the usefulness of cognitive restructuring in building a flexible appraisal style rather than in having a strategy that can calm and relax the client. They point to the fact that cognitive restructuring, if used in states of heightened negative emotions, can serve as an emotional avoidance strategy, which can be problematic from a longer-term perspective. Therefore, they recommend working on reappraisal prior to the situations that evoke problematic emotions, so that the overall flexibility of the appraisal style can be enhanced regardless of the anxiety evoked in specific situations.

The majority of authors and Beck et al.'s (1979) original approach use cognitive restructuring as a technique that can be learned and then applied by the client outside the therapy session, and then reviewed in the session. For that purpose, forms such as the Daily Records of Dysfunctional Thoughts are used (Beck et al., 1979; Young et al., 2008) (see Table 7.2). The forms are first used for monitoring and identifying negative automatic thoughts and then for combating them.

TABLE 7.2 *The Daily Record of Dysfunctional Thoughts (adapted from Beck et al., 1979; Možný & Praško 1999; Young et al., 2008) Adapted with permission from Guilford Press.*

Date and time	**Situation:** 1. Describe the event leading to unpleasant emotion or 2. Describe stream of thoughts, daydream or recollection leading to unpleasant emotion	**Emotion:** 1. Specify emotion: e.g. sadness, anxiety, anger 2. Rate the degree of unpleasantness on a scale of 0–100%	**Thought:** 1. Write automatic thought(s) connected with the emotion 2. How much do you believe in it (on a scale of 0–100%)?	**Rational response:** 1. Write adaptive response to automatic thought(s) 2. How much do you believe in it (on a scale of 0–100%)?	**Result:** 1. Re-rate belief in automatic thought (on a scale 0–100%) 2. Specify and rate emotions (on a scale of 0–100%) 3. What can I do?

As mentioned above, cognitive restructuring can also target the underlying assumptions (primary assumptions; Beck et al., 1979) from which the problematic automatic thoughts originate. These are basic assumptions (beliefs) about oneself and the world.

In the case of depression, for which cognitive therapy was originally developed, these assumptions, together with cognitive errors, were the triggers of depression. Cognitive restructuring of these primary assumptions (beliefs) follows a similar course to the work with automatic thoughts. They need, however, to be identified first.

Cognitive restructuring is a well-established and widely used method, typically as a part of cognitive and cognitive-behavioural therapies. Despite the fact that it is widely used, there is not much evidence about its relative contribution to otherwise effective cognitive-behavioural therapies. Studies (see Ahn & Wampold, 2001) often do not find an added benefit in cognitive restructuring compared to other aspects of cognitive-behavioural treatment. However, a study of Dobson et al. (2008), comparing cognitive-behavioural therapy to behavioural activation in the treatment of depression, suggests that there may be a delayed additional effect of cognitive restructuring. Cognitive restructuring can thus be an important skill that clients can learn.

Behavioural techniques

Behavioural techniques are an important part of behavioural and cognitive-behavioural approaches. There exist a range of behavioural techniques that are used on the basis of a particular case conceptualisation, targeting the problem that brought the client to therapy. They include systematic desensitisation, planning of activities, different forms of rehearsal, graded task assignments, assertiveness training and so on (see Beck et al., 1979; Westbrook et al., 2007; Bennet-Levy et al., 2004). I will focus on the three most often used techniques: (1) behavioural experiments that are linked to cognitive restructuring; and two well researched techniques: (2) behaviour activation for mood improvement; and (3) exposure to anxiety-provoking stimuli.

Behavioural experiments

Behavioural experiments are used primarily in cognitive-behavioural therapy. They are used in the service of cognitive restructuring. They stem from a cognitive case formulation and may be used:

(1) to test particular problematic beliefs;
(2) to test newly formulated adaptive beliefs; or
(3) as a means of obtaining further data for cognitive formulation (Bennet-Levy et al., 2004).

Cognitive therapy puts a lot of emphasis on linking the sessions' process with the actual client behaviour outside the session. Any cognitive work uses data obtained on the basis of observing one's cognitive processes in an everyday action. Any work on cognitive restructuring is supported by gathering evidence in reality and testing newly formulated beliefs in it. For example, a client with social anxiety and the fear of being observed and judged negatively by fellow travellers on the train (belief) may (a) observe what he sees on the train and how he responds to it experientially (gathering data), (b) may then test his belief by gathering evidence that speaks for and against this belief, and finally, hopefully later in successful therapy, (c) test a new belief that fellow travellers are benign and do not pay much attention to him.

Behavioural experiments may need to be used creatively. They need to be collaboratively and carefully constructed so that they support the client's involvement in therapy. They should also be regularly reviewed and reflected on (see Chapter 6). Many valuable practical tips are outlined, for example, in the work of Westbrook, Kennerley, & Kirk, (2007).

Behaviour activation

Behaviour activation (BA) is an important component of cognitive-behavioural therapy for depression (e.g. Beck et al., 1979). It can also be found as a stand-alone therapy (Dimidjian et al., 2008). The roots of this intervention are in the work of Ferster (1973) and Lewinsohn (1974) on behavioural therapy for depression (see Hopko et al., 2003) and in the work of Beck and colleagues in their cognitive therapy for depression. The empirical work of Jacobson et al. (1996), who tested whether the effectiveness of CBT could be explained by BA, was also influential.

Behaviour activation is embedded in a behavioural case conceptualisation. The main idea is that behaviour is linked to mood, and promoting mood-improving behaviour and overcoming behavioural avoidance leads to a change in the depressive mood (Dimidjian et al., 2008). Behaviour activation first needs to be explained to the client (Dimidjian et al., 2008). The therapist explains that there is a link between an event in the client's life and his or her feelings. A thorough functional analysis of the client's behaviour is conducted. This is done through a careful monitoring of daily activity (Dimidjian et al., 2008) (see Table 7.3). Case conceptualisation of what contributes to depression is performed. The link between the mood and activity is established and activities that enhance pleasurable, positive emotions are assigned. Also, activities that are avoided due to worry or fear are addressed, so that the avoidance is targeted and overcome. The homework is carefully planned, including positive or negative contingencies that will reinforce the enactment of prescribed activity (see details in Dimidjian et al., 2008).

Graded task assignment (Beck et al., 1979) may also be used so that the plan can be achieved. This means that an activity is broken down into small, manageable steps and achieved gradually, while progress is constantly reviewed. Special attention is focused on avoidant behaviour and the motivation behind the avoidance. Trouble-shooting

TABLE 7.3 *Weekly Activity Record (adapted from Dimidjian et al., 2008). Adapted with permisssion from Guilford press.*

Hour	Monday	Tuesday	Wednesday	Thursday	Friday	Saturday	Sunday
6–8							
8–10							
10–12							
12–2							
2–4							
4–6							
6–8							
8–10							
10–12							

and problem-solving strategies are used to overcome the avoidance (Dimidjian et al., 2008). Rumination, so typical in depression, is combated by promoting full experiential engagement with different activities (for details, see Dimidjian et al., 2008). Every step of behaviour activation is carefully monitored and reviewed, with frequent contact between the therapist and client in-between the sessions. Also, sessions are scheduled twice a week at the onset of therapy (for details, see Dimidjian et al., 2008).

There is very good evidence pointing to the power of BA. Behaviour activation has been shown to be as effective as the full package of CBT for depression (Jacobson et al., 1996; Dimidjian et al., 2006; Dobson et al., 2008), with potentially better effectiveness in the acute phase of the treatment (Dimidjian et al., 2008) and somewhat lower effectiveness in the follow-up (Dobson et al., 2008).

Exposure

Exposure is an imaginary or real (*in vivo*) exposing of oneself to the triggers of anxiety. A special form of exposure is an interoceptive exposure, in which the client is exposed to his or her own bodily symptoms (e.g., feeling dizzy after spinning), which resemble anxiety symptoms (Barlow & Craske, 2007; Craske & Barlow, 2008). Typically, exposure is part of the cognitive-behavioural package, but it can also be a stand-alone behavioural treatment. The effectiveness of exposure is well established and it is probably the most researched and most effective psychological intervention (Woody & Ollendick, 2006).

Exposure is the most frequently used technique in the treatment of the variety of anxiety disorders. For example, in the treatment of panic disorder, with or without agoraphobia, interoceptive exposure is used so that the client can overcome his or her own misappraisal of the bodily symptoms of anxiety (see Barlow & Craske, 2007; Craske & Barlow, 2008). This treatment also uses exposure *in vivo* so that the client can learn to overcome situations that he or she avoids because he or she expects the onset of a panic attack. The *in vivo* exposure is performed in a gradual manner, starting from the least anxiety-provoking and moving towards the most anxiety-provoking situations that the client avoids (Craske & Barlow, 2008). In the case of obsessive-compulsive disorder (see Franklin & Foa, 2008), exposure can be used in its imaginary form (where the client stays in the imagined situation that brings on anxious obsessions) and in its *in vivo* form (where the client engages in the activities that produce the obsessions). Again, a hierarchy of obsessions-triggering situations is used. Exposure, in the case of working with obsessive-compulsive disorder, is complemented with ritual prevention (RP), which prevents the client from acting upon the compulsions (actions responding to obsessions) that reduce the anxiety.

In the case of PTSD (Foa, Hembree, & Rothbaum, 2007; Resick, Monson, & Rizvi, 2008), exposure is used in its *in vivo* form, where the client is exposed to fear-evoking stimuli. The imaginary form is used as well, and the client is exposed to trauma-related memories. The client visualises and recounts the traumatic event, which is recorded so that the client can repeatedly listen to this account (Foa, Hembree, & Rothbaum, 2007).

A relatively new use of exposure is in the treatment of Generalised Anxiety Disorder (Brown, O'Leary, & Barlow, 2001), where the client is exposed to ruminative worries, evoking the fear-related consequences without interrupting them (Brown, O'Leary, & Barlow, 2001). A group version of exposure may be used in the therapy of social anxiety, in which individual clients serve as partners in a role play of challenging social situations (Turk, Heimberg, & Magee, 2008). In all these different forms, exposure can be and often is complemented with the other CBT techniques, such as cognitive restructuring.

Description of exposure technique

The basic principles of exposure, which are used, for instance, in the treatment of panic and agoraphobic, simple phobic and OCD symptoms, are described below (see Craske, Antony, & Barlow, 2006; Craske & Barlow, 2008; Franklin & Foa, 2008).

Exposure is always preceded by a careful assessment of the anxiety-provoking situations or bodily symptoms in the case of panic. The hierarchy is constructed on the basis of the level of anxiety in different situations. The hierarchy for bodily symptoms, in the case of panic, is accomplished through the monitoring of anxiety during exercises that produce physiological reactions similar to panic symptoms (see Craske & Barlow, 2008). In the case of OCD, the strength of the compulsion to do the rituals which alleviate the anxiety triggered by different obsessions is also assessed (Franklin & Foa, 2008).

With the agreement of the client, exposure to situations that are somewhat challenging begins (the least anxiety-provoking situations can be skipped). In some approaches, such as that of Franklin and Foa (2008), the client may be exposed to the situation in his or her imagination first and then, as homework, to the same situation *in vivo*. In imaginary exposure, the therapist asks the client to close his or her eyes and try to vividly imagine the anxiety- or obsession-provoking situation. The client is then asked to stay in the situation. The level of anxiety and the level of tendency to escape from the situation, or in the case of OCD, the level of tendency to do the compulsion, is monitored (charts or tables can be used for this purpose). The client stays in the imaginary situation until the anxiety is somewhat reduced. Anxiety typically recedes after 20–30 minutes, though it may vary among clients and depending on the situations to which they are exposed. In the initial reaction, the anxiety may even grow as this may be the first time that the client has stayed in the situation that he or she has avoided for a long time. Therefore, if we do *in vivo* exposure, we need to plan the situation so that the client does not escape from it and thus becomes even more fearful. An accompanying person who can be instructed (e.g. a relative) or the therapist may initially be in the situation with the client. It is important that the accompanying person serves as an understanding coach, who tries to increase the client's autonomy and engagement with the situation. Potential problems with avoidance and dependence on the other person have to be reflected upon, monitored and not supported.

Exposure can be undertaken in doses, meaning that there can be a break and then it can be repeated a few times (until the anxiety is reduced). The break may be used to distract or relax the client. During the exposure, techniques such as cognitive restructuring or relaxation (e.g. breathing; for more, see below), which help to sustain exposure, may be used as well. However, this has to be done carefully so that it does not represent safety behaviour, and thus actually enhance the avoidance of anxiety that the client needs to become accustomed to. On the other hand, anxiety may be raised in the imagination purposefully by instructing the client to stay with the most anxiety-provoking thoughts and images.

Doses of exposure are undertaken until the situation is much less anxiety-provoking. If the reduction of anxiety does not come in one 'dose' of exposure, it can be interrupted and then repeated. It can be repeated several times until the reduction of anxiety is achieved. It will eventually as it is a physiological phenomenon. If the anxiety is not reduced, it typically means that the client is involved in some avoidance strategies that interrupt the anxiety, so that it cannot get to its natural peak and achieve the subsequent reduction. These avoidance strategies (e.g. worries) need to be detected.

If we start with imaginary exposure, any reduction in anxiety can be consolidated by following it up with *in vivo* exposure to the same situation. Once this is handled successfully, we can move down the list and do the exposure with another situation on the list. Usually, one situation is tackled in the session. If it is a key anxiety-provoking situation, it can be the focus of several sessions. Once the whole hierarchy of anxiety-provoking situations has been gone through, the client can be encouraged to devise his or her own exposure strategies for any new situations that cause anxiety. This can be monitored in the follow-up sessions.

Exposure can have different forms. Craske and Barlow (2001) distinguish between therapist-led and client-led exposure, intensive (a few hours a day) or less intensive exposure, graded exposure (as described above) or flooding exposure (starting at the top of the list with the most difficult situation), exposure with a planned interruption or without an interruption, focused exposure (the client pays attention to anxiety) and distracting exposure (the client tries to distract him or herself). When conducting exposure, it is essential that it is not compromised by safety behaviours that allow emotional avoidance (see Allen et al., 2008). Allen, McHugh, & Barlow (2008) identify three types of emotional avoidance: (1) subtle behavioural avoidance (e.g. avoiding eye contact); (2) cognitive avoidance (e.g. worry); and (3) safety signals (e.g. carrying a mobile phone). It is important that during exposure the client is not engaged in some sort of subtle emotional avoidance, as the new 'emotional learning' that the anxiety-provoking situation is not that dangerous may be compromised by attributing it to the safety-promoting behaviour.

Exposure for anxiety disorders is probably the most effective psychological technique that currently exists (Emmelkamp, 2004; Woody & Ollendick, 2006). Its mechanism is, however, still not clear. It seems that the original explanation – that it is gradual habituation and extinction – is not fully true. Current research, using neuroimaging, suggests that anxiety is still present in anxiety-provoking situations (amygdala activation indicates this), but that the therapy makes it more likely that this susceptibility is inhibited, and that the prefrontal cortex is involved in this process (Grawe, 2004; McNally, 2007).

Relaxation techniques

Cognitive-behavioural therapies utilise a range of different relaxation techniques. These typically consist of muscle relaxation techniques and breathing techniques. The most common relaxation technique is the Jacobson's progressive muscle relaxation. This relaxation can, at first, be taught by the therapist. The therapist instructs the client, who has closed eyes, to tighten and relax different muscles (see Wolpe & Lazarus, 1966). The client is typically sitting in a relaxed manner and is asked to clench his or her fists and then relax them, and to observe the difference in the experience. Similarly, the client is asked to tighten the lower and upper arms, respectively, and then relax them, and to observe the difference in the experience. The same is repeated with facial muscles, the neck, the upper back, then the chest and stomach muscles, and finally the bottom, thighs, calves and feet. The procedure is excellently described in Wolpe and Lazarus's (1966) book on behaviour therapy.

In German-speaking countries, the most popular method of relaxation is Schultz's autogenic training (Schultz & Luthe, 1959). In this procedure, clients, with their eyes closed, are coached to imagine that:

(1) their hands are heavy, their legs are heavy, their whole body is heavy;
(2) their hands are warm and relaxed, their legs are warm and relaxed, their whole body is warm and relaxed;
(3) their heartbeat is calm;
(4) their breathing is calm and regular;
(5) their stomach is soft, warm and relaxed;
(6) and their forehead is cool and light.

This is done at a slow pace over 5–10 minutes. The method has different versions. Both autogenic training and progressive muscular relaxation can be used as a technique to supplement therapy or in the session itself to create a relaxed state. They have to be practised over several weeks before the client masters them and can benefit from them fully. Typically, they are taught in a gradual manner. Initially, only the first step is taught. Then the second step is added, then the third, and so on.

Current CBT relies heavily on different breathing techniques that bring about a relaxed state. An example is diaphragmatic breathing, which teaches the client to deepen and slow inhalation and that exhaling is relaxing. A good description can be found in Barlow and Craske (2007; see Box 7.2 for a brief account).

Box 7.2 A description of diaphragmatic breathing (adapted from Barlow & Craske, 2007)

(1) Take breath down to your stomach (the stomach expands while chest stays more or less without movement).
(2) Breathe in normal amounts of air (not too much and not too little).
(3) Count when you breathe in (e.g. 'one') and mentally say the word 'relax' when you breathe out.

Relaxation is used to reduce the client's overall tension. The client can also be taught to use relaxation techniques in anxiety-provoking situations. However, this has to be done with caution so that they are not perceived as safety-bringing behaviour, because they could then serve as an emotional avoidance function and thus contribute to the overall anxiety problems.

Though there exist many self-help books and audiotapes providing instructions on how to do them, relaxation techniques are typically taught by the therapist, as some clients experience difficulties in either learning relaxation or experiencing it as bringing relief. As with other activities, it may take some time until the client learns to relax and use the procedure competently and successfully. In general, however, the methods are easy to use and learn.

Relaxation procedures are also used in integrative approaches to therapy or by professionals who are otherwise not using the full CBT package. There also exist relaxation techniques that do not have their origin in behavioural therapy. An example would be the clearing-a-space technique from emotion-focused therapy (see Elliott, Greenberg, & Lietaer, 2004). This technique is inspired by one of the steps of the focusing technique (see below) of Eugene Gendlin (1996). When the client feels tension, he or she can be asked to focus on the part of the body where the tension is felt. The quality of the feeling is described and named, also taking into account what in the client's life the tension relates to. For instance, I feel uneasy in my body because I have a difficult conversation with my boss tomorrow. I can label the tension and heaviness in my stomach as a 'boss conversation'. If the client labels his or her experience in such a way, then the client can be asked to put that labelled feeling away in his or her imagination (e.g. to the corner of the room, to the next room). Once this has been successfully achieved, the client can redirect attention back to the named part of the body to see how he or she feels. If the client is still not relieved, the procedure is repeated and the client is asked to identify the feeling that prevents him or her from feeling relaxed, to name it and put it away. The procedure may be repeated several times. The detailed description can be found in Elliott, Greenberg, and Lietaer (2004). An example is also provided in Chapter 8 in the section discussing working with overwhelming feelings.

Similar to relaxation techniques are mindfulness meditation techniques (Kabat-Zinn, 1996; Segal, Teasdale, & Williams, 2002; Bishop et al., 2004). These techniques do not focus on bringing about a relaxed state, but rather teach the client to pause and have an observational, non-judgemental stance in which the client notices thoughts, feelings, bodily experiences, but accepts them rather than reacts to them. It focuses on the client's *awareness* of inner experiences of the inner and outside world, being attentive to them without immediately acting on them. Different mindfulness instructions can be found, for instance, in Kabat-Zinn's work (1996).

Experiential techniques

A number of experiential techniques are used in psychotherapy. They were originally developed within different approaches (e.g. Gestalt therapy, psychodrama, solution-focused therapy). In recent years, some of them were redressed and used in the empirically-informed emotion-focused therapy (see Elliott, Greenberg, & Lietaer, 2004). Here I will present a few well-studied 'experiential tasks' of this form of therapy together with the description of when they can be suitably used in therapy.

Focusing

Experiential focusing is a method developed by a client-centred and experiential therapist Eugene Gendlin (1978, 1996). Though it is not directly empirically developed, it stems from empirical investigations of client-centred therapy. Later it was studied with regard to its usefulness in deepening the client's experience (see the review of Hendricks, 2002). Greenberg, Rice, and Elliott, (1993) use their version of focusing in cases where they want to explore unclear feelings. They identify three features of an unclear feeling that this task is suitable for (see Elliott, Watson, Goldman, & Greenberg, 2004: 181):

(1) the client makes a reference to a particular inner experience;
(2) the client has difficulty in articulating this experience; and
(3) this experience is disturbing.

The actual procedure of focusing is as follows (see Gendlin, 1996; Elliott, Watson, Goldman, & Greenberg, 2004):

(1) The client pays attention to the bodily experience of the feeling and allows it to unfold.
(2) The client is invited to observe what label (word or image) captures the quality of the feeling.
(3) The client is asked to see whether the label fits the experience (this is repeated with step 2).
(4) The client is asked to check how his or her body responds to this labelling and whether the felt quality changes; (steps 2 and 3 are repeated until all different aspects of the experience are labelled).
(5) As all aspects of the (changing) experience are named, the feeling should become clearer and experientially felt relief should be observed. The client is invited to observe and appreciate the felt difference. Elliott, Watson, Goldman, and Greenberg (2004) also suggest an in-session or outside-session consolidation of this felt change by exploring with the client what the client can do to support the felt difference.

Focusing can be used as a stand-alone technique, but aspects of it can be used through the therapy (see Chapter 5) to help the client pay attention to bodily aspects of experience. Focusing may also be used for accessing important emotions that are suppressed or not noticed (see Greenberg, 2002).

There is a lot of material on the focusing method, by both the originator of the method, Gendlin (1978, 1996) and by other authors (Cornell, 1996; Leijssen, 1998). The method is promoted by the Focusing Institute (www.focusing.org). The 'emotion-focused' version of focusing can be found in the work of EFT writers such as Greenberg, Rice, and Elliott (1993) and Elliott, Watson, Goldman, and Greenberg (2004).

Systematic evocative unfolding for puzzling experiences

Another experiential technique used in emotion-focused therapy is systematic evocative unfolding for problematic client experiences that leave the client puzzled (Greenberg, Rice, & Elliott, 1993). The technique was developed by Laura Rice (see Rice & Saperia, 1984), who studied client-centred therapy, where the focus of exploration was the description of situations in which the clients' reactions left them puzzled as to why they reacted as they did. Elliott et al. (2004) suggest that this task can be used when the client describes a situation to which the client responded with a problematic feeling or behaviour that is puzzling to the client.

The task consists of several steps (Greenberg, Rice, & Elliott, 1993; Elliott, Watson, Goldman, & Greenberg, 2004) (see Figure 7.1). The main idea is to get the client back into the problematic situation (e.g. a description of the client's row with his wife) by presenting it to the therapist as if it was happening right now. This can be done by starting with the broader context of the situation (e.g. when the client came home after a difficult day at work) and moving slowly to the main problematic part. In this process, the therapist is slowing the client down and asking the client to stay with different aspects of the situation (stimuli) and check what sort of reaction they trigger in the client's experiencing. When a particular trigger (a salient aspect of the situation) is identified, the specific qualities (e.g. a look of disdain from the wife at a particular part of the row) that the client responded to (e.g. a sudden bout of depression) can also be examined. The exploration can then focus on the particular 'meaning' of the stimulus that was perceived and which triggered the puzzling and problematic reaction (e.g. the bout of depression). When this specific perception is recognised, the reaction is not only more understandable, but it is also clearer why it was so salient (Rice uses the term 'meaning bridge' for this connection). It usually pertains to a central aspect of the client's vulnerabilities that can then be examined further in therapy. Good descriptions of systematic evocative unfolding can be found in Rice and Saperia (1984), Greenberg, Rice, and Elliott (1993), and Elliott, Watson, Goldman, and Greenberg (2004).

Systematic evocative unfolding is a good example of the refinement of an otherwise 'non-specific' client-centred interviewing style. As with 'focusing', these techniques can be used throughout therapy when we want to see how external stimuli and their perceptions impact on inner emotional experiencing.

Two-chair dialogue for resolving self-depreciation

A very central technique of emotion-focused therapy is the two-chair technique for resolving the client's self-criticism (self-depreciation). The technique, which originally comes from Gestalt therapy, was refined and further developed by the programmatic research of Les Greenberg (1984). The task is suitable for exploring, reliving

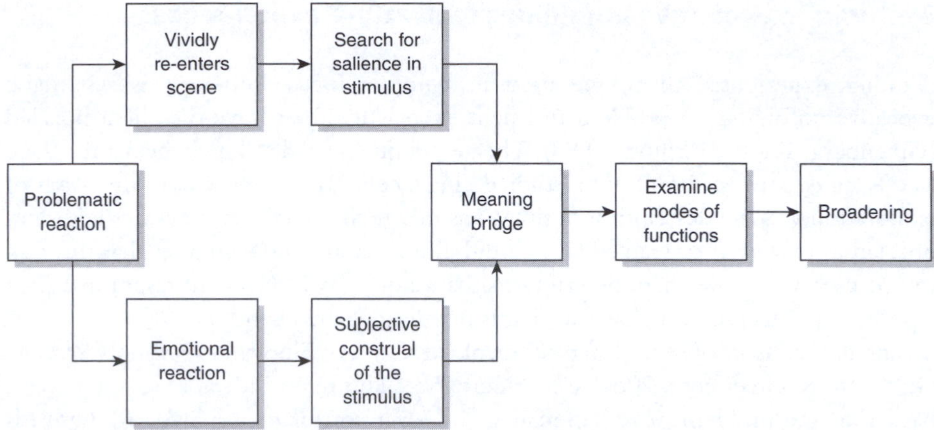

FIGURE 7.1 *The model of systematic evocative unfolding (Rice & Saperia, 1984). Adapted with permission by Greenberg (2006)*

and resolving intense feelings of self-hostility and self-disgust typical in depression, and also 'self-scaring' processes in anxiety disorders, etc. (see Elliott, Watson, Goldman, & Greenberg, 2004). The task is enacted as a dialogue between two parts of the self, the critical one and the impacted one.

In the task, feelings (often disgust) of a self-critical part of the self are evoked and directed towards the self. The emotional impact of such criticism is then accessed (these are usually hurt feelings, and a vulnerable, sad despair). Accessing and expressing this vulnerability often triggers a softening of the criticism and greater self-compassion. The need to protect oneself from the critical part is helped to come to the fore and self-protective anger is experienced and then expressed to the critic. Thus, the following sequence is observed (see Greenberg, 1984; Greenberg, Rice, & Elliott, 1993; Elliott, Watson, Goldman, & Greenberg, 2004):

1 Disgust at self expressed by the critic.
2 Access and expression of hurt by the criticised part.
3 Access and expression of self-compassion by the critic towards the criticised part.
4 The recognition of the need for self-protection and access and expression of self-protective anger by the criticised part.
5 Acknowledgement of the hurt and anger of the criticised part by the critic.

When this sequence is accomplished, more reflection, a clarification of the motives of the critic and more consideration of outside-session implications follow.

The above sequence is facilitated by the therapist, who is familiar with the model of resolution. However, the therapist constantly monitors the true feelings of the client at any moment of the dialogue. At the start of the dialogue the client is asked to express the self-disgust or other forms of self-criticism that led to the initiation of the task. Then the therapist asks the client to change chairs and together with the client looks at the emotional impact of the criticism. The client then accesses it and expresses it to the critic in the other chair. The dialogue then continues following the sequence: identifying the impact of the other part's expression, experiencing it and expressing it. The therapist monitors emotional arousal and coaches the client to fully access and express emotions. Any avoidance of emotional involvement is monitored and brought to the client's awareness as it is considered to hinder emotional resolution and the building of a more self-compassionate and empowered self.

The whole two-chair dialogue is a sophisticated technique and requires in-depth training and supervision. The escalation of self-depreciation at the beginning of the dialogue paradoxically brings fresh hurt that evokes self-compassion and self-protective anger, which in turn evokes respect and acknowledgement. The process usually takes the whole session and needs to be repeated over several sessions. The whole task therefore has to be firmly embedded in emotion-focused case formulation (see Chapter 3). An excellent guide to the task is provided in Greenberg, Rice, and Elliott (1993) and Elliott, Watson, Goldman, and Greenberg, (2004).

An empty chair dialogue for resolving an interpersonal injury

Another empirically-based experiential technique used in emotion-focused therapy is an empty chair dialogue for resolving an interpersonal injury (Greenberg, Rice, & Elliott 1993; Elliott, Watson, Goldman, & Greenberg, 2004). The task comes from Gestalt therapy and was further developed after its successful use in therapy by Greenberg and Foerster (1996). The task is typically used within the emotion-focused case conceptualisation and targets key, unresolved interpersonal issues. Greenberg, Rice, and Elliott (1993; see also Elliott, Watson, Goldman, & Greenberg, 2004) distinguish three main features of the marker (the client's experience), for which this task is especially suitable. The client has (Elliott, Watson, Goldman, & Greenberg, 2004: 245):

- unresolved lingering feelings of hurt and resentment;
- the feelings are related to a significant person;
- the feelings are currently experienced and there is a sign that they are being restricted or interrupted.

The technique again consists of a dialogue between the client and the enacted other person in the empty chair. The task starts with the client expressing the problematic feelings. They are usually a response to a specific behaviour of the other (e.g. rejection by the other). At the beginning of the dialogue the most hurtful aspects of the other's behaviour are enacted by the client, who sits in the other chair and plays out those aspects of the other's behaviour. This is done so that the hurting aspects can be brought to awareness and also to bring forth their emotional impact in the client. The client is then asked to sit in the original chair and observe the emotional impact of the hurtful behaviour. This emotional impact is then accessed and expressed to the imagined other in the empty chair.

The main focus is on differentiating feelings in the client (typically, hurt and anger for being violated). The client is coached by the therapist to access and express those feelings. The fact that these feelings are often unresolved for a long period of time suggests that a restriction or interruption of them is present in the client. In the task, this avoidance often comes to the fore. If it happens, the client is asked to have a dialogue with him or herself and enact the interrupting part in the other chair so that the manners and motives of the interrupting can be expressed. The emotional impact of the interruption is then accessed by putting the client into the original chair and observing how the interrupting processes impact on him or her. Usually, they raise tension. If this is so, the client is coached to observe and experience this tension and to identify a need that is being obstructed by the interruption. Often, it is a need to express either hurt (sadness) or anger stirred by the violation done by the significant other. The expression of primary emotions of anger, hurt and sadness then continues.

Greenberg and his colleagues (Missirlian et al., 2005; Greenberg, Auszra, & Herrmann, 2007) observed that if the primary emotions of sadness and protective anger are freshly accessed and expressed, they then lead to the sense of resolution that is often accompanied by a changed view of the other (it is more comprehensive and more understanding). The experienced and expressed sadness and anger is also accompanied by a clearer awareness of the unmet need originally violated or not fulfilled by the other. The need can then be attended to in new ways or it can be let go. The process of this task is nicely depicted in Greenberg's model (2006) of the resolution of unfinished business (see Figure 7.2).

As already mentioned, the empty chair dialogue for resolving interpersonal injuries is well studied. More recently, it was also studied as a tool for promoting forgiveness and letting go in interpersonal injuries (see Greenberg, Warwar, & Malcolm, 2008). This task, just like the two-chair dialogue, requires a lot of skill and experience. It may be used in emotion-focused therapy as a central task for restructuring the underlying problematic emotion scheme. Thus it has to be firmly embedded in the proper case conceptualisation. A good description of the task is provided in Greenberg, Rice, and Elliott (1993) and Elliott, Watson, Goldman, and Greenberg, (2004). The American Psychological Association produces a DVD of Les Greenberg demonstrating the use of both tasks in two sessions (Greenberg, 2007).

Working with dreams in psychotherapy

Having presented cognitive, behavioural and experiential techniques, I will now focus on a technique defined by the material at its core. I refer to a technique developed

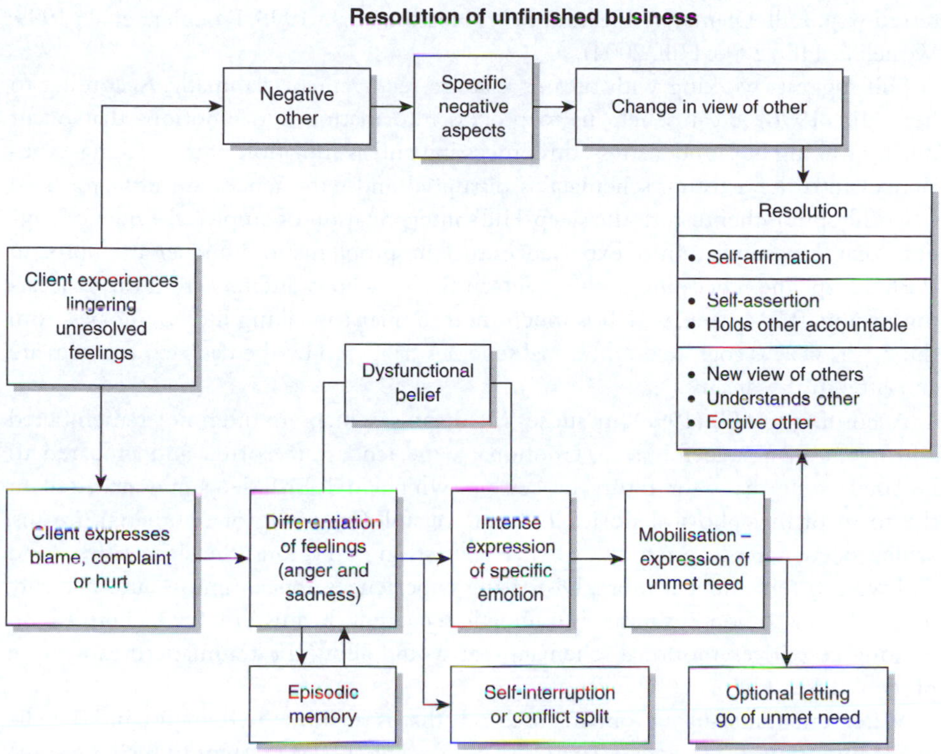

Resolution of unfinished business

Client experiences lingering unresolved feelings

Negative other

Specific negative aspects

Change in view of other

Resolution
- Self-affirmation
- Self-assertion
- Holds other accountable
- New view of others
- Understands other
- Forgive other

Dysfunctional belief

Client expresses blame, complaint or hurt

Differentiation of feelings (anger and sadness)

Intense expression of specific emotion

Mobilisation – expression of unmet need

Episodic memory

Self-interruption or conflict split

Optional letting go of unmet need

FIGURE 7.2 *The research-based model of the resolution of interpersonal unfinished business adapted from Greenberg, Rice, and Elliott. Adapted with permission from Guilford press (1993).*

by Clara Hill (1996) for working with recurrent dreams, nightmares or sleep terror. Though the work with dreams is not so central to current mainstream psychotherapy, I am including this particular technique as it is informed by extensive programmatic research by Clara Hill and her colleagues. It is also easily applicable within an integrative approach to therapy and thus fits this book well.

Work with dreams in psychotherapy has a long tradition, starting with Freud (2007/1900). It is still a mainstream focus of psychoanalytic therapy. In her work, Hill draws on psychodynamic origins but also incorporates experiential elements (e.g. from Gestalt therapy or focusing techniques) and behavioural elements (in changing the dreams). Hill's model (she uses the term cognitive-experiential model) consists of several steps: exploring the dream content and emotional experience in it; facilitating insight into aspects of the dream and the dream as a whole; and enabling an action that changes the dream or behaviour/life aspects reflected in the dream. The model is based on an empirical knowledge of dreams and has been extensively tested (e.g. Hill, Diemer, & Heaton, 1997; Heaton, et al., 1998; Rochlen, et al., 1999; Wonell & Hill, 2000; Hill, 2004).

Hill suggests working with dreams that are recurrent or traumatic. According to her (Hill, 1996), dreams help us to process information and emotions that occur during waking life. Under stress, this processing and assimilation of the waking experiences into the 'existing schemata' is disrupted and experiences are not processed smoothly, but rather disturb the sleep. Hill's interpretation of empirical evidence suggests that the assimilation of experiences that are problematic is further attempted in REM sleep. The processing of the events in REM sleep is different from the processing in non-REM sleep, which is much more similar to waking life. Memories from the day as well as cognitive-emotional schemes triggered by the day's experiences are activated in the dreams.

According to Hill (1996), in 'successful' dreams, which are often not remembered and occur in a peaceful sleep, emotional experiences are sorted and prepared to be used as the basis for future processing, which in REM sleep presents itself in the form of metaphorical stories. In 'unsuccessful' (recurring or traumatic) dreams, which occur when we worry or experience strong emotions, the sleep is less solid and we can remember it more. Distressing experiences appear almost automatically in the dreams. A good example is traumatic recurrent dreams in PTSD. There are no existing cognitive-emotional schemata that would allow the traumatic dream to be processed (see Hill, 1996).

When encountering a problematic dream that is seen by the therapist and the client as important for therapy, Clara Hill (1996) suggests several steps (which are summarised in Box 7.3). First, the therapist asks the client to recount the whole dream in the present tense as if it was happening right now (the client can also close his or her eyes). This is done so that the emotional experiences and the content of the dream become more vivid and less distant. The therapist also focuses on the client's immediate feelings about the dream when he or she woke up. The therapist asks the client to go through the most significant parts of the dream and to access and express the emotions that the client experiences at those parts. The therapist also encourages the client to freely associate about the particular significant images from the dream (*What comes to your mind when you stay with this picture?*). If, for example, the client dreamt about being in a corridor, the therapist might ask: *What is specific about this corridor? Does it remind you of anything? How do you feel being in this corridor? Where does this corridor lead?* And so on. When emotions are being tracked, the client may be asked to slow down and to stay with the emotional experience (e.g. *Stay with that sadness that you are describing*). The client may also be asked to be a part of his or her dream (this is a Gestalt influence; see Perls, 2008). For example: *Be that corridor. How do you feel as this corridor?* The idea behind this is that the dream images represent a part of the client's experience which can thus be brought to awareness. The exploration phase of working with a dream may also ask for associations with recent waking-life events. The therapist explores the different parts of the dream, but tries not to lose the overall meaning of the dream.

Box 7.3 Cognitive-experiential model of working with recurrent or traumatic dreams (adapted from Hill, 1996)

Exploration stage

- The therapist asks the client to recount the dream as if it was happening right now.
- The therapist asks the client to go through the dream images sequentially and express emotions experienced in those images. The client is also asked to freely associate to those images.
- The client is asked to slow down when attending to emotions or he/she may be asked to enact some images or parts of them as if the client was those images.
- The therapist also explores whether the dream images remind the client of anything from recent days.

Insight stage

- The therapist encourages the client to look at the meaning of the dream, using expressed associations as a base.
- The therapist, together with the client, interprets the dream, considering four perspectives: (1) the dream on its own; (2) the dream in relation to recent waking events; (3) the dream in relation to past experiences; (4) the dream in relation to different parts of the client's self.

Action stage

- Changing the dream in the imagination or by waking up and imagining it going differently so that it is not traumatic.
- Further work on understanding the dream.
- Changing in real life, based on the knowledge gained from working on, exploring and understanding the dream.

In the second phase of working with a dream, Hill attempts to promote insight into the dream. The focus is on the meaning of the dream, taking into account the generated associations. The dream is looked at on four levels: the dream itself (learning about the self from the dream), its connection to waking events, its connection to the past and its connection to the parts of the client's self. The therapist is trying to enable the client to come up with his or her own self-understanding. However, the therapist may contribute with some suggestions that may shape insight as well. The therapist's prior knowledge of the client can contribute to this.

Finally, Hill recommends several possibilities for promoting an active approach to change based on the achieved insight. The focus may be on changing the dream or to change aspects of the waking life that could not be processed originally and transpired in the dream. With regard to changing the dream, Hill suggests changing it in the imagination. The therapist may ask the client to evoke the dream in his or her imagination and change it in the way the client wishes. This can also be done at home in the case of a reappearing recurrent dream. The client may learn to wake up during the problematic dream and tell him or herself before they fall asleep again how they would like to have the dream changed. This approach can foster the client's sense of agency. The action stage can also be used to promote a further elaboration of understanding. This stage can focus on how the client can apply the learning about the self and recent past experiences to his or her everyday waking life.

I have presented in this chapter several research-informed techniques that are used as more comprehensive therapeutic strategies. These techniques attempt to achieve respective goals that respond to the client's presentation. They are typically firmly embedded in a particular case conceptualisation. There are many other techniques in these approaches (see Leahy, 2003, for many CBT techniques) and some other approaches rely on the use of strategic interventions that can be considered as 'techniques' (e.g. solution-focused and systemic therapies).

Recommended reading

A more detailed description of the techniques described here can be found in:

Elliott, R., Watson, J.C., Goldman, R.N., & Greenberg, L.S. (2004). *Learning Emotion-focused Therapy: The Process-experiential Approach.* Washington, DC: American Psychological Association.

Hill, C.E. (1996). *Working with Dreams in Psychotherapy.* New York: Guilford Press.

Westbrook, D., Kennerley, H., & Kirk, J. (2007). *An Introduction to Cognitive-behavioural Therapy: Skills and Applications.* London: Sage.

Part III
Adjusting Therapeutic Strategy

The general strategy that the therapist employs when working with a client is based on the client's presenting issues, their understanding as formulated in case conceptualisation, but also on the here-and-now presentation of the client. In the next two chapters we will look at the therapist's responsiveness (see Stiles et al., 1998) to the client's here-and-now presentation and to some aspects of the overall treatment strategy which depend on the central problems that bring the client to therapy. The chapters do not provide an exhaustive and detailed account of the situations and problems, but are rather attempting to sensitise the reader to the complexity of the therapeutic process.

Eight
Specific Situations in the Process of Therapy

Abstract
This chapter describes specific situations that may arise in the therapeutic process. These situations include discussion of interpersonal patterns as they are present in the relationship with the therapist, intense emotions present in the session, silence in therapy, crying in therapy, anger expressed towards the therapist, the presence of hallucinations, delusions and dissociations, etc. Research-informed responses to these situations will be discussed.

There is a number of situations that ocurr in therapeutic process that the therapist has to respond to immediately (Stiles et al., 1998). We will now look at some of them and examine how the therapist can respond.

Working with interpersonal issues in the psychotherapeutic process

Psychodynamic approaches, in particular, look at problematic interpersonal patterns (see Luborsky & Crits-Christoph, 1990, 1998) as the main focus of therapy because they assume that the client's psychopathology lies in an unsuccessful compromise resolution of the client's inner conflict, which is linked to the client's needs in relation to others. Working with interpersonal patterns in an interpretative way, mostly through exploring and interpreting their manifestation in the transference relationship with the therapist, is one of a therapist's basic aims in psychodynamic approaches (see Chapters 1, 2, 3 and 5). The empirically-confirmed fact that the client's interpersonal style presents itself in the relationship with the therapist underlines the importance of being aware of the client's interpersonal patterns in the process of therapy (see Luborsky & Crits-Christoph, 1990). However, an interpersonal aspect of the client's presentation may come to the fore in different ways in different therapeutic approaches.

The client's interpersonal stories are a natural focus of psychodynamic, but also other approaches, to therapy. The link between those stories and the actual interaction with the therapist is obvious. The therapist can thus either explore or interpret the client's interpersonal patterns on the basis of the stories the client tells about relationships with other people or on the basis of their mutual interaction. Van Kessel and Lietaer (1998), person-centred theorists, emphasise that the therapeutic relationship either has an implicit healing function, which is present in the therapist's effort to offer the client an optimal supportive relationship, or provides an option for explicit work on exploring, understanding and potentially altering the client's interpersonal patterns. In the second case, according to these theorists, the therapist observes the following principles in order to use the client–therapist interaction to increase the client's insight into his or her interpersonal patterns (Van Kessel & Lietaer, 1998: 160–165):

(1) The therapist focuses on the interpersonal issues in the relationship in the sense that the therapist is sensitive to the interpersonal connotations in the client's narrative and to its parallels with the therapist–client relationship. The therapist is also sensitive to the implications of what the client is trying to communicate about others for their own mutual relationship, etc.
(2) The therapist does not respond in the same way as others in the client's usual interpersonal patterns. This way of responding breaks the usual social reciprocity. For instance, if the therapist is accused of something, the therapist does not automatically start responding in self-defence, but is rather interested in understanding the client.
(3) The therapist focuses on the clarification of interaction patterns. The therapist uses good opportunities for highlighting the interaction patterns tentatively, and in their historical or more general interpersonal context (other past or current relationships).
(4) The therapist uses the therapeutic relationship as a medium for therapeutic change by using the focus on interaction, outlined in the first three principles, for stimulating a new way of relating and for experimenting in the therapeutic relationship.

An application of the outlined principles may look like this: The client is talking about how hard it is for her to say something negative in the relationship with her husband. The therapist may offer his observation that it has happened in the therapeutic relationship too, that it was hard for the client to speak about some negative things she had experienced towards the therapist. The therapist encourages the client to look at the fears that obstruct her expression of anger. As these are brought into the open, it may be clearer that it is out of a fear of being attacked. This being something that regularly happened to the client when she wanted to be assertive in her family of origin. The therapist may then encourage the client to express her dissatisfaction in their own therapeutic relationship, so she can build up her justifiably angry and assertive part.

Psychodynamic approaches also highlight the fact that the therapist becomes a model for the client, showing the client how to cope with interpersonal conflicts surrounding the fulfilment of a need that is obstructed by a fear (see Weiss, Sampson, and Mount Zion Psychotherapy Research Group, 1986; see Chapter 3). As Weiss, Sampson, and Mount Zion Psychotherapy Research Group (1986) suggest, the client may be testing the therapist to see whether the therapist is able to put up with difficult interpersonal interaction. The therapist's emotional stability is then central. Similarly, psychodynamic approaches emphasise the function of the therapist's countertransference, which, in an optimal case, helps the therapist to understand the emotional experiencing of the client and eventually to understand the experiencing of people exposed to interaction with the client (see, for example, Giovacchini, 1989; Casement, 1999).

Working with silence in the psychotherapeutic process

Due to the fact that therapeutic interviewing does not follow the norms of typical conversation, silences are not exceptional. It is especially so in exploratory therapeutic approaches. In such approaches, the therapist typically allows for silences in the hope that the client pauses and reflects on his or her own experience. However, in reality, silences may be spent in different ways. For example, in the early sessions, the clients may pause because they do not fully understand what is expected from them. In such a case, silence may also provoke anxiety (see Dale, Allen, & Measor, 1998). On the contrary, in productive therapy moments, the client may use the silence for thinking, reflecting and focusing on his or her own experiencing. Another form of silence can be experienced when the client feels hopelessness and gives in to a feeling of depression and lacks the energy to continue in the dialogue with the therapist.

An interesting study into the functions of silences in therapy was undertaken by Heidi Levitt (2001). She interviewed seven clients of four different therapists (of different theoretical orientation) about silences in their sessions (sessions were taped and reviewed). She found that silences could be divided into productive, neutral and obstructive silences (see Figure 8.1). In productive pauses, the clients experienced emotions, formulated ideas and reflected on their experience. In neutral silences, the clients either retrieved information or associated inwardly. In obstructive silences, the clients were either disengaged or were focusing on the interaction with the therapist as the alliance seemed to be under threat.

The therapist's way of treating a silence obviously depends on the type of silence. When the therapist encounters an obstructive silence the focus should be on improving the alliance. For instance, at the beginning of exploratory therapy, the client may be confused about what is expected. When a silence occurs at this stage and the client is uncomfortable about it, the therapist may coach the client in the use of silence. For

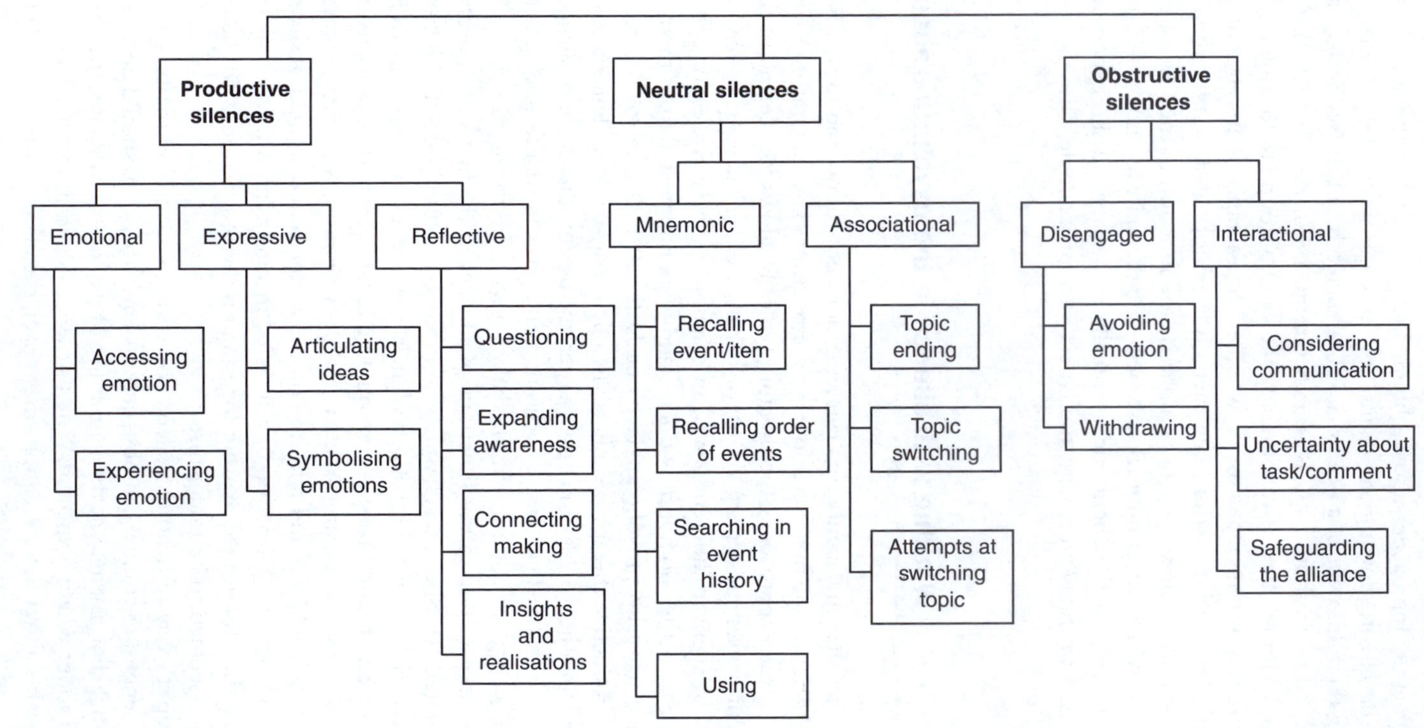

FIGURE 8.1 *Pausing experiences found in the study of Levitt (2001: 300). Reproduced with permission by Taylor & Francis Ltd (www.informaworld.com).*

example: *I am staying silent so I can allow you to focus on your inward experience and reflect on it. There is no need to rush. Maybe you can just stay with what is happening inside of you, what you feel and what is going through your mind.* The therapist may also check after the client was silent and explicitly ask how the client experiences silences and offer an explanation of how they can be used if they are problematic.

Silences may also be promoted by the therapist differently depending on a particular task of therapy. For instance, when the client is working on developing a hierarchy of anxiety-provoking situations, it may well be suitable to encourage the client to pause and search in their memory for different anxiety-promoting situations. In cases when the client is using silence for an emotional exploration, it is important that the therapist is in contact with this process and checks what is happening with the client (e.g. *What is happening in you right now?*). Sometimes, when a silence is painfully overwhelming (e.g. because of deep sadness or emotional pain), it is important that the therapist tries to empathically respond to that experience in order to provide a holding presence which breaks the existential isolation. In such instances, the therapist also conveys his or her presence by making eye contact and speaking with a concerned and compassionate quality of voice, all of which stem from a genuine concern and care for the client.

The use of silence is an important therapeutic skill. Silences bring an important quality to the therapeutic process. They provide a space for the client to stay with their experience. They also allow the therapist to use a pause for the purpose of reflection on the therapeutic process. It may be in such silences that the therapist formulates a new question or strategy that can be offered to the client.

Working with severe psychotic or dissociative symptoms in the psychotherapeutic process

Psychotic symptoms such as hallucinations and delusions, which are accompanied by very pronounced anxiety, disorientation and confusion, may be encountered, for instance, by therapists working with psychotic clients or clients with dementia. Such states are characterised by a loss of contact with reality. Similar symptoms may be displayed by clients who experience very intense emotions (e.g. anxiety). They may have experiences of panic, dissociation and depersonalisation. The main, immediate goal of the therapist encountering such a presentation in the session is to contain the client's experience, as it can be uncomfortable and frightening. Clients with more severe difficulties (e.g. acute psychotic disorder) may present with paranoid experiencing and demonstrate potential distrust towards the therapist.

As the main problem of clients with such experiences is their loss of contact with their surroundings and reality, the therapist's responses may focus on the strengthening of it by explicitly referring to the current reality (environment) and placing the client in it. Different interventions can be used to orientate the client, such as *You are here with me in my office talking to me....* The therapist can offer a calm presence, such as *I am here with you in this difficulty, I will try to assist you in finding appropriate help....* The therapist can strengthen the coherence of the client's experience by verbalising it in a coherent and clarifying way, such as *You feel like that because....* Gary Prouty (1994), a person-centred therapist, developed a pre-therapy approach that targets confusion in such clients and provides holding and meaning for them. Prouty suggested several interventions targeting the client's contact function:

(1) *Situational reflections* – the therapist orientates the client, for example: *Now we have our regular session in X facility.*
(2) *Reflections of the client's facial expressions* – the therapist can respond to the facial expression, for example: *You seem to be frightened....*
(3) *Word-for-word reflections* – the therapist repeats the client's statements word for word, so the client's expressions can be acknowledged and reflected back to the client, meaning the client can stay in touch with the verbal expressions of his or her experience.
(4) *Reflections of the body* – the therapist may non-verbally or verbally reflect the body posture of the client, so the client's experience can be mirrored in this way as well.
(5) *Recurrent reflections* – the therapist repeats those reflections to which the client responded, as these were the expressions that developed conversation and the contact with the therapist.

The goals of the therapist's interventions when working with the client's disorientation and confusion is to contain it and give it a meaning. Thus the frightened state can be 'survived' by the client and instead of experiencing other people as threatening, the client can see other people as helping him or her to cope with the difficult state. This, however, may be difficult with acutely psychotic clients, who can experience the presence of the therapist as contributing to the frightening experience. It is especially so if the client feels disrespected and manipulated by the therapist into making choices (such as being admitted to hospital) that the client does not see as viable, but rather as potentially traumatic. In such cases, the therapist has no other option but to be patient and attempt to collaboratively ensure the client's safety.

Working with crying in the psychotherapeutic process

Crying is often present in the therapy process. It can be an expression of various emotions and experiences, such as sadness, sorrow, being moved, hopelessness, despair, but also happiness, etc. In general, it accompanies variations of sadness. When crying is part of the expression of primary adaptive emotion such as normal grief (see Greenberg,

2002; also Chapter 3), it can be a catalyst for relieving (physiological and mental) tension. On the other hand, crying can also be experienced as painful, embarrassing and as something that does not bring any positive physiological effect (see Cornelius, 2001). The latter is the case when crying is an expression of secondary hopelessness or primary maladaptive unresolved grief. In such instances, crying may be tiring and may not bring any relief. Its containment and regulation (e.g. by breathing) or using it to access primary adaptive emotions may be more appropriate (see Greenberg, 2002). The therapist therefore needs to be able to determine whether the emotion that goes with the crying is primary and adaptive.

The therapist needs to allow the client to cry in the session as it is an important aspect of the expression of felt experience. Emotion-focused therapists may also facilitate crying explicitly (e.g. when the client is on the verge of tears, they may point this out, give permission and invite the client to cry: *These are important tears. Let them come*. See Greenberg 2007). Permission may also be communicated by the presence of tissues in the room, although this may be seen by clients who are avoidant of emotional experience as pressure to cry. The therapist also has to be mindful of the fact that crying may be considered by some clients as an 'embarrassing' thing, showing their inability to cope (especially for some male clients). The therapist may normalise this by responding to crying as to other emotional expressions. Some inexperienced therapists may feel a need to comfort the crying client immediately when the client starts to cry, as it is often considered socially appropriate in such a situation. However, to the client, it may signal that the therapist is disturbed by the client's crying and wants to stop the client's discomfort (experience). Therefore, though the therapist may show compassion and empathy, it is important that it is done in a way that validates the client's experience, does not want to stop the client from crying and wants to help its expression or containment. In this, an important role is played by empathic responding, which captures the client's experience in words that show the therapist's experiential understanding of the client's state.

Working with overwhelming and suppressed emotions in the psychotherapeutic process

There are two main problems in relation to the client's emotional experiencing in therapy. The client's emotion may be either overregulated, i.e. the client is restricted, tense and not experiencing or aware of an emotion(s), or underregulated, i.e. overwhelmed and flooded by emotion (see Greenberg, 2002).

With regard to the overregulation of emotions, the main therapeutic strategy is to bring avoidance to awareness by pointing it out or asking the client to enact avoidance so the client is more aware of how he or she avoids the emotion and what experiential impact it has (see Greenberg, Rice, & Elliott, 1993). For instance, when the client reports a flat emotional state but experiences tension, the client may be asked to create tension purposefully and thus to stop his or her own emotional processing and observe how he or she is doing it and what experiential impact it has on him or her. This may increase awareness of the fact that the client is doing it and it may also help to uncover the function of it, which is generally protection from being emotionally hurt or traumatised. The restriction and avoidance typically obstructs a need, such as to get appropriately angry when violated. The localisation of such a need, together with an increased awareness of the avoidance, may sometimes be sufficient to overcome the overregulation and bring the experience and expression of the emotion to the fore. However, if emotional avoidance is pervasive and is the central problem of the client, this process has to be repeated and the client may need a lot of coaching in accessing the obstructed needs and experiencing and expressing the emotions linked to them.

On the other hand, during the therapeutic process there may occur moments when intense emotions are experienced as overwhelming, unpleasant, leaving the client too vulnerable and unclear. Those moments are frequently characterised by high agitation linked to the problematic experiences that are not yet assimilated and are still painful. The client may feel helpless in regulating such experiences, threatened by their uncontrollability and not fully focused or integrated. The therapist may help the client to regulate such experiences by either suggesting slow breathing or using the 'clearing a space' technique or other relaxation-producing interventions (see Chapter 7 and Box 8.1), but mainly through offering an empathic verbalisation of the client's experience. This may have a holding and containing effect. The therapist's attempts to symbolise the client's experience may bring a meaning to it but also convey the sense that it is possible to understand and label it. The therapist's firm presence is also calming, as it conveys that the therapist is not overwhelmed by intense emotions. The therapist's sensitivity and caring presence may also help to dissipate the client's embarrassment about being exposed to vulnerable and uncontrollable states in front of the therapist. The therapist's empathic attempts to understand the client's experience may also encourage self-empathy in the client (see Watson, Goldman, & Vanaerschot, 1998), which has a regulating function as well. Finally, the therapist's empathic attempts to symbolise the client's experience also help the client to unravel the plethora of information contained in such emotional experiences.

Box 8.1 A version of the 'clearing a space' method of Leijssen (1998). Adapted with permission from Guilford Press and the author

An experiential therapist, Mia Leijssen (1998: 131–132), provides a good example of regulating emotional experience through the 'clearing a space' technique. She describes working with a client who is afraid of dying.

C: *There is a terrible pressure here (indicating her breastbone); I cannot take it any more ... It is such a strong counterforce preventing me from living ... I can hardly go on breathing!*

T: *Could you try to push this counterforce a bit further away?*

C: *I wouldn't know how to do it.*

T: *Could you give me an idea of how you experience it? Apart from preventing you from living, how are you getting along underneath it or what sort of feeling does it give you?*

C: *It is an enormous, heavy block of concrete on top of me; I don't get any air under there!*

T: *OK. Now I understand that you cannot push away something like that! We'll leave the heavy block where it is, and you may try to imagine that you yourself step back ... Try to imagine making a step that gets you from under this block. (Client nods while therapist suggests it; such small bodily signs are an indication that we are on the right track.)*

C: *Yes, that feels good (deep sigh) ... I can breath again (silence) ... and all of a sudden I also see that the block of concrete is my mother, who always prevented me from living!*

When working with emotions it may be important to assess them differentially (Greenberg & Safran, 1989; Greenberg, 2002). As Greenberg recommends, it may be more meaningful to respond to primary emotions as they contain the most valuable information. This may be relevant when overwhelming experiences contain several emotions, some of which are primary and some of which are secondary. For example, if the client's response to being abandoned by a partner is interminable despair, the empathy communicated towards the hurt and the sense of being unjustly hurt may provide more meaning to the client than just the acknowledgement of despair of a trauma caused by the abandonment. Also, it may be important to differentiate between productive and unproductive overwhelming and unresolving emotions (Greenberg, Anszra, & Herrmann, 2007). While productive emotions may need to be attended to, the unproductive emotions may need to be regulated so they can be used in a productive way (for more, see Boxes 8.2 and 8.3).

Box 8.2 Differentiation of emotions (Greenberg, 2009)

Emotions

1 Primary
Adaptive – productive (e.g. fresh and new, in the moment, in response to shifting circumstances, change when circumstances change, feel good even if not happy, bring relief/changes)

(Continued)

(Continued)

Maladaptive – productive (e.g. difficult but bearable and contained; it is possible to work with them further so they can be transformed) or unproductive (e.g. feel bad, stuck in it, familiar old feeling, overwhelming, feel as bad as the last time, deep, distressing, sobbing, can include tantrums or ranting)

2 Secondary
Maladaptive – unproductive (e.g. obscure, reactive, diffuse, emotion in response to an emotion, upset, hopeless, confused, inhibited, low energy, whining, complaining)

3 Instrumental
Maladaptive – unproductive (e.g. emotional expressions aimed at eliciting a certain response from others, such as crocodile tears)

Box 8.3 Features of in-session productive emotional experience (Greenberg, Anszra, & Herrmann, 2007).

Productive emotions are characterised by a specific manner of processing that involves:

- attention to the emotion;
- symbolisation of it;
- congruence between verbal and non-verbal aspects of experiencing emotion;
- acceptance of emotion;
- optimal regulation of emotion;
- experienced agency in emotional experiencing; and
- differentiation of different aspects of emotional experiencing.

Working with hopelessness in the psychotherapeutic process

Depression is one of the most common problems that therapists encounter (I will focus on therapeutic work with depression more in Chapter 9). So are the experiences of hopelessness and helplessness that are so common with this disorder. Experienced hopelessness and helplessness are examples of overwhelming emotions. The difficulty with them is that they are painful and inhibit productive emotional experiencing and expression. Hopelessness and helplessness, as well as other depressive symptoms, manifest themselves in, for instance, the client's slow pace of verbal expression and overall demeanour, sometimes a silent voice, non-specific sadness, despair, proneness to feelings of guilt, irritation (anger) with the self and/or others, loss of perspective, fear of the future, etc.

To provide containment, holding, experiences of support and validation, the therapist needs to adjust his or her own communication to the client's pace and respect the client's 'slowness'. The therapist needs to be patient in helping the client to differentiate aspects of the emotional experiencing. In this, the therapist may need to move beyond secondary hopelessness (Greenberg & Watson, 2006) and into more primary emotions related to specific aspects (narratives) of the client's life situation. There is a great difference between feeling down generally and feeling put down by a specific comment of a boss in front of other colleagues. The therapist may feel spontaneous compassion towards the client's clearer and idiosyncratic experiences of hurt than towards an unspecific universal distress.

As the client's pace is slow, it may be up to the therapist to move actively in the client's world and to differentiate emotional experiences and their meanings. It is important that the therapist also responds to the nuances of difficult and painful emotions (e.g. sadness, powerlessness, despair, anger). The therapist may need to respond to aspects of the client's experience that are unclear to the client (Gendlin, 1984). An important skill is the capability to recognise the client's needs that are not being met and affirm the client's right to have them met and actively pursued.

All the above-mentioned suggestions aim at providing a supportive presence that hopefully enables the client to be able to sustain those difficult emotional experiences. An empathic presence can thus offer not only relational and emotional support, but also help to name aspects of the difficult experience and in this way make them more comprehensible (Watson, Goldman, & Vanaerschot, 1998; Watson, 2002). Especially important is an increase in the awareness of unmet needs that need to be attended to.

Working with suicidal risk in the psychotherapeutic process

Suicidal behaviour in clients is the most worrying situation for every therapist. According to Westefeld et al. (2000), 97% of psychologists in the USA worked at least once with a suicidal client, 29% had at least one client who attempted suicide and 11% had at least one client who committed suicide. This just underlines the significance of the suicidal threat in therapeutic work.

The worst aspect of a suicide attempt lies in the fact that it can lead to the loss of life or serious injuries. This loss is a loss for the client's loved ones too. Furthermore, the suicide or suicidal attempt is a huge trauma for all involved. The trauma includes the regrets of close ones, thoughts about whether it could have been prevented or whether one contributed to it. Following a suicide attempt, the guilt of the survivors for traumatising others and the trauma of one's own despair also need to be taken into account. The therapist is part of this too, as he or she may be haunted by a professional conscience and legal responsibility. All of this must be realised within the context of knowing that, straight after an unsuccessful suicide attempt, the majority of survivors are happy about the fact that they survived (Chesley & Loring-McNulty, 2003).

Suicidal behaviour is most typically present in difficulties that can be classified as mental health disorders, such as bipolar disorder, certain forms of personality disorders (especially borderline personality disorder), schizophrenia and depression (see Westefeld et al., 2000). The potential suicidal risk may have different qualities ranging from a vague and general talk about the possibility of suicide (suicidal ideation) to a determined expression of an intentional decision to kill oneself (suicide planning). Suicidal ideation typically stems from a range of painful emotions that the client wants to avoid, such as shame, guilt, trauma. These may be unbearable and mixed with helplessness and hopelessness that these emotions are not resolving. Suicidal ideation is often an expression of the wish to avoid them. The actual planning of the suicide often comes after a period of emotional suffering, when the thought of suicide is experienced as a solution. The suicidal attempts, however, can also be sudden, when the option of suicide comes to the fore of awareness out of the unbearable emotional pain felt at that moment. This often happens when judgement is impaired by substances (alcohol) or overwhelming emotions.

The risk of suicidal behaviour needs to be routinely assessed as a part of basic intake information. For example, if, after asking about the client's problems and suffering, there exists any hint that the client may have thoughts of suicide or plans for attempting it, it needs to be explicitly explored. The same applies if the state of the client, who originally did not seem to be at risk, deteriorates. When working with potential suicidal behaviour the therapist first has to assess its risk properly. Both ideation and suicide plans are assessed. Experts in the area suggest asking explicit questions on ideation and suicidal plans. For example, *Have you been feeling so badly lately that you have thought about harming yourself?* (see Westefeld et al., 2000: 453). The therapist assesses not only the current level of ideation and plans, but also asks the client how it is in situations when the client is at his or her lowest. The client's impulsivity also needs to be assessed, as well as the potential triggers of an unbearable emotional state and the environmental conditions that may contribute to suicidal behaviour.

Established psychological tests can be used in this assessment. Many screening measures, such as Beck Depression Inventory (Beck, Steer, & Garbin, 1988) or the Clinical Outcome in Routine Evaluation – Outcome Measure (Evans et al., 2000) contain items measuring suicidal ideation or plans. Specific measures solely devoted to suicide risk assessment exist as well (e.g. Scale for Suicide Ideation – Beck et al., 1979; Suicide Behaviour Questionnaire – Linehan, 1996; Suicide Status Form – Jobes et al., 1997).

A knowledge of risk factors (and of their possible combination) may be helpful for the therapist. Westefeld et al. (2000), in their thorough review of suicide risks, consider the following:

- mental disorder (e.g. depression, schizophrenia, personality disorder, bipolar disorder);
- reduced ability to regulate affect;
- hopelessness, helplessness, perfectionism;
- abuse histories and lack of social support;
- drug and alcohol consumption;
- previous suicide attempts;
- chronic pain or chronic illness;
- age (i.e. adolescents and the elderly);
- gender (men are four and a half times more likely to commit suicide than women; see Centers for Disease Control and Prevention, 2007);
- minority status (ethnic or sexual).

The assessment also includes the client's current stress factors, available environmental support and capability of constructive coping (see Westefeld et al., 2000). As the risk of misjudgement of suicide urgency is considerable (Westefeld et al., 2000), it may be prudent to evaluate the suicidal risk more conservatively. If the risk exists, assessing its acuteness is also important. An immediate, acute threat of suicide may warrant the therapist suggesting hospitalisation and this is something that the therapist can collaboratively explore with the client in the session. An alternative could be mobilising appropriate relatives to monitor the client, although issues of confidentiality would have to be carefully discussed with the client and the breach of confidentiality should be a last resort (always done transparently with the client).

If the client is in crisis, but there is not an immediate threat of him or her attempting suicide, the therapist may suggest increasing the frequency of sessions. This not only provides support for the client, but it also allows the therapist to monitor the client's emotional state and risk behaviour. An intervention that is often considered when an attempt is not immediately imminent is contracting around suicidal behaviour (see Bond, 1993; Westefeld et al., 2000; Bateman & Fonagy, 2004). Contracting is typically performed in writing. It includes not only the commitment of the client not to commit suicide, but also outlines the steps the client can take when in crisis. Such a contract is explicit about its timeframe, commitments and the steps to be followed in the circumstances of a suicidal urge. However, the 'Practice Guidelines for the Assessment and Treatment of Patients with Suicidal Behaviours' of the American Psychiatric Association (2003) point to the limitations of suicidal contracts and caution clinicians not to overestimate them.

A suicide ideation and wish to die is always explored in therapy. It often has a clear meaning (e.g. unbearable emotional pain, unbearable shame). The therapeutic work therefore needs to focus on these underlying vulnerabilities that lead the client to consider suicide as a resolution of suffering. The therapist's understanding of suicidal behaviour in the context of the client's overall difficulties is crucial. The suicidal ideation may be different for an adolescent who has broken up with a girlfriend than for a client with schizophrenia who is haunted by a delusion that he is going to be tortured so he has to kill himself. With regard to interventions used at times of crisis, a skilful, containing and supportive presence may be essential. Suicidal clients are sensitive to the respect and validating presence of the therapist (Paulson & Worth, 2002). The therapist's firmness is also recommended by some (Fujimura et al., 1985). Outside the therapy session, it is important that the therapist engages the client's social support network (Westefeld et al., 2000; see Chapter 9), if one is available. The client's activity for days of crisis can be planned as well. When appropriate, a referral can be considered as well as other forms of care or treatment (e.g. medication).

Excellent sources on the issues of suicide include Westefeld et al. (2000), Bongar (2002) and 'Practice Guidelines for the Assessment and Treatment of Patients with Suicidal Behaviours' of the American Psychiatric Association (2003).

Working with deliberate self-harm in therapy

Deliberate self-harm – behaviour aiming to harm or destroy body tissue and cause physical injury (e.g. Gratz, 2001) – just like suicidal behaviour, presents serious risks for clients in therapy. It is especially so as it may already be present in clients of adolescent age (Hawton et al., 2002). Deliberate self-harm may be present in the client with affective and personality disorders (Haw et al., 2001). Work with clients who deliberatly self-harm, just as in the case of suicide risk, requires careful case management strategies, such as proper assessment and contracting, when it comes to addressing this behaviour during the therapy. Especially in the case of adolescents, issues of confidentiality and its limitation needs to be addressed. The safety of an adolescent is of utmost consideration.

What is especially important is to explore what the deliberate self-harm is an expression of. This behaviour can be linked with suicidal behaviour (see Rodham, Hawton, & Evans, 2004). Often it can be an expression of anger directed towards the self. It can also be an attempt to override emotional distress by an act that brings attention to the physical pain. However, it can also be an interpersonal act of trying to communicate despair and the extent of emotional distress. In other cases, it can be an attempt to impress others (see Rodham, Hawton, & Evans, 2004; Hawton & James, 2005, for the variety of reasons; see also Box 8.4). The reasons need to be examined so that an appropriate therapeutic strategy can be employed. In a case where it is an expression of emotional disregulation and/or anger towards the self, emotion regulation strategies can be developed (see Linehan, 1993; Menin, 2004). If the self-harm has interpersonal connotations, these can be unfolded and healthier ways of communicating can be worked on. Linehan (1993), in her dialectical behaviour therapy, presents many useful suggestions for learning how to contain the urge to self-harm (e.g. distracting strategies) (see Low et al., 2001; McKay, Wood, & Brantley, 2007). However, with young clients, the work on changing self-harming behaviour may involve more strategic interventions that include their environment, which may be contributing to the reasons for such behaviour. More on self-harm with adolescents can be found in Fox and Hawton (2004).

Box 8.4 Potential reasons for self-harming according to Hawton and James (2005)

- To die
- To escape from unbearable anguish
- To change the behaviour of others
- To escape from a situation
- To show desperation to others
- To change the behaviour of others
- To 'get back at' other people or make them feel guilty
- To gain relief of tension
- To seek help

Reproduced from Hawton & James (2005) with permission from BMJ Publishing Group Ltd.

Encountering manipulation in the psychotherapeutic process

Occasionally, the therapist may encounter a client who follows specific, undisclosed goals that the client does not reveal to the therapist. For example, the client may be involved in a court battle with an ex-partner (e.g. for custody of their children), engages in counselling and in the middle of counselling requests a written report from the therapist. The therapist is then in a difficult position. The therapist may not like the situation that the client has got him or her into but still has to respond to the client's needs. In such cases, the therapist has to make his or her own judgement about whether preparing the report would be within their competence, whether such a report can be seen as corresponding with the contract the therapist had with the client, and whether it would be ethically sound to provide it. The therapist also has to examine his or her own feelings in such a situation – not only what would be appropriate professionally, but also personally.

Similarly, the therapist may be caught in an ethical dilemma when a client reports how he or she manipulated somebody they describe in their story. The therapist may then focus the work on highlighting and acknowledging the ethical aspect of the client's account of his or her interpersonal behaviour (see Chapter 4). Furthermore, some clients reveal so-called instrumental emotions, that is they intentionally or unintentionally express emotions so that they elicit an excepted response from the therapist (e.g. crocodile tears to elicit comfort) (Greenberg & Safran, 1989). As Greenberg, Rice, and Elliott (1993) nicely present it, in such cases it is important for the therapist to acknowledge it and to look for the underlying primary emotional experiences that need to be responded to (e.g. fear of loneliness if I don't 'moan' enough).

Different intentional or unintentional manipulation may be encountered in the psychotherapy process. It may be more characteristic when working with people with certain types of problem (e.g. personality disorders such as histrionic, narcissistic and borderline). One must therefore remember that the different strategies often employed by clients either towards therapists or towards other people in their stories are led by anxiety, fear, and their own insecurity. It is this vulnerability that the therapist needs to attend to most in such instances. Therapeutic strategies should focus on how to therapeutically address those vulnerabilities and build resilience towards them in the client.

Working with anger directed at the therapist

Clients often express anger during the psychotherapeutic process. Mostly, it is anger aimed at a third person not present in the therapist's office. Occasionally, it can also be anger aimed at the therapist. It can be expressed directly or indirectly. Research shows that the client's expression of anger is very difficult for therapists, especially if it is a direct expression of anger (Hill et al., 2003).

I showed some examples of anger directed towards the therapist and the ways of dealing with it in Chapter 2, which was devoted to solving a conflict in the therapeutic alliance (see the models of Safran & Muran, 2000). The initial step in the therapist's dealing with the client's expression of anger towards the therapist is that the therapist will not start to be defensive. Though the therapist may share the impact the anger has on him or her, it is important that the therapist is also able to stay with the client's anger and explore and unfold the reasons for it. Often it is important to acknowledge the therapist's own share of responsibility for the client's anger, though at times it may be more to do with the client's 'dynamic' (see Hill et al., 2003). If the anger is not directly expressed, it may be important to facilitate the client to express it more directly (Safran & Muran, 1996, 2000). The therapist may also explore what hurt and vulnerable emotional experiences in the client underlie the anger. These need to be responded to and looked after (see Chapter 2). Indeed, in the case of some clients (especially the ones with certain types of personality disorder) this may be a central issue to work on in therapy.

The danger of instances of expressed anger in therapy is that they may signal a threat to the therapeutic alliance and may indicate a risk of a premature termination of therapy. Hill et al. (2003), in their study, showed that in cases where the directly expressed anger was not resolved, it was more typical of situations in which the therapists felt anxious and when the anger stemmed from the client's personality. In cases of indirectly expressed anger, it seems that helping the client to express the anger more directly was crucial for the resolution.

Working with attitudes and beliefs related to the client's problem

Therapists encounter clients with different beliefs and attitudes. Some of them sometimes seem to be not conducive to mental health. Typically, it is not the attitudes or beliefs themselves, but rather their rigid experiencing that can be an expression of a mental health difficulty. Occasionally, clients may come with problems linked to beliefs and attitudes that appear delusional or based on hallucination. In some instances, there exists an 'unspoken' consensus among professionals that something is delusional; in other cases (often religious and spiritual beliefs) there is no consensus. For instance, an elderly female client may be convinced that the devil is threatening her. For a secular therapist, this may be very difficult to follow. A male client may be uncertain whether his parents' belief in UFOs is a sign of their problem or not, as he himself is not sure whether there are indeed aliens among us or not. Clients' attitudes and beliefs as well as their worldview may differ from those of the therapist in many instances. When those beliefs or attitudes are central to the therapeutic work, it may be necessary to work with them. The therapist has to respect the client's autonomy and free will, while at the same time the therapist may consider some beliefs or attitudes as harmful to the client. Finding the balance when approaching a client with a hopefully informed view that a certain belief or attitude may contribute to the client's problem is very difficult to do.

There are good models in the area of multicultural counselling that can be used when working with the 'personal culture' of a specific client. It is important that the therapist understands the client's attitudes and beliefs and explores with the client how they are connected to the experienced difficulties that brought the client to therapy. The therapist may also use the client's beliefs and support the healthy elements of those beliefs. For example, an OCD client of Catholic denomination who feels sinful five minutes after confession may be helped to distinguish between a healthy attitude towards living an honourable life and an expression of anxiety in the self-condemning attitude 'I am sinful as I had a bad thought, a thought of anger towards somebody'. Therapeutic work typically focuses on the experience of beliefs and attitudes and whether they lead to unhealthy psychological and physical distress, rather than the content of such a belief. The therapist therefore needs to be knowledgeable about different 'cultures' or at least be prepared to learn about them. The therapist also needs to monitor his or her own respect of others and any countertransferential reactions that can prevent the therapist from working with the client in the therapeutic framework. If the therapist allows him or herself to get to the client's world from the inside, the therapist can then adjust his or her own approach to the client's worldview. In Box 8.5 I describe a tentative model of working with spiritual and religious issues in therapy that may serve as an example of the principles of working with clients' beliefs and attitudes when they are intertwined with their psychological problems.

Box 8.5 A tentative model of working with spiritual and religious issues in therapy (Davis & Timulak, 2008)

Core assumptions:

- Spirituality can be a resource in dealing with psychological distress.
- Spiritual difficulties can contribute to psychological distress.
- Some clients want spiritually sensitive help as their spirituality may not be separate from their psychological well-being.

The religion- and spirituality-sensitive therapist will have an awareness of the following in his or her practice of therapy:

- The effects of religion and spirituality on mental health and its relevance for psychotherapy.
- Personal spirituality and religiosity and any biases they may have.
- The limitations to their expertise.
- Training and supervision needs which include an understanding of the major religions, the difference between religion and spirituality, and the role these may play in an individual's life.

The client in religion- and spirituality-sensitive therapy will be aware that:

- Their spiritual/religious beliefs and practices may be a source of support which helps them to cope with mental health issues.
- Their spiritual/religious beliefs and practices may be relevant to their psychological distress.

The therapeutic relationship:

- The therapist is congruent, gives unconditional positive regard for the meaning of the client's beliefs (working within an *ecumenical* framework of spirituality) and is empathic.
- The dangers are transference/countertransference.

Assessment:

- During the assessment process, alongside other background information, a question regarding the role of religious/spiritual beliefs and practices in the client's life can be included to establish whether or not the client perceives this to be relevant to the therapeutic process.
- If this is done in an open and accepting manner, then the client will know that the therapist is willing to explore these issues alongside any other issues that the client wishes to bring to therapy.

Interventions:

- Interventions which accommodate the client's beliefs are most helpful when they are requested by the client and agreed on by the client and therapist mutually. It is essential that the client's autonomy is respected during any intervention. The therapist will endeavour to understand the way these beliefs impact/work out in the client's life and tailor the intervention accordingly.
- Examples of these interventions will be guided meditations within the client's religious/spiritual framework. Also some mainstream therapies have manualised versions for highly spiritual or religious clients.
- Religion- and spirituality-sensitive psychotherapy can also accommodate an exploration of aspects of the client's beliefs which they consider to be either helpful or unhelpful to their psychological well-being.

Referral:

- The therapist needs to be mindful of his or her own limitations in terms of expertise and personal bias. When assessing what the client needs, it may be appropriate, in collaboration with the client, to refer him or her either for additional support from a spiritual/religious advisor or to a more explicit religious/spiritual psychotherapist.

There are a vast number of situations that the therapist may encounter in the therapeutic process. I have selected just a few to bring a flavour of the complexity of the therapeutic process and the expectations put on the therapist. The situations and the therapist's response to them may be quite similar among therapists, irrespective of the therapist's overall strategy or therapeutic orientation. In the next chapter we will deal with more strategic issues when encountering typical problems and disorders for which counselling and psychotherapy are used.

Recommended reading

There is no single textbook that deals with the different situations in the therapeutic process, but I could recommend some of Yalom's books as they nicely describe the immediacy of the psychotherapeutic process. For example:

Yalom, I.D. (2002). *Gift of Therapy*. New York: Harper Collins.

Nine

Specifics of Psychotherapy and Counselling for Some Psychological Disorders and Difficulties

Abstract

This chapter covers commonly recognised psychological difficulties that are being classified in the mainstream psychiatric classification systems such DSM–IV and ICD–10. Mood disorders, anxiety disorders, personality disorders, substance-related disorders, eating disorders and psychotic disorders are covered. Information on their characteristics, etiology, prevalence and treatment are provided. The main focus of this chapter is on principles of empirically-informed psychological therapy for these types of problem.

Psychotherapy and counselling can be seen as professional activities that are used for addressing and overcoming human suffering (Miller, 2004). They involve psychological (social, intrapersonal and interpersonal) processes. Psychotherapy and counselling were often developed as generic professional activities for alleviating various forms of psychological suffering. In some instances (e.g. behavioural therapy), some forms of psychotherapy and counselling were also developed as specific procedures for specific problems. These problems could usually be classified so that a cohort of professionals could understand what kind of problem was being described.

Although counselling and psychotherapy are interventions for many psychologically based general problems in life, they are also recognised as suitable interventions for what is currently conceptualised by mainstream medicine and psychology as distinct psychiatric and psychological disorders. Classification systems such as DSM–IV and ICD–10 are used to classify similar psychological, physiological, and interpersonal features/symptoms in people. This classification, though often seen as controversial (e.g. Bentall, 2003, 2009; Miller, 2004), is used as a main communication system among mental health professionals for describing common features of typical problems, but also their prevalence, common course, potential etiology, and so on.

This chapter will outline the main principles and references for working with the typical problems/disorders that psychotherapy is used for. I will roughly use the general mainstream classification of psychological disorders. While focusing mostly on the description of the therapeutic strategy and principles that are empirically found to be linked to successful outcomes, I will also examine other interventions beyond psychotherapy or counselling that may be either more primary or used in addition to psychotherapy or counselling in addressing a given problem.

Specifics of psychotherapy and counselling for adjustment disorders

Adjustment disorder is a very broad DSM–IV category that covers symptoms of emotional distress such as anxiety and low mood which can be connected to stressful events of a various nature (family problems, relational difficulties, occupational stress, etc.). The experienced distress is typically in excess of what would be expected with regard to the stressor and should cause social and occupational impairment (see American Psychiatric Association, 2001). As this category is very broad and often refers to the distress clearly linked to a stressor, it was not studied as to the relative effectiveness of specific therapeutic approaches in the form of currently popular randomised controlled trials. However, it is safe to say that most psychotherapy and counselling, as developed through tradition and also through research was conducted with this broad category of problems. Therefore, all the main approaches, from psychodynamic, humanistic and cognitive-behavioural traditions, and the skills and strategies presented in the previous chapters of this book are perfectly applicable to this type of problem. Naturally, they have to be embedded in an idiosyncratic case conceptualisation that is flexibly adjusted in the course of therapy. As the problems covered by this broad category often represent an emotional response to life events and situations, the conceptualisation may need to involve practical steps in addressing the problematic situation. For example, if 'adjustment' disorder is an emotional distress linked with a demotion at work, the therapist may need to examine practical steps which the client has to take to resource him or herself. These may include social support provided from close relatives or friends, consideration of another form of career, diversifying interests so they are not centred solely on work, learning from the experience for the future, reassessing priorities in life, etc.

Social support

Social support may play an important role in overcoming any adjustment difficulties. Therapists may actively explore the client's social milieu and encourage the use of contact with relevant family members or friends. In many cases, a more formal support may be considered. For example, support groups for the unemployed may be used in the case of unemployed clients. Such groups can show that the client is not alone with the problem. They may offer emotional support, but also practical steps in facing unemployment.

Social support may be especially important for clients with a minority status, for example, migrants, ethnic minorities, sexual orientation minorities, religious minorities, etc. The experienced isolation may be overcome by the possibility of meeting people of the same status or at least with a more in-depth understanding of minority issues. Social support may also play an important part as a component of therapy. In specific cases, and with the client's consent, the therapist may involve an appropriate significant other (e.g. spouse) and explore with him/her and the client the ways in which this person can support the client.

Self-help materials and other helping materials or interventions

Self-help materials, such as books, leaflets and relevant websites for specific problems that may belong under the heading of problems leading to adjustment disorder, may be of assistance. For example, some educational institutions (e.g. universities) provide mental health portals that contain a lot of relevant information on mental health issues and many suggestions of what to do in various situations. Online interventions such as self-administered computer programs are starting to become available as well. The most well-established research evidence is for self-help books (Marrs, 1995) and, more recently, for diverse online interventions (Marks, Cavanagh, & Gega, 2007). I will focus on some of them in the section discussing therapy for depression and anxiety disorders (see below).

Leisure activities and sport

Therapists working with clients with a variety of problems covered by the broad category of adjustment disorder may consider exploring the utilisation of leisure activities and sport with the clients. These can be a very useful resource for coping with adversity. The client's interests may vary, from the more artistic pursuits (e.g. reading, theatre, movies) to more physical ones (hiking, running, biking, etc.). Activities that are performed in a group format may, at the same time, fulfil the function of social support.

Psychopharmacology and referrals

Since many situations that lead to adjustment problems may elicit quite acute symptoms of low mood, anxiety, tension, sleeplessness, etc., and clear impairment of everyday functioning, if the client agrees, the therapist may organise an appropriate referral to a GP or psychiatrist who may in turn consider medication. It is important to recognise the client's preferences and also the level of distress, previous experience with psychological difficulties and the means by which these were addressed (e.g. whether the client was on any medication in the past). The prescribing physician may then consider possible alternatives that could ameliorate the client's symptoms. The physician considers an appropriate treatment also on the basis of the client's general health and response to treatment in the past. Often antidepressants or, for a short period of time, other medication, such as benzodiazepines for anxiety symptoms, or sleep-improving medications may be prescribed. From the perspective of a psychological therapist, it is important to consider how the client sees the interplay of drug treatment and psychological therapy, how he or she understands each of them may contribute to the resolution of the problems. The therapist also needs to familiarise him or herself with the effects of the medication on mood and emotional experiencing (and in some cases, even on cognitive function), and should have an understanding of potential side-effects and withdrawal symptoms when the client finishes with the medication, as this may have a significant influence on the emotional experiencing that is important for therapy. Currently, there is a number of books that serve as a guide for the therapist (e.g. Beitman et al., 2003; Patterson et al., 2006).

Specifics of psychotherapy and counselling for depression

The *Diagnostic Statistical Manual* of the American Psychiatric Association recognises several mood disorders, such as major depressive disorder (characterised by one or more major depressive episodes), dysthymic disorder (typically, at least two years of depressive mood) or bipolar disorder (either type I or II depending on whether it is a manic or mixed episode or a depressive episode that is to the fore) (for diagnostic details and other mood disorders see DSM–IV, American Psychiatric Association, 2001). Mood disorders represent a significant subgroup of mental health difficulties, with their yearly prevalence higher than 5% (see Narrow et al., 2002). Lifetime prevalence may be much higher, with major depressive disorder present in more than 15% of the population (Kessler, 2002). Mood disorders often precede, follow or co-occur with anxiety disorders, but in general, depressive symptoms may be present in any other disorder. People with mood disorders need to be routinely assessed for suicide risk, with approximately half of clients being suicidal (Stolberg, Clark, & Bongar, 2002).

Defining features of depressive symptomatology (major depressive episode) are the presence of several depressive symptoms, such as depressed mood, loss of interest, weight loss or gain, insomnia or hypersomnia, psychomotor agitation or retardation, fatigue, feelings of worthlessness or inappropriate guilt, diminished ability to think or concentrate and recurrent suicidal ideation. More than five of these symptoms (including one of the first two) have to be present over more than a two-week period and several exclusion criteria have to be ruled out (see DSM–IV, American Psychiatric Association, 2001; see also Box 9.1). If fewer than five symptoms are present, DSM–IV recognises a tentative category of minor depressive episode (disorder).

Although there is a number of psychological, developmental and social factor theories of depression, biological factors seem to be important in establishing vulnerability to depression (Gotlib & Hammen, 2002). Biological factors include genetic susceptibility, which transpires in the functioning of neurotransmitters such as serotonin, though structural aspects of the brain are also taken into consideration. Psychological, social and developmental factors focus on early adversity, parental psychopathology and social environment stressors (for more, see Gotlib & Hammen, 2002).

Box 9.1 Mood disorders according to DSM–IV and their main features (American Psychiatric Association, 2001: 345–346). For full diagnostic criteria, please consult DSM–IV

Major depressive disorder – characterised by one or more major depressive episodes (i.e. at least two weeks of depressed mood or loss of interest plus other symptoms).

Dysthymic disorder – characterised by at least two years of depressed mood on more days than not.

Depressive disorder not otherwise specified – disorders with depressive features that do not meet the criteria for other depressive disorders.

Bipolar I disorder – characterised by one or more manic or mixed episodes, usually accompanied by major depressive episode.

Bipolar II disorder – characterised by one or more major depressive episode accompanied by at least one hypomanic episode.

Cyclothymic disorder – characterised by at least two years of numerous periods of hypomanic symptoms and numerous periods of depressive symptoms.

Bipolar disorder not otherwise specified – disorders with bipolar features that do not meet criteria for any specific bipolar disorder.

Several different psychotherapeutic approaches, especially cognitive therapy for depression (Beck et al., 1979; Beck & Alford, 2008) and interpersonal therapy for depression (Klermann et al., 1984; Weissman, Markowitz, & Klerman, 2000) were extensively studied. Other approaches, such as behavioural therapy (e.g. Dimidjian et al., 2008) and emotion-focused therapy (Greenberg & Watson, 2006) were also studied. It seems that all major approaches, with the exception of behavioural therapy, recognise two main forms of depression: *self-critical* (identity-based) depression that can be summarised by the belief 'I am worthless', and *relational* depression (experiencing abandonment), characterised by the position 'I am not lovable'. This theoretical distinction was developed by Sidney J. Blatt, who recognises anaclictic (relational) and introjective (self-critical) personality leanings in different people that also transpire in depressive symptomatology (Blatt, 2008; Blatt, Shahar, & Zuroff, 2002). These two features can also be predictive of the effectiveness of therapy, with self-critical depression, often typified by a high level of perfectionism, being harder to treat (Blatt et al., 1998). Some approaches showed empirically that the two types of depression are closely linked – i.e. 'I am worthless and therefore nobody loves me' – and it is difficult to find a clear type that distinguishes the two forms (see Greenberg & Watson, 2006).

While CBT approaches conceptually understand the two forms of depression as characterised by two different sets of problematic core beliefs, emotion-focused therapy sees them as problematic core emotion schemes characterised by fear, shame and sadness that typically correspond with the attachment (I am not loved) or identity (I am worthless) domain. Psychodynamic theorists (Blatt, 2008) see the two dimensions of depression as an expression of personality structure. Whichever approach is taken, therapy is focused on the restructuring of beliefs, schemes or personality structures: in the case of CBT, by cognitive restructuring (see Chapter 7); in the case of EFT, through the transformation of maladaptive emotion schemes by assessing adaptive emotion schemes (self-compassion, protective anger, expression of adaptive grief) (see Pascual-Leone & Greenberg, 2007); and in the case of psychodynamic therapies, by working through the personality structure by exploring and looking for insight into interpersonal functioning, especially in the relationship with the therapist.

Some therapies for depression also focus on other aspects of combating symptoms. CBT makes heavy use of behaviour activation (see Chapter 7) to boost the client's engagement in positive emotion triggering activities. Interpersonal therapy (Weissman, Markowitz, & Klerman, 2000) focuses on the exploration of interpersonal aspects of depression (in one of the domains, such as grief, role transitions, interpersonal disputes and interpersonal deficits) and building or allowing for an appropriate interpersonal response to the interpersonal aspects of the client's situation.

Other therapies, such as classical client-centred therapy, build on the provision of a caring relationship that offers the needed support and possibility of emotional and cognitive processing of difficult experiences. Some versions of CBT focus on promoting self-compassion in clients (e.g. Gilbert, 2007).

With regard to bipolar disorder, much less is known about an effective therapy for this problem. Psychotherapies often focus on improving medication (mood stabilisers) compliance, prevention of further episodes (especially of depression), and decreasing the time needed for stabilisation after an episode (Miklowitz, 2008). A number of therapies, mostly cognitive-behavioural but also other therapies, were studied for this disorder (Miklowitz & Craighead, 2007). For instance, interpersonal and social rhythm therapy focuses on helping clients to function in their social and interpersonal context, which is impacted by mood difficulties, and to see how their social and circadian rhythms are influencing and influenced by mood, so the clients can be more in control of their functioning (Frank & Schwartz, 2004). Cognitive-behavioural therapies conceptualise the idea that negative self-evaluation and problematic core beliefs contribute to sudden changes in mood and therefore need to be targeted in therapy. Mania is also targeted by teaching tempering when there is a pull for manic behaviour (see Leahy, 2004).

One of the more promising treatments seems to be the family-focused treatment (Miklowitz & Craighead, 2007). This form of therapy consists of three main strategies: psychoeducation, communication enhancement training and problem-solving skills training (Miklowitz, 2008). The client's immediate family is part of the treatment. Psychoeducation, which lasts for up to seven sessions, focuses on discussing symptoms and the course of the disorder, the etiology of the disorder and the discussion of treatment. The second part of family focused treatment is the teaching of four communication skills: expressing positive feelings, active listening, making positive requests for changes in others' behaviour and giving negative feedback. This part of therapy lasts for about seven or eight sessions (Miklowitz, 2008). Finally, the third part of therapy consists of problem-solving skills training and again lasts for seven or eight sessions. Problem-solving skills training focuses on non-adherence to medication, repair of damage done during manic episodes, and relationship conflicts (Mikowitz, 2008). As is clear from this description, this therapy (and similarly other therapies for bipolar disorder) treats psychotherapy as an adjunct treatment that focuses on the quality of life with the bipolar condition rather than on full recovery from this serious difficulty.

In general, several therapeutic processes were found to be important in empirical findings on the factors influencing the effectiveness of psychological therapies for mood disorders (see Beutler, Castonguay, & Follette, 2006). They relate to client factors, therapist factors, relationship and technique factors. Some of them are presented in Box 9.2.

Box 9.2 Examples of empirically-informed principles of working with mood disorders (Beutler, Castonguay, & Follette, 2006: 112–115)

Client factors:

- The more severe patients have worse prognosis.
- Patients with co-morbid personality disorders have worse prognosis.
- The patient-perceived level of social support is an important predictor in treatment effectiveness.

Therapist factors:

- Therapist flexibility in changing strategies, adapting to patients' presentations, tolerance and creativity are related to improvement.

Relationship factors:

- A positive working alliance enhances therapy.

Techniques and interventions:

- Advantageous techniques directly focus on presenting problems and concerns.
- Techniques focus on an adaptive way of feeling and being.
- An intensive therapy may be beneficial; also non-individual interventions (e.g. family therapy).

From the therapist's perspective, when working with people with depression, what may be especially challenging is the level of hopelessness the clients with depression experience. Especially in the case of recurrent or dysthymic depression, the client's despair may be difficult to face by the therapist as the therapist may feel under pressure to relieve the client. It is even more pronounced in the work with clients with a high level of perfectionism and hostility (Blatt et al., 1998), features not uncommon in clients with depression (Wiebe & McCabe, 2002). Furthermore, the instability of bipolar clients requires close collaboration with a prescribing physician and good knowledge of the limitations of medications. The relapses, and their unpredictability, may be very difficult to bear for therapists as well. Bipolar disorder is also characterised by non-compliance and denial of the problems, especially in the acute manic phase, which may be challenging for the therapist (Basco, Merlock, & McDonald, 2004). Suffering may also lead to a lot of frustration that may be directed towards the therapist (Basco, Merlock, & McDonald, 2004). The role of supervision and peer team support is therefore irreplaceable. The therapy should be a real team effort and requires multidisciplinary work, so it is not possible for it to be led in an isolated private practice. The same applies to work with severe depression.

Psychopharmacology and other biological interventions

Mood disorders are currently also treated by biological means. It is important for the therapist to be familiar with these treatment options as they can often overlap, supplement or be more primary to psychotherapy. The advantage of a multidisciplinary approach is currently being recognised more and more. Many therapists work in a multidisciplinary setting and many of those that are in a more individualistic setting collaborate with other professionals. The awareness of other forms of treatment and the issues that go with it is therefore important for therapists (e.g. Patterson et al., 2006).

Antidepressants are routinely considered in the treatment of depression. This is so in the case of moderate and, especially, more severe depression. A number of antidepressants, in general affecting neurotransmitting in the brain, exist (e.g. see Patterson et al., 2006). They are used in the acute phase of depression, but also in the maintenance phase. The prescription and dosage depends on many factors, such as the number of depressive episodes, the lifetime course of depression, etc. In general, however, they are prescribed for months or more. For instance, in the case of the first episode, they may be prescribed for three months of an acute phase and the following six months of the maintenance phase (Patterson et al., 2006). They may also have various side-effects (affecting the central nervous system, the gastrointestinal system, sexual functioning, the cardiovascular system) that need to be carefully monitored. Furthermore, the withdrawal symptoms may also be unpleasant and important to monitor. Finally, given the risk of suicide, the level of toxicity needs to be taken into consideration when prescribing (for more, see Beitman et al., 2003; Patterson et al., 2006). The effectiveness of antidepressants is debatable, ranging from a 60% recovery rate to much lower (Elkin et al., 1989; Patterson et al., 2006; Boren, Leventhal, & Pigott, 2009). There definitely exists a critical mass of non-responders to antidepressant medication (see project STAR*D in Rush et al., 2006) who do not respond even to changing the course of antidepressants.

For the therapist working with depressed clients on antidepressant medication, many issues may arise. For instance, the use of antidepressants may interfere with therapy as the clients may not feel confident that psychological therapy is responsible for any changes achieved. On the other hand, clients may be ambivalent about taking medication and its side-effects, and this may become an important focus of therapy (Beitman et al., 2003). Furthermore, the withdrawal phase when finishing medication may be crucial for psychological therapy, as the client, apart from experiencing the withdrawal symptoms, may experience anxiety about the return of depression.

In the case of bipolar disorder, antidepressants may induce hypomania or mania (Patterson et al., 2006), which is important information for therapists. Mood stabilisers, such as lithium or atypical antipsychotics, are used in acute manic phases. Mood stabilisers are also used in the maintenance phase, sometimes combined with antidepressants (see Patterson et al., 2006). In the therapy of bipolar clients, it is important to bear in mind that mood stabilisers such as lithium have serious side-effects, a very high toxicity and strong withdrawal symptoms (see Patterson et al., 2006).

Electroconvulsive treatment is sometimes used in the treatment of mania or depression. It is usually employed if other forms of treatment have failed or cannot be used (see American Psychiatric Association, 2001). The main side-effect that has an implication for psychological therapy is amnesia (in various degrees).

Social support

Apart from biological treatment, there are other resources that can be important for tackling mood difficulties. The therapist may plan their use with the client or encourage the client to consider them. Research suggests that deficits in perceived parental support among adolescents proved to be a predictor of depression (Stice, Ragan, & Randall, 2004). This was not the same for perceived peer support, which seemed not to have an impact (Stice, Ragan, & Randall, 2004). The perceived lack of social support also seems to be related to depression in the elderly (Koizumi et al., 2005). Furthermore, it seems that the onset of depression leads to a decrease in social relations, which further decreases social support (Stice, Ragan, & Randall, 2004). Therefore, it may be crucial for any approach to depression to consider how social support can be mobilised for the client. This is often done through adjunct therapy, where a partner or others close to the client with depression are involved in therapy (see Beach & Jones, 2002). The role of community support (e.g. social clubs, church-based activities) may be an important source of social support as well.

Self-help materials and other helping materials or interventions

The use of self-help books (e.g. Greenberger & Padesky, 1995) can be useful in fighting depression (Cuijpers, 1997; Floyd et al., 2004). It can be especially so in a form of adjunct therapy, when books are used in addition to psychological therapy (Floyd, 2003). More recently, online interventions and computer-based programs have started to appear. Many follow the CBT model (e.g. Beating the Blues – Proudfoot et al., 2004), some are integrative (Deprexis – Meyer et al., 2009). They seem to be beneficial for mild to moderate forms of depression, especially for the populations that would otherwise be hard to reach (Marks, Cavanagh, & Gega, 2007).

Leisure activities and sport

Though some studies show otherwise (e.g. De Moor et al., 2008), it is often suggested that leisure activities and exercise are good for people with depression (Strohle, 2009). Even if not directly, then as a part of behaviour activation interventions (see Chapter 7), pleasure-increasing activities are clearly beneficial in fighting depression (see Dimidjian et al., 2008).

Recommended reading

A classical text of CBT for depression is:

Beck, A.T., Rush, A.J., Shaw, B.F., & Emery, G. (1979). *Cognitive Therapy of Depression*. New York: Guilford Press.

A newer version is:

Beck, A.T. & Alford, B.A. (2008). *Depression: Causes and Treatment* (2nd edition). Philadelphia: University of Pennsylvania Press.

A well-studied interpersonal therapy for depression is presented in manual form in the following books:

Klerman, G.L., Weissman, M.M., Rounsaville, B.J., & Chevron, E.S. (1984). *Interpersonal Psychotherapy of Depression*. New York: Basic Books.

Weissman, M.M., Markowitz, J.C., & Klerman, G.L. (2000). *Comprehensive Guide to Interpersonal Psychotherapy*. New York: Basic Books.

Behavioural activation therapy is described in the following chapter:

Dimidjian, S., Martell, C.R., Addis, M.E., & Herman-Dunn, R. (2008). Behavioral activation for depression. In D.H Barlow (ed.), *Clinical Handbook of Psychological Disorders : A Step-by-step Treatment Manual* (4th edition) (pp. 328-364). New York: Guilford Press.

A manual of humanistic therapy for depression can be found in:

Greenberg, L.S. & Watson, J.C. (2006). *Emotion-focused Therapy for Depression*. Washington, DC: American Psychological Association.

Specifics of psychotherapy and counselling for anxiety disorders

Another form of common difficulties that people seek therapy for are anxiety disorders. Anxiety disorders are defined by two major sets of symptoms: panic attacks and agoraphobia (American Psychiatric Association, 2001). Panic attacks are characterised by symptoms such as a pounding heart, sweating, trembling/shaking, shortness of breath, a feeling of choking, chest pain, nausea, dizziness, fear of losing control, fear of dying, hot flushes, etc. (American Psychiatric Association, 2001). A number of those symptoms must be present at a given time to meet the criteria for a panic attack. Panic attacks can be understood as a sudden intense fear reaction without a presence of real danger. Agoraphobia is characteristic by avoidance of places or situations from which escape may be difficult (American Psychiatric Association, 2001).

The Diagnostic and Statistical Manual of Mental Disorders (DSM–IV, American Psychiatric Association, 2001) distinguishes several forms of anxiety disorders: panic disorder (with and without agoraphobia), specific phobia, social phobia (anxiety), obsessive compulsive disorder (OCD), post-traumatic stress disorder (PTSD), acute stress disorder, and generalised anxiety disorder (GAD). The main features of these different forms of anxiety disorders are presented in Box 9.3.

Box 9.3 Anxiety disorders according to DSM–IV and their main features (American Psychiatric Association, 2001: 429–430). For full diagnostic criteria, please consult DSM–IV

Panic disorder – recurrent and persistent panic attacks about which the patient is persistently concerned; can be with and without agoraphobia.

Specific phobias – clinically significant anxiety triggered by a feared object or situation accompanied by agoraphobic behaviour.

Social anxiety – clinically significant anxiety triggered by social situations accompanied by avoidant behaviour.

Obsessive compulsive disorder – presence of obsessions that trigger anxiety and/or compulsions, a ritual behaviour that neutralises anxiety.

Post-traumatic stress disorder – re-experiencing of an extremely traumatic event accompanied by increased arousal and avoidance of stimuli associated with the trauma; symptoms present more than a month after the trauma.

Acute stress disorder – similar to PTSD, but present immediately after the trauma.

Generalised anxiety disorder – persistent anxiety and worry lasting more than six months.

The reported prevalence of anxiety disorders varies depending on the criteria used (e.g. DSM–III vs. DSM–IV) and the methodology of a given study. A very conservative assessment suggests that within a given year almost 12% of the American population has some anxiety disorder (Narrow et al., 2002), with almost 8% simple phobias, 3% social phobia, almost 4% PTSD, 3% GAD, 2% OCD and 1% panic disorder. There is a high co-morbidity among anxiety disorders themselves. Furthermore, anxiety disorders often co-occur with depression and avoidant dependent personality disorders (Hazlett-Stevens, Pruitt, & Collins, 2009; for more about personality disorders, see below). In the case of OCD, it is obsessive-compulsive personality disorder (Mathews, 2009).

The etiology of anxiety disorders is, just like other psychological disorders, very complex and multi-determined. Biological proneness or vulnerability (see Barlow, 2002) involves the functioning of neurotransmitters, as is also the case with depression. It is also well established that certain parts of the brain, such as amygdale, are hyperactive in people with anxiety problems (for more, see Antony, Federici, & Stein, 2009). With regard to the psychological aspects of anxiety disorders, Barlow (2002) recognises a general vulnerability, characterised by a diminished sense of control, and specific vulnerability that is linked to specific anxiety-provoking triggers such as somatic symptoms or social situations. Specific parenting styles (e.g. overprotective behaviour or neglect) and peer victimisation are currently being widely investigated and it is hypothesised that they play a role in the development of anxiety disorders (see Antony, Federici, & Stein, 2009; Hudson & Rapee, 2009).

A number of therapeutic approaches to anxiety disorders have been studied. The majority of them are cognitive-behavioural therapies (see Antony, Federici, & Stein, 2009). The main features of those treatments are: psychoeducation, relaxation training, different forms of exposure and cognitive restructuring (Antony, Federici, & Stein, 2009; see also Box 9.4). Psychoeducation usually focuses on the explanation of anxiety disorders, anxiety symptoms and the role of avoidance in maintaining them. Relaxation training focuses on the clients learning how to relax by themselves. Different forms of exposure help the clients to learn that their anxiety is bearable and survivable. Exposure also builds resilience when facing anxiety-provoking situations. It is also a strategy that leads to the overcoming of avoidant (e.g. agoraphobic) behaviour. Finally, cognitive restructuring is used for clients learning to recognise the role of their thinking and appraisal in escalating anxiety. Furthermore, clients are to change their thoughts and appraisal so that these can be benign and calming.

Box 9.4 Empirically well-established therapeutic strategies for anxiety disorders (Antony, Federici, & Stein, 2009: 13)

Panic disorder – psychoeducation, cognitive restructuring, interoceptive exposure, *in vivo* exposure.

Specific phobias – *in vivo* exposure, applied tension.

Social anxiety – psychoeducation, cognitive restructuring, *in vivo* exposure, stimulated exposure (role plays), social skills training.

Obsessive compulsive disorder – exposure and prevention of rituals, cognitive restructuring.

Post-traumatic stress disorder – *in vivo* exposure, exposure in imagination, cognitive restructuring, progressive muscle relaxation.

Generalised anxiety disorder – cognitive restructuring, progressive muscle relaxation.

We discussed all of these strategies in Chapter 7. There are a number of CBT manuals that have been empirically validated. A good overview is provided in Barlow (2008). Several publishers, for example Oxford University Press, also publish a series of validated treatment manuals (e.g. Craske & Barlow, 2007). These are typically accompanied by workbooks for clients. There are also a few studies of non-CBT therapies, but their evidence is only starting to be accumulated (e.g. Teusch & Bohme 1999).

With regard to our current empirical knowledge about factors that are important for the successful psychological therapy of anxiety disorders, it seems that exposure to fearful stimuli and overcoming of avoidance is crucial (see Newman et al., 2006). It is also important to note that anxiety can reappear easily. The transfer of learning from exposure is difficult if the situations to which the client is exposed are not similar to the situations provoking fear in reality (Ohman & Ruck, 2007). Research also suggests that anxiety disorders may be quite resistant and may have a high relapse rate (see Westen & Morrisson, 2001). What is also interesting is that the content of anxious thinking (worrying) in some disorders, such as GAD, often focuses on the underlying fears of failure, inadequacy or incompetence (Hazlett-Stevens, Pruitt, & Collins, 2009), which may suggest that general therapeutic strategies focused on such underlying vulnerabilities used in humanistic (emotion-focused) and psychodynamic therapies may also be useful (see the section on depression). Newman et al. (2006) reviewed existing empirical evidence and selected therapeutic principles that the research suggests are important for the effectiveness of psychological therapies for anxiety disorders. Their examples are presented in Box 9.5.

Box 9.5 Examples of empirically-informed principles of working with anxiety disorders (Newman et al., 2006: 190–195).

Client factors and therapist factors:

- Greater severity, chronicity as well as co-morbid depression, personality disorder and substance abuse predict poorer outcome.
- Therapy is less effective if the client perceives his/her social structure as hostile and critical.
- Therapy is less likely to be effective if the client reports negatively perceived parenting.
- Therapy is less likely to be effective if the client has low internal attributions of control or high negative self-attributions.

Relationship factors:

- A strong therapeutic alliance enhances therapy.

(Continued)

(Continued)

Techniques and interventions:

- Therapists help clients to be aware of inaccurate perceptions.
- Therapists engage clients in a corrective emotional experience in which clients are directly confronted with and face their fear and learn to cope with anxiety.
- Therapists help clients develop the skills for handling feared situations.

From the therapist's perspective, an important feature of anxiety disorders is the client's primary focus on the symptoms of anxiety. It is at times difficult to get the focus of therapy beyond that as the clients are often so preoccupied with their safety that anything other than immediate relief from anxiety and reassurance is a much lower priority. Furthermore, the clients may easily relapse and thus lose faith in full recovery. They may also see therapy as a threat as it requires them to get outside their safety zone. Clients with anxiety disorders can also become clingy to their therapist and deteriorate towards the end of therapy when they are required to function independently (see Teusch & Finke, 1996). Therefore, to build a high-quality working alliance that focuses on the agreement on the goals and tasks of therapy is a priority.

Psychopharmacology and other biological interventions

Therapists have to be aware that in the case of most anxiety disorders medication is also an option, especially in the case of more severe conditions. However, some studies show the superiority of cognitive-behavioural therapy over medication (e.g. for panic disorder – Barlow et al., 2000). This issue may be more complex if the longer-term perspective and sequential treatment is taken into account, where medication may be an important part of a successful treatment. Antidepressant medication is typically used for those purposes (Patterson et al., 2006; Antony, Federici, & Stein, 2009). Benzodiazepines are also used in the treatment of various anxiety disorders (see Antony, Federici, & Stein, 2009). They have proven to be effective (see Roy-Byrne & Cowley, 2007), although there is a risk that clients can become addicted to them, plus they have significant withdrawal symptoms. Furthermore, when used concurrently with CBT, they may serve as an avoidance mechanism and thus actually feed into the anxiety (Craske & Barlow, 2008). Therefore, any prescription should be given in collaboration with the therapist. The evidence of the effectiveness of various medication (e.g. antipsychotic medication) is growing (see the relevant chapters in Nathan & Gorman, 2007 and Antony & Stein, 2009). An important question for any therapist is whether the combined treatment (medication and psychotherapy) yields better results. Although, in general, it seems to be common-sense thinking, there is only a small amount of evidence supporting this (see Thase & Jindal, 2004; Otto et al., 2009).

Social support

Empirical evidence suggests that social support may be an important preventative factor in the development of some anxiety disorders (Brewin, Andrews, & Valentine, 2000). Indeed, it may be useful to have collaborating significant others in the treatment of anxiety disorders. New treatments that involve family members are being tested (e.g. for OCD, Franklin & Foa, 2007). In many countries formal self-help groups exist as well (e.g. Anxiety Disorders Association of America). Not much is known about their effectiveness, but there is no doubt that they can help to break social isolation and the stigma of having an anxiety problem. Tailored groups may exist for specific groups, such as war veterans with PTSD, which provide support.

Self-help materials and other helping materials or interventions

There is a number of self-help books for people suffering from anxiety disorders (see Mansell, 2007). Some have been found to be more helpful, some less so. Mansell (2007) presents a survey undertaken by a UK-based organisation, No Panic, which found that, on the positive side, readers find some of the books easy to read, compassionate, encouraging and optimistic, explaining why avoidance makes things worse, etc. On the other hand, some books are seen as patronising, impersonal or distant, pertinent to a small range of anxieties, with goals not relevant to the reader. Among newer books, one can find CBT-informed books such as Leahy's *The Worry Cure* (2006), or mindfulness-based books such as Brantley's *Calming Your Anxious Mind* (2003).

Many CBT manuals contain a client workbook that is a natural part of the therapy and that contains plenty of information for the client (e.g. Barlow & Craske, 2007). The client may also use these types of book after the therapy finishes as a support in maintaining the effects of therapy. There are also specifically tailored bibliotherapy approaches to relapse prevention (see Wright et al., 2000).

A number of computer or internet-based programmes for anxiety exist as well (see Marks, Cavanagh, & Gega, 2007). They are used either as a complementary treatment, a preventative treatment, a first-line treatment in a step-cared model or as the only available treatment if the clients cannot avail face-to-face services. Virtually all of them are CBT based. They are currently mostly in the development phase (see Marks, Cavanagh, & Gega, 2007).

Leisure activities and sport

Research evidence suggests that physical activities may be helpful for people suffering from anxiety disorders (Strohle, 2009). Not much is known about the usefulness of other leisure activities, but common sense would suggest that overall life balance should be helpful when dealing with any adversity, not to mention stress-related anxiety problems.

Recommended reading

The fourth edition of Barlow's edited book has many chapters written by leading CBT therapists and researchers developing therapies for anxiety disorders that show what the actual therapy looks like:

Barlow, D.H. (ed.) (2008). *Clinical Handbook of Psychological Disorders: A Step-by-step Treatment Manual* (4th edition). New York: Guilford Press.

David Barlow also edits Oxford University Press's Treatments that Work series, which brought out several manualised, empirically-based therapies for anxiety disorders. They are also typically accompanied by guides for clients that are used by clients in therapy. Some of the therapist's guides are:

Craske, M.G., Antony, M.M., & Barlow, D.H (2006). *Mastery of Your Fears and Phobias*. New York: Oxford University Press.

Craske, M.G. & Barlow, D.H (2007). *Mastery of Your Anxiety and Panic*. New York: Oxford University Press.

Foa, E.B., Hembree, E.A., & Rothbaum, B.O. (2007). *Prolonged Exposure Therapy for PTSD: Emotional Processing of Traumatic Experiences*. New York: Oxford University Press.

Hope, D.A., Heimberg, R.G., & Turk, C.L. (2006). *Managing Social Anxiety*. New York: Oxford University Press.

Zinbarg, R.E., Barlow, D.H., & Craske, M.G. (2006). *Mastery of Your Anxiety and Worry* (2nd edition). New York: Oxford University Press.

Specifics of psychotherapy and counselling for personality disorders

What is currently classified as 'personality disorders' often represents the most complex problems that therapists encounter. Personality disorders are characterised by 'an enduring pattern of inner experience and behaviour that deviates markedly from the expectations of the individual's culture, is pervasive and inflexible, has an onset in adolescence or early adulthood, is stable over time, and leads to distress or impairment' (American Psychiatric Association, 2001: 685). This pattern has to be manifested in two or more areas, such as cognition, affectivity, interpersonal functioning and impulse control, and should not be better accounted for by another disorder, substance influence or general medical condition (see American Psychiatric Association, 2001: 689). The different personality disorders and their main features are presented in Box 9.6.

Box 9.6 Personality disorders according to DSM–IV and their main features (American Psychiatric Association, 2001: 685). For full diagnostic criteria, please consult DSM–IV

Paranoid personality disorder – a pattern of distrust and suspiciousness; others are seen as malevolent.

Schizoid personality disorder – a pattern of detachment from social relationships and a restricted range of emotional expression.

Schizotypal personality disorder – a pattern of acute discomfort in close relationships, cognitive and perceptual distortions, and eccentricities of behaviour.

Antisocial personality disorder – a pattern of disregard and violation of the rights of others.

Borderline personality disorder – a pattern of instability in interpersonal relationships, self-image, affects and impulsivity.

Histrionic personality disorder – a pattern of excessive emotionality and attention seeking.

Narcissistic personality disorder – a pattern of grandiosity, need for admiration and lack of empathy.

Avoidant personality disorder – a pattern of social inhibition, feelings of inadequacy, and hypersensitivity to negative evaluation.

Dependent personality disorder – a pattern of submissive and clinging behaviour related to an excessive need to be taken care of.

Obsessive-compulsive personality disorder – a pattern of preoccupation with orderliness, perfectionism and control.

There is a lot of debate and controversy around the conceptual issues and classification of personality disorders (as there is with the rest of the DSM–IV classification). The criticism focuses on the lack of theoretical foundation, lack of reliability among different assessors, significant overlap among the categories, the claim that the assessment of personality disorder is falsely independent of Axis I disorders (e.g. mood disorders, anxiety disorders), etc. (see Livesley, 2001). The prevalence of personality disorders in the community is estimated at between 5% and 9%, depending on the classification system used (DSM or ICD) (Samuels et al., 2002; see also Mattia & Zimmerman, 2001). Different personality disorders tend to co-vary together (25–50% co-occurrence) and are co-morbidly present in more than 60% of Axis I diagnoses (e.g. depression, anxiety disorders) (Mattia & Zimmerman, 2001).

Hypothesised etiology is very complex (Livesley, 2001). The studies look at the role of neurotransmitter levels, such as serotonin and norepinephrine, in relation to some aspects of some personality disorders, such as impulsivity or aggression (Coccaro, 2001). Similarly, dopamine is investigated in relation to psychotic-like symptoms in schizotypal personality disorders (Coccaro, 2001). Neurobehavioural dimensional models of personality disorders (see Clonninger, 1987; Depue & Lenzenweger, 2001) postulate an interplay of several biological factors that influence several relevant dimensions such as extraversion agency (dopamine, for instance, plays an important biological role here), affiliation (the role that hormones play), fear (anxiety circuits in which amygdala and some neurotransmitter levels play a role), constraint/inhibition (e.g. modulated by serotonin) (see Depue & Lenzenweger, 2001).

In psychosocial theories, the role of early attachment is particularly stressed (Bartholomew, Kwong, & Hart, 2001; Bateman & Fonagy, 2001). Some attachment styles can be over-present in some personality disorders, such as preoccupied attachment style in histrionic and borderline personality disorders, fearful attachment style in avoidant personality disorders, dismissive attachment style in antisocial personality disorder (Bartholomew, Kwong, & Hart, 2001). Early adversity in people with personality disorders was also studied extensively. It seems that factors such as parental psychopathology and traumatic childhood experience (e.g. sexual and physical abuse) may play an important role (see Paris, 2001).

Apart from studies that focused on the *post hoc* analysis of the impact of the presence of a personality disorder in the treatment of other disorders such as anxiety disorders or depression (see Reich, 2003), there have not been many high-quality therapy outcome studies on personality disorders. Studies of other primary problems, such as depression, suggest that the presence of a personality disorder predicts a worse response to therapy on the part of the client (Crits-Christoph & Barber, 2007). Of the therapies that were specifically developed for people with personality disorders, dialectical behaviour therapy (Linehan, 1993), which focuses on explicitly teaching skills of emotional regulation, and mentalisation-based psychoanalytic therapy (Bateman & Fonagy, 2004) proved to be promising in addressing some of the symptoms of borderline personality disorders (Crits-Christoph & Barber, 2007). Other disorders were studied to a much lesser extent and often in studies that did not differentiate between different personality disorders.

Broader research evidence from different types of studies suggests that psychotherapeutic work with clients who demonstrate personality problems is typically longer (Crits-Christoph & Barber, 2007). Following the review of empirical studies on personality disorders, Critchfield and Smith Benjamin (2006) conclude that personality disorders present a unique challenge to the therapeutic relationship and the therapist, and that the ability of both participants to work those challenges out to a positive resolution seems to be crucial for therapy to work. Several other therapeutic principles were identified in the review of empirical research studies examining the psychotherapy of personality disorders. They are presented in Box 9.7.

Box 9.7 Examples of empirically-informed principles of working with personality disorders (Critchfield & Smith Benjamin, 2006: 255–262)

Client factors related to outcome:

- Level of impairment and corresponding treatment intensity.
- Willingness and ability to engage with treatment.
- History of positive attachment.
- Match between client's resistance level and intervention type.

Therapist factors related to outcome:

- Comfort with long-term, emotionally intense relationships.
- Patience.
- Tolerance of own feelings regarding the client.
- Specialised training.
- Open-minded, flexible and creative in approach.

Relationship factors related to outcome:

- Strong alliance.
- Relatively highly active therapist.
- Therapist structuring treatment and setting boundaries.

Technique factors:

- Therapist availability.
- Early formulation and identification of problems.
- Therapist honesty and explicitness regarding his/her own limits.
- Focused, theoretically coherent, consistent and well co-ordinated treatment.
- Balance between the focus on change and empathic support.
- Focus on increasing adaptive functioning vs. maladaptive functioning.
- Support for therapist through ongoing supervision.

In general, countertransferential reactions on the therapist's part can be significant when working with clients showing signs of personality disorders. The clients have challenging features that are of an interpersonal nature. For instance, clients with borderline difficulties may present a constant threat of instability that can oscillate between anger and despair (see Bateman & Fonagy, 2004), which may in turn be challenging for the therapist's stability. Clients with histrionic features may also display strong emotions that the therapist may not have a natural, compassionate response to, as they may be too strong for the context to which they relate. Clients with schizoid features may be very distant and overly cognitive, which may be difficult for the therapist who wants to focus on their emotional experience. Dependent clients may be overly clingy and intrude on the therapist's boundaries, etc. Management of countertransference and the work on problematic interpersonal patterns can thus be crucial for therapy (for interpersonal ways of working with different personality disorders see, for instance, Benjamin, 1996). The role of adequate support and good supervision for the therapist is crucial when working with challenging clients with personality difficulties.

A chronic suicidal threat may be a part of the presentation of some personality disorders (especially in borderline personality disorder – see Paris, 2007). Similarly, dangerous self-harm behaviour may be present (Gerson & Stanley, 2002). Paris (2007), as well as other authors, points to the fact that in working with such behaviour in the context of a personality disorder, it is important to maintain the overall structure of treatment so it can be predictable for patients. This may be important as some of the clients with personality difficulties may challenge therapeutic boundaries. They may require extra care, closeness, and the presence of the therapist (e.g. in the extreme case by stalking – Mullen & Purcell, 2007). This stresses even more the importance of having support from colleagues, peers and a supervisor when working with challenging clients.

On a more technical level, one must also bear in mind that clients with a low quality of object relations (who are often clients who have undergone severe trauma and may have developed some of the personality disorders) may not be responsive to relational interpretations and may find them hostile (Crits-Christoph & Connolly Gibbons, 2002). The quality of interpretation and its strategic use, balanced with work on the alliance, may be central in such cases (Gabbard & Horowitz, 2009). The fragility of some clients (e.g. those with borderline features) may require a lot of supportive presence that may sometimes be challenging for the therapist to sustain if the client is also hostile towards the therapist.

Other forms of treating personality disorders, self-help materials and other helping materials or interventions

When addressing personality difficulties, other forms of help can be considered. For instance, medication may address some symptoms. Usually the medication that is prescribed for other disorders with similar symptoms is used. For example, psychotic-like symptoms in schizotypal or borderline personality disorders may be addressed by antipsychotic medication. Affective symptoms, such as in the case of borderline personality presentations, may be addressed by antidepressants or mood stabilisers (for more, see Koeningsberg, Woo-Ming, & Siever, 2007).

Ruiz-Sancho, Smith, and Gunderson (2001) reviewed a number of psychoeducational approaches that can be used in addressing personality difficulties. Many of them include not only the client, but also the family. These approaches incorporate information about personality disorder, practical guidelines and management strategies to cope with difficulties and support (see Ruiz-Sancho, Smith, & Gunderson, 2001). Some therapeutic approaches, such as dialectical behaviour therapy (DBT), contain a strong psychoeducational element as well. Self-help groups, bibliotherapy and online materials may also be useful complements to psychological therapy. The link among some personality difficulties and a complex socio-economic background (e.g. Cohen et al., 2008) may in some cases suggest collaboration between a social worker and the therapist. Often, a real deprivation in life goes hand in hand with more complex problems, such as the ones present in people with personality difficulties (e.g. borderline personality disorder). A more comprehensive social intervention may then be required.

Recommended reading

The two most-studied therapies for borderline personality disorders are mentalisation-based psychoanalytical therapy and dialectical behaviour therapy. Here are their respective manuals:

Bateman, A. & Fonagy, P. (2004). *Psychotherapy for Borderline Personality Disorder: A Mentalization-based Treatment*. New York: Oxford University Press.

Linehan, M.M. (1993). *Cognitive Behavioral Treatment of Borderline Personality Disorder*. New York: Guilford Press.

Specifics of psychotherapy for substance use disorders

Another area of problems typically addressed by counselling and psychotherapy are problems related to substance use. DSM–IV (American Psychiatric Association, 2001: 197–199) recognises several substance use-related types of disorder. It can be:

(i) **A substance dependence** – a maladaptive pattern of substance use characterised by the presence of three or more symptoms, such as increased tolerance or diminished effect of the substance; withdrawal symptoms; consumption of larger amounts of substance than intended; persistent desire or unsuccessful efforts to control substance intake; time spent on obtaining, using or recovering from a substance; reduction in social, occupational, or recreational activities; the use is continued despite recurrent physical or psychological problems.

(ii) **A substance abuse** – a maladaptive pattern of substance use leading to clinically significant impairment or distress (at the same time not meeting the criteria for substance dependence), as manifested by one (or more) of the following: recurrent substance use resulting in a failure to fulfil work, school, or home obligations, recurrent substance use in situations in which it is physically hazardous; continued substance use despite the recurrent social or interpersonal problems.

(iii) **Substance-induced disorders** – substance intoxication, substance withdrawal, and substance-induced mental disorders.

An American study (Stinson et al., 2005) showed an approximately 9% yearly prevalence of substance use disorders in the USA (see also Winnick & Norman, 2005). This estimate suggests that it is a widespread mental health problem. The etiology of substance use disorders is, as with other mental health problems, multifactorial. There seems to be a genetically-based vulnerability to the development of addictions (Gardner, 2005; Lin & Anthenelli, 2005), currently to a great extent attributable to aberrations in the brain's dopamine system as it relates to the reward function (see Gardner, 2005). The importance of experienced reward (the level of pleasure and the enjoyable effects obtained) can thus be biologically based, which can also transpire when the person is reintroduced to the effects of a substance (see Gardner, 2005). Dopamine systems seem to play a role in the experience of craving, and the depletion of these systems is seen in chronic drug use, thus requiring higher and/or continuous doses in order to achieve the same effect from the drug as at the beginning of its use (Gardner, 2005). The biological mechanisms may further vary for different substances (see Lowinson et al., 2005).

Psychological understanding of the use of substances often looks at it as a distress-regulating strategy (Khantzian, Dodes, & Brehm, 2005). Many social and environmental factors, including the availability and characteristics of a specific substance, then contribute to the complex dynamic between the users and the substance (Johnson & Golub, 2005). Early adversity, family background deficiencies, the influence of peers, social networking, including the functioning of subcultures, all play a role in the development of problematic substance use (Sussman, Skara, & Ames, 2008).

Several psychological therapies have been established as effective in addressing substance use problems. Different cognitive-behavioural strategies were examined empirically, focusing on psychoeducation, coping skills training (including coping aimed at managing the antecedents and contingencies of substance use – see Najavits, Liese, & Harned, 2005), self-control training and especially social skills training that targets deficient interpersonal skills which play a role in the problematic substance use

(Finney & Moos, 2007). Therapy usually includes multiple possibilities (outpatient, inpatient and day treatments) and may include the management of detoxification (see McCrady, 2008). The options are tailored to the client's difficulties, the level of support available, the stage of change, motivation for treatment, etc. (McCrady, 2008). Often, significant others are included in the treatment as well. A community reinforcement approach (e.g. Higgins, Sigmon, & Heil, 2008) that uses many behavioural strategies is well studied. This approach focuses on the functional analysis of addictive behaviour, the development of a functional social network and leisure activities, many types of skills training and different forms of therapeutic support, including couple therapy, but also practical help in the area of employment (see Higgins, Sigmon, & Heil, 2008). These can also be combined with medication. Medication either prevents the use of a substance (e.g. disulfiram, which causes a negative reaction if combined with alcohol), or substitutes for its effect by replacing an illicit drug use that is often connected to antisocial behaviour (e.g. methadone treatment in opioid addictions).

Another well-studied intervention for addictions (especially alcohol abuse) is motivational interviewing (Miller & Rollnick, 2002; see also Chapter 6). There is a number of outcome studies, mostly RCTs (Burke, Arkowitz, & Dunn, 2002), monitoring its effectiveness, and recently also process studies (e.g. Moyers & Martin, 2006). Motivational interviewing (Miller & Rollnick, 2002) is based on several principles, such as the therapist's empathy, the development of discrepancy concerning where the client is and where he or she wants to be, the avoidance of argumentation by trying not to 'convince' the client about the need for change, rolling with the client's resistance to change and supporting the client's self-efficacy. In the first phase of treatment, the therapist and the client work together on building motivation for change. The therapist attempts to elicit the client's self-motivational statements, is empathic, and explores and offers personal feedback on the severity of drug abuse, drug-connected problems, etc. In the second phase of treatment (Miller, 1995), the therapist and the client focus on strengthening the commitment to change. The client plays a major role in drawing up the plan of change and the therapist contributes with his or her own knowledge about combating the drug usage. The therapist and the client then monitor the client's progress and try to renew motivation. Significant others are often involved in therapy as well.

Substance-related disorders are often addressed by multiple and varied means of help, as mentioned above. Very important are various self-help groups (Horvath, 2005). The most famous of them is Alcoholics Anonymous, which inspired other self-help movements (such as Narcotics Anonymous and Gamblers Anonymous). Alcoholics Anonymous (e.g. Nace, 2005) is a self-help movement of autonomous groups subscribing to the 12 steps to recovery (e.g. admittance of powerlessness over alcohol, trust in and giving oneself to the power of God, which can restore sanity, admittance of all wrongs committed). The groups, which often meet weekly, but also more often, follow the same structure of following the 12 steps through the mutual sharing of experiencing life with alcohol (fellowship) and also provide one-to-one support (through having a sponsor). There are now also professional programmes, developed on the basis of this model, which encourage attendance of AA meetings regularly and these have proved to be very effective in treating alcohol abuse (Babor & Del Boca, 2003).

Other approaches, such as drug counselling (Mercer & Woody, 1999; Daley, Mercer, & Carpenter, 2002), were successfully tested empirically for different addictions. They often use a combination of individual, group and self-help treatment. They often focus on providing information about addiction, working on increasing awareness of the problem, the provision of support and engaging the clients in offering support for their fellows in the recovery process, as well as the learning of recovery coping skills in the cognitive, behavioural and interpersonal domains (see Daley, Mercer, & Carpenter, 2002). In one of these approaches (Mercer & Woody, 1999; Daley, Mercer, & Carpenter, 2002), a combination of individual and group drug counselling proved to be superior to cognitive behavioural and psychodynamic therapy supported by group drug counselling for cocaine addiction (see Crits-Christoph et al., 1999). The main features of the work of the counsellor in the individual format of drug counselling are shown in Box 9.8.

Box 9.8 Goals of the addiction counsellor in the individual drug counselling programme for cocaine addiction (Mercer & Woody, 1999: Chapter 6)

1. Help the patient to admit that he or she suffers from the disease of chemical addiction.
2. Point out the signs and symptoms of addiction that are relevant to the patient's experience.
3. Teach the addict to recognise and re-channel urges to use drugs.
4. Encourage and motivate the patient to achieve and sustain abstinence.
5. Monitor and encourage abstinence by using objective measures, such as urinalysis and Breathalyzer® tests.
6. Hold the chemically addicted person accountable and discuss any episodes of use and strongly discourage further use.
7. Assist the patient in identifying situations where drugs were used to cope with life's problems and in understanding that using drugs to cope with or solve problems does not work.
8. Help the addict to develop new, more effective problem-solving strategies.

9. Introduce the patient to the 12-step philosophy and strongly encourage participation in Narcotics Anonymous, Alcoholics Anonymous and/or Cocaine Anonymous.
10. Encourage the chemically addicted person to develop and continue with a recovery plan as a lifelong process.
11. Help the addict to recognise and change problematic attitudes and behaviours that may stimulate a relapse.
12. Encourage the patient to improve self-esteem by practising newly acquired coping skills and problem-solving strategies at home and in the community.

Working with people who have problems with the use of substances may be challenging for therapists in several ways. One of the challenges is the denial of some people who have substance use problems (e.g. see Substance Abuse and Mental Health Services Administration, 2002). This requires that the work with these people has to be done in a setting that allows for objective monitoring for the presence of the substance. The denial issue may be especially relevant if the client has a history of denying the problem. The therapist without objective information may often be in doubt whether the client is taking the substance. Denial may also be relevant in some cases when the client does not have an internal motivation for treatment as he or she does not see the negatives of substance use, although these are perceived by relatives, friends or colleagues at work. Building internal motivation by focusing on the discrepancy between reality and perception may then be a very important step (Miller & Rollnick, 2002).

Another challenge for therapists working with people with substance use problems is the likelihood of relapse, which may be demoralising for the client as well as the therapist. Understanding that relapse is a natural part of the treatment is important. Also, work on preventing relapses must be central. In preventing the impact of relapse, it is especially important to identify relapse risk factors, understand relapse as a process, understand substance cues and cravings, understand social pressures, have supportive social networks, develop emotion regulation, etc. (Daley & Marlatt, 2005).

The multiple health issues that people using substances have also dictate the provision of complex health care within a setting. Social issues may be relevant as well, so the inclusion of social workers and other relevant professionals is needed. Withdrawal symptoms may require medical care. Furthermore, as mentioned above, therapy may be complemented by medication that either prevents craving, substitutes for the illicit drug or is used to prevent consumption of the substance.

Another major issue in the therapy of substance-related problems is that people using substances problematically may have co-morbid difficulties. The most common problems are depression, anxiety disorders, schizophrenia and personality disorders (Grant et al., 2004a, 2004b). Psychological therapy then also needs to focus on the co-morbid problems, which are often underlying factors in the substance-related problem (Denison, 2005).

McCrady, Haaga, and Lebow (2006) summarised the empirical evidence on the key principles behind effective therapy of substance use problems (see Box 9.9). They came to a conclusion that specialised treatment is crucial. They also concluded that motivation and readiness to change are essential. What is clear from their overview is that there are multiple ways of tackling substance use problems, but the client's own responsibility for his or her treatment is significant. Also very important is a comprehensive intervention that targets the social environment, as the social environment plays a key part in the development of, but also recovery from, addiction. According to their review, increasing the client's awareness of patterns involved in substance use and the development of emotion regulation strategies other than the use of substances seem to be important as well (for more, see Box 9.9).

Box 9.9 Examples of empirically-informed principles of working with substance use disorders (McCrady, Haaga, & Lebow, 2006: 342–346)

Contextual factors:

- Positive social contexts are important in dealing with substance use disorders.
- Continuity of care is important.
- Specialist treatment is required.

Client factors related to outcome:

- Clients with positive expectancy are more likely to benefit from therapy.
- Greater readiness to change is a good predictor.
- Severity of substance use disorder is a negative predictor.

Technique factors:

- Involvement of significant others and the provision of social support is positively linked with outcome.
- Focus on motivation is an important part of successful therapy.
- Focus on helping the client to develop awareness around the substance use.
- Building of emotion regulation strategies seems to be important.
- Recognition of contingencies (conditioning) involved in the use of substances.

Interacting factors:

- Matching the level of confrontation to the client's ambivalence is important.
- The use of the social environment should depend on whether it contributes to addiction or to recovery.
- Attention needs to be devoted to co-morbid problems.
- Treatment intensity should match the level of severity of the problem.
- Multiple needs-addressing treatments are effective.
- Gender-specific interventions may be considered.

Recommended reading

The American National Institute of Drug Abuse offers free access to several empirically tested manuals for working with addictions on its webpages (see www.drugabuse.gov).

An important book on motivational interviewing is:

Miller, W.R. & Rollnick, S. (2002). *Motivational Interviewing: Preparing People to Change Addictive Behavior* (2nd edition). New York: Guilford Press.

CBT for substance use is presented in an older volume:

Beck, A.T., Wright, F.D., & Liese, B.S. (1993). *Cognitive Therapy for Substance Use*. New York: Guilford Press.

Specifics of psychotherapy for eating disorders

Eating disorders share some of the features of addictive behaviours. Their common thread is an attempt to prevent weight gain and concerns about body shape linked to negative self-evaluation. Though DSM–IV recognises three distinct disorders (anorexia nervosa, bulimia nervosa, and eating disorder otherwise not specified), in reality these three categories often overlap in time (a person moves from one category to another) for people with problematic eating. The main features of these three diagnostic groups are given in Box 9.10. Eating disorders typically concern females more than males (only 5–10% of clients with eating disorders are men – Hoek, 2002; Hoek & van Hoeken, 2003). The yearly prevalence is between 0.3% (anorexia) and 1% (bulimia) (Hoek, 2002; Hoek & van Hoeken, 2003). Eating disorders often co-occur with other problems, such as depression and anxiety disorders (especially OCD and social anxiety) (see Bulik, 2002; Halmi, 2003). Several symptoms of anxiety may co-occur, such as obsessional thinking, worrying and social anxiety, while purging behaviour can also have an anxiolytic effect (Bulik, 2002). Other problems, such as substance use-related problems or personality disorders, may co-occur as well (Wilson, 2002; Wonderlich, 2002; Halmi, 2003).

Box 9.10 Eating disorders according to DSM-IV and their main features (American Psychiatric Association, 2001: 583, 589, 594). For full diagnostic criteria, please consult DSM-IV.

Anorexia nervosa – the main characteristics are refusal to maintain normal body weight, fear of weight gain and distorted perception of own body shape. There are two types: restricting food or binge eating – purging type.

Bulimia nervosa – the main characteristics are binge eating and involvement in compensatory behaviour preventing weight gain. There are two types: purging and non-purging.

Eating disorder not otherwise specified – symptoms overlapping with the above, but meeting none of them fully.

The onset of eating disorders is in mid or late adolescence (American Psychiatric Association, 2001). Eating disorders present a serious problem because anorexic behaviour may cause death in some cases (due to chronic problematic eating patterns as well as suicide). It is a chronic problem with only 50% of anorexic and 70% of bulimic clients achieving recovery within 10 years of the onset of the problem (Sullivan, 2002). It seems that the dynamic involved in eating disorders centres around personality traits of perfectionism, obsessionality, negative self-evaluation and extreme compliance (Schmidt, 2002). These can be influenced by biological as well as social-environmental factors.

Anorexic behaviour is characterised by a very high level of control that is absent in more bulimic behaviour, but is restored through compensatory behaviour. This control serves as a protection against negative self-evaluation or control by others (especially if they want the client with the eating disorder problem to change (see Fairburn et al., 2008; Dolhanty & Greenberg, 2009)). In a sense, it is a form of self-harming behaviour that paradoxically, in the short term, brings relief and a boost by achieving 'thinness'. This form of achieving or striving for thinness brings with it a sense of self-efficacy that has potentially dangerous consequences.

There is a number of psychological therapies that have been studied as a means of addressing eating disorders. It is important to be aware that this therapy normally requires collaboration with a medical team. A number of serious complications may develop (some of them life-threatening), such as renal and electrolyte abnormalities, cardiovascular problems, and gastrointestinal, endocrine, metabolic and dermatologic problems (see Pomeroy & Mitchell, 2002). Inpatient, outpatient and day treatment care may be involved in addressing eating disorder problems. With regard to the empirical evidence, bulimia has been studied much more than anorexia (due to the low prevalence of anorexia – see Wilson & Fairburn, 2007). Cognitive-behavioural therapy (Fairburn, Cooper, & Shafran, 2003) is the most studied and relatively efficacious therapy (eliminating binge eating and purging in 30–50% of clients). The second most studied therapy is interpersonal therapy (IPT) for bulimia, which from a longer-term perspective seems to be equally as effective as CBT, although CBT seems to have an earlier response rate (Wilson & Fairburn, 2007) whereas IPT seems to have a better retention.

Anorexia has been studied much less, with CBT again dominating. However, other approaches have also been studied, such as family-based treatment. The results are, in general, very modest (e.g. less than 15% recovering fully – Wilson & Fairburn, 2007). Binge eating disorder, which is now being recognised as a specific type of problem, also attracted some outcome research attention (Wilson & Fairburn, 2007). Due to overlapping depressive and anxiety symptoms, eating disorders are treated with antidepressant medication, which seems to be beneficial, although for bulimic problems in particular it seems less beneficial than CBT (Wilson & Fairburn, 2007). Guided self-help programmes and psychoeducation groups may also be useful (Wilson & Fairburn, 2007). The first preventative programmes delivered online are now being developed and tested (Newton & Ciliska, 2006).

The main features of the most studied cognitive-behavioural therapy for eating disorders are as follows (Fairburn, 2008; Fairburn et al., 2008). The therapy consists of several stages. In the first stage (which is delivered across four weeks, twice a week), the focus is on the engagement of the client in therapy, proper assessment and idiosyncratic case formulation of the difficulty, which is prepared jointly with the client. During this stage, the client is educated about eating problems, is taught to monitor his or her own eating and his or her experiences around it, and regular eating patterns are also established. Weekly weighing is introduced and significant others are involved in therapy. In the second stage, the therapy process is reviewed and the case formulation refined. The focus may now be on problems with mood intolerance, perfectionism, low self-esteem and interpersonal difficulties, if any of those contribute significantly to the eating problem (Fairburn, Cooper, & Shafran, 2003). The third stage typically consists of around eight weekly sessions. During this stage, the over-evaluation of shape and weight is targeted. This is achieved through increased awareness, by refocusing on other aspects of life besides body and weight, through overcoming constant body checking and/or body avoidance, by targeting 'feeling fat' experiences and building skills to contain them, and by understanding the origins of over-evaluation. Also during this stage, the therapy focuses on dietary restriction and its replacement by regular eating. This stage focuses on understanding how eating-related behaviour is linked to triggering events, and the skills of responding differently to difficult events are tackled through teaching problem-solving strategies. Finally, stage four of therapy (approximately three sessions across several weeks) focuses on the consolidation of any changes achieved and the prevention or acceptance of the possibility of relapse (for more about therapy, see Fairburn, 2008).

Other forms of therapy that are studied much less may focus on the role of interpersonal difficulties or emotion regulation in the development and course of eating disorders (Fairburn et al., 2008; Dolhanty & Greenberg, 2009). It is well recognised that clients may use eating control as a way of controlling emotional and interpersonal difficulties that they are not able to face otherwise. For instance, family tensions may intensify resistance to eating and dieting may represent a displaced attempt at control (Fairburn, Cooper, & Shafran, 2003). With regard to emotional regulation, eating disorders can be seen as an expression of negative self-evaluation that is displaced to feeling fat (ugly) (see Dolhanty & Greenberg, 2009). This may bring intolerable shame (about appearance). The problematic affect may also have an interpersonal connotation of using controlled eating as a boundary against the other (parents), or as a goal (to please others), or as a control of an otherwise uncontrollable experience of the other, etc. In all interpersonal and emotional strategies, the enhanced control of eating brings in the short term a sense of relief and a sense of protection. Only from a long-term perspective do the damaging aspects of this control become visible.

Working with clients with eating problems may present several countertransferential issues. The therapist may over-invest, having power struggles around the control, may have feelings of being helpless, may not be able to go beyond the symptoms focus, etc. (e.g. Satir et al., 2009). This is amplified by the seriousness of the problem and the health and life risks involved. With perfectionist clients, the therapist may be under pressure and may find him or herself being judged regarding his or her body shape. On a more positive note, the therapist may be drawn to be caring with the client (also because many clients are at an adolescent age) (see Satir et al., 2009). Anorexic clients are especially challenging and frustrating, with therapists being more frustrated and helpless and less connected and engaged than with bulimic clients (Franko & Rolfe, 1996). The constant presence of a potential relapse may also be challenging, with the therapist losing a sense of his or her own effectiveness. Therefore, it is not surprising that supervision is seen as a major resource when working with this group (see Franko & Rolfe, 1996).

Recommended reading

Several therapeutic approaches are described in the book edited by Timothy Brewerton:

Brewerton, T.D. (ed.) (2002). *Clinical Handbook of Eating Disorders: An Integrated Approach*. New York: Marcel Dekker.

A comprehensive cognitive-behavioural therapy manual is provided in a book edited by Fairburn and one from a group from King's College London:

Fairburn, C.G. (2008). *Cognitive-behavioural Therapy and Eating Disorders*. New York: Guilford Press.

Waller, G. et al. (2007). *Cognitive Behavioral Therapy for Eating Disorders*. Cambridge: Cambridge University Press.

Specifics of psychotherapy for schizophrenia

Schizophrenia and related psychotic disorders is one of the most debilitating mental health problems. The common features of these disorders are psychotic symptoms that include hallucinations, delusions, disorganised speech and behaviour, and catatonic behaviour. The main features of these disorders are summarised in Box 9.11. There are between 0.3 and 0.7 % of people with schizophrenia at any given time in the USA (Castle & Morgan, 2008). Some sources (e.g. DSM–IV) use 0.5–1.5% as a life-time estimate of the prevalence of schizophrenia. It appears that there are several risk factors that increase the likelihood of schizophrenia and related problems. These include genetics, obstetric complications, external environmental factors during pregnancy, urbanicity, childhood stressors such as separation of parents, abuse, trauma, etc. (Castle & Morgan, 2008). Biologically, some structural changes to the brain (such as a smaller size of some parts of the brain) as well as neurotransmitters dysregulation (e.g. the dopamine system or glutamate receptor) are observed (though it does not say anything about what factors are responsible for it) (Downar & Kapur, 2008). Stressful life events and a critical and hostile family or other interpersonal environment often serve as a trigger for the onset or relapse of schizophrenia (Bebbington & Kuipers, 2008). The mechanism that is proposed is that stressful events raise anxiety which is difficult to contain and brings changes to thinking (more paranoid thinking and negative self-evaluation) (Bebbington & Kuipers, 2008). The lack of a supportive confidant also seems to be an important feature (Bebbington & Kuipers, 2008).

Box 9.11 Schizophrenia and related psychotic disorders according to DSM–IV and their main features (American Psychiatric Association, 2001: 298). For full diagnostic criteria, please consult DSM–IV.

Schizophrenia – is a disorder that lasts at least six months and includes at least one month of active-phase symptoms such as hallucinations, delusions, disorganised speech or behaviour, catatonic behaviour and negative symptoms (e.g. affect flattening).

(Continued)

(Continued)

Depending on dominating symptoms, different subtypes can be classified such as paranoid, disorganised, catatonic, undifferentiated and residual. There is deterioration in social and occupational functioning.

Schizophreniform disorder – symptomatic presentation is similar to that of schizophrenia, but lasts less than six months, plus there is no deterioration in social and occupational functioning.

Schizoaffective disorder – a mood episode occurs together with active-phase symptoms of schizophrenia, with symptoms of hallucinations and/or delusions preceding or following the mood episode.

Delusional disorder – at least one month of non-bizarre delusions.

Brief psychotic disorder – psychotic symptoms lasting less than a month.

The course of schizophrenia and related disorders varies. Negative symptoms may be quite stable and positive symptoms occur in an episodic manner (Haffner & An Der Heiden, 2008). At the onset, the period between the first positive symptoms and their peak may be about a year (Haffner & An Der Heiden, 2008). Depression and co-morbid use of substances is often present and there is an elevated risk of suicide (Haffner & An Der Heiden, 2008; Wohlheiter & Dixon, 2008).

Schizophrenia is normally treated multidisciplinarily. An antipsychotic medication is routinely used. Typical (targeting positive symptoms by blocking dopamine receptors) and more recently atypical (targeting both positive and negative symptoms and effecting receptors differentially) and third-generation antipsychotic medication (also targeting cognitive symptoms) are used (Downar & Kapur, 2008; Kutscher, 2008). An acute phase, characterised by the presence of hallucinations and/or delusions, that is not responsive to medication is sometimes also treated by electroconvulsive therapy (ECT) (e.g. McClintock, Ranginawala, & Hussain, 2008). However, biological treatments also have many undesirable side-effects (weight gain, diabetes, a risk of blood disease in case of clozapine, memory problems in case of ECT – see Patterson et al., 2006; Dolder, 2008) and are not welcomed by many clients. It is also recognised that they prevent the occurrence of new positive symptoms or make them milder rather than overcoming them, so it is psychological therapies that have to make sense of the symptoms or balance their potentially disturbing effect (Downar & Kapur, 2008).

There is a wide array of psychosocial approaches that are used in addressing the problems and experiences of people with schizophrenia or similar problems. It is well recognised that the client and preferably the client's significant others have to be involved in planning the overall care. A number of psychosocial interventions have been empirically tested and are considered to be helpful in the tackling of schizophrenia and related problems. They are typically used in conjunction and by one multidisciplinary team so that they can be co-ordinated and tailored to a specific client (Miller & Velligan, 2008). The client's preferences should play an important role in this tailoring of therapy. The interventions vary from supported employment through environmental supports to a formal psychological therapy.

Environmental supports (Velligan & Miller, 2008) represent specific steps that target the client's difficulties in everyday functioning (such as dressing, shopping or cooking, etc.). Supports are provided for and tailored to the client (e.g. reminders or organisation of the wardrobe). Sometimes electronic devices are used (e.g. monitoring and administering medication). Another form of important help is supported employment, which represents a specific form of vocational guidance (Becker, 2008). Clients are encouraged and helped to find a competitive employment fitting their interests as opposed to the often simple jobs that such clients were doing in the past. The support is provided on an ongoing basis and individually so that the client can not only be in an appropriate and interesting job, but also to have support in it.

Since homelessness and housing is a potential risk for people with schizophrenia or similar problems, supported housing is another form of help (Ridgway, 2008). Supportive housing is client-centred. Accommodation is organised so that it matches healthy controls and the client's preferences. Clients are not secluded, but integrated into their natural environment and get the level of help that they need, not more. This type of intervention prevents homelessness and dramatically increases the quality of life (Ridgway, 2008). Another intervention that is routinely considered is cognitive rehabilitation, which targets cognitive deficits since some clients may have different cognitive difficulties (Wykes, 2008).

All of these interventions are usually complementary to psychological therapies that are tailored to the client and provided by one multidisciplinary team (e.g. Assertive Community Treatment – Kopelowicz, Liberman, & Zarate, 2007). Psychological therapies include psychoeducation, family intervention, social skills training, stress management and coping skills training and often cognitive-behavioural interventions (see Kopelowicz, Liberman, & Zarate, 2007; Muesser & Jeste, 2008). Psychoeducation focuses on a knowledge of the disorder, its course, its symptoms, a potentially effective coping mechanism and treatment options, and mechanisms of functioning. A specific focus is on relapse prevention and recognition of the starting difficulty. It often includes work with significant others and family. Working with the family concentrates on the provision of information, removing blame from the family and the client, giving support to (the often drained) relatives, the creation of realistic expectations and enhancement of the support that relatives can offer (Barrowclough & Lobban, 2008). A specific focus of social skills training is on improving social perceptions, social reasoning and social performance (Bellack et al., 2004; Tenhula & Bellack, 2008). Social skills training (Tenhula & Bellack, 2008) is a structured educational procedure that breaks the desired behaviour into small steps that are then taught and rehearsed in role plays with the provision of shaping and positively framed feedback. It teaches basic social skills, conversation skills, assertiveness skills, conflict management skills, communal living skills, friendship and dating skills, health maintenance skills, vocational skills and substance use-related skills (Bellack et al., 2004).

There is also a number of cognitive-behavioural therapies (e.g., Morrison et al., 2004; Tarrier, 2008) targeting schizophrenia and related problems that have been more or less successfully tested (sometimes the results of those therapies are controversial – e.g. Tarrier et al., 2000). These approaches may vary in their formulation or emphasis, although they all use (though somewhat differently) the established cognitive and behavioural techniques. Morrison et al.'s approach (Morrison et al., 2004; Morrison, 2008) looks at psychosis as a traumatic experience which, when interpreted in a culturally unacceptable way, is not seen as meaningful. This interpretation is seen as accounting for distress and disability. The therapy focuses not necessarily on the reduction of psychotic symptoms, but rather on achieving the goals the client has in addressing the problems of living. Psychotic symptoms are seen as responses to stressful life events that may be partially functional or were functional in the past.

The cognitive therapy of Morrison et al. (Morrison et al., 2004; Morrison, 2008) uses an idiosyncratic formulation that incorporates the client's early experiences in offering an understanding of how the client's current problems developed. The problem maintenance conceptualisation is also established. As in classical cognitive therapy (see Chapters 3 and 7), the link is established between the thought processes, feelings, physiological experience, behaviour and triggering events/situations. Cognitive restructuring is used to address voices that provoke fear and distress and the negative beliefs related to the self or others. Evidence is gathered for and against their validity. The focus is on being able to generate alternatives, some of which are benign and have a distress-reducing impact. A lot of normalisation of the client's experience is used. Beliefs and their alternative explanations are further tested in carefully designed behavioural experiments (that promote win-win situations). Safety behaviour is brought to awareness and overcome. Some forms of CBT (e.g. Tarrier, 2008) also focus on behaviour activation that counteracts the negative symptoms. All CBT approaches attend to the prevention of relapses by educating clients about them and by working on skills that can be used by clients once they start to encounter the acute problems again. The focus, however, is also on the promotion of personally relevant goals and valued social roles that improve the quality of life (Morrison, 2008).

Working with a client who has psychotic difficulties may be challenging in several ways. First, it is imperative that any psychological therapy is part of a more comprehensive and multidisciplinary approach as it is well known that a client suffering from those difficulties may have problems in several areas. Furthermore, the therapist needs sufficient support from his or her colleagues as the client's suffering may often be very distressing for the therapist. Suicide risk may be elevated for clients suffering from this problem, which may increase the therapist's anxiety. To build a relationship with clients suffering from psychotic symptoms is extremely challenging. First, clients are very distressed and want to experience relief, which puts many expectations on the therapist. But secondly, they are also very vulnerable and can experience the therapist as potentially threatening or harmful, which can increase the therapist's feelings of guilt. The therapist's anxiety may also be increased when the client is more acutely showing positive symptoms as the therapist may then become part of the hallucinations or a delusional presentation. On the other hand, negative symptoms are characterised by monotony and a level of emotional withdrawal, which is often also impacted by antipsychotic medication, and this is draining and repetitive for the therapist. Supervision, collegial peer support, working as part of a multidisciplinary team and personal therapy for the therapist may be invaluable for preventing burn-out and personal distress when working with these types of problem.

Recommended reading

The edited book of Mueser and Jeste (2008) provides an excellent overview of issues involved in schizophrenia. Beck et al.'s (2008) book provides rich information that forms a basis for CBT for schizophrenia. Morrison et al.'s (2004) and Bellack et al.'s (2004) books represent step-by-step manuals for working with schizophrenia.

Mueser, K.T. & Jeste, D.V. (eds) (2008). *Clinical Handbook of Schizophrenia.* New York: Guilford Press.

Beck, A.T., Grant, P., Rector, N.A., & Stolar, N. (2008). *Schizophrenia: Cognitive Theory, Research, and Therapy*. New York: Guilford Press.

Morrison, A.P., Renton, J.C., Dunn, H., Williams, S., & Bentall, R.P. (2004). *Cognitive Therapy for Psychosis: A Formulation-based Approach.* London: Routledge.

Bellack, A.S., Mueser, K.T., Gingerich, S., & Agresta, J. (2004). *Social Skills Training for Schizophrenia: A Step-by-step Guide.* New York: Guilford Press.

Counselling and psychotherapy for other problems

Although I have presented here problems recognised by DSM–IV and ICD–10 as distinct mental health disorders, there is a huge variety of psychological, social and interpersonal difficulties that are being addressed by counselling and psychotherapy. Especially in a non-medical setting, the problems are recognised on the basis of their idiosyncratic relevance for the client. For instance, the client may have problems in a specific relationship that he or she needs to resolve. There may not be any need for an assessment of the diagnostic condition if the therapist and client come to a case conceptualisation that fits the client's presentation and serves as a basis of successfully evolving therapy. Indeed, even DSM–IV (American Psychiatric Association,

2001) recognises a variety of clinically relevant problems, such as psychological factors related to a medical condition, relational problems, problems related to abuse or neglect, bereavement, academic difficulties, occupational difficulties, identity problems, religious or spiritual problems, acculturation problems, and problems connected to specific phases of life (e.g. retirement). Counselling and psychotherapy in their generic form, as presented throughout most of this book, are well suited to assisting these problems. The case conceptualisation that shapes therapeutic strategy for any given problem is then idiosyncratically based on either problematic emotion schemes (e.g. in emotion-focused therapy), problematic interpersonal patterns (in psychodynamic therapy), problematic cognitive and behavioural schemes (in CBT) or a mixture of them in integrative approaches. Some of these problems have also attracted research attention that examined a number of clients with similar difficulties so that typical features could be formulated. An example would be bereavement (e.g. Larson & Hoyt, 2007) or unresolved interpersonal issues (Greenberg, Warwar, & Malcolm, 2008).

In fact, as I mentioned at the beginning of this chapter, with the exception of cognitive-behavioural therapies, which were traditionally developed as a distinct approach for distinct problems, other therapeutic traditions were developed as generic therapies which are adjusted to idiosyncratic problems. It is therefore no surprise that the focus on specificity of the therapeutic strategy for a specific disorder has been met with much scepticism among therapists of those other orientations. The formulation of general principles of therapy, which are then refined for a specific client's inner dynamic, is thus still seen as an acceptable standard for practice and training. Interestingly, cognitive-behavioural approaches are starting to move in this direction as well by developing uniform protocols for emotional disorders (Allen, McHugh, & Barlow, 2008) or transdiagnostic approaches (e.g. Fairburn, Cooper, & Shafran, 2003 for eating disorders). A tension will probably persist between looking at idiosyncratic client processes versus more universal commonalities in problems and presenting symptoms.

Another important issue that needs to be considered is that counselling and psychotherapy often may be just one of the interventions that can be helpful for the client in tackling the problem. The therapist therefore needs to consider what other help should be encouraged or organised for the client. Biological/physiological, social, interpersonal, spiritual or self-help interventions may sometimes be an important adjunct to therapy or counselling, and in some cases they may indeed be the more primary interventions targeting the problem.

Afterword

Counselling and psychotherapy are complex activities, informed by tradition and by clinical experience communicated in numerous books and papers as well as by thorough and inventive research. This book has sought to bring together, in a succinct form, the important features of this exciting and rewarding work for beginning therapists, while emphasising especially generated research knowledge. I hope that readers will find much useful information in this book. However, I would still urge readers to be cautious because counselling and psychotherapy cannot be taught from a book. The actual training in the skills, practical experience under supervision and constant feedback are far more crucial than a text that captures only a limited aspect of this complex experience.

Further caution is necessary with regard to the integrative nature of this book. The presentation of therapy as a relatively uniform, generic activity, which can easily draw on and switch from one theoretical framework to another, exaggerates similarities across those frameworks and suppresses existing tensions and contradictions. The reader must therefore be aware when using this book that his or her preferences, or the orientation of a particular training programme, may emphasise some of the interventions and strategies presented here over others. Nevertheless, I believe it is valuable to be knowledgeable about the theoretical and clinical conceptualisations and therapeutic strategies of various approaches, especially the ones that have undergone sufficient rigour in generating research findings that inform those conceptualisations and strategies.

Finally, any book of this nature has to be selective in its scope. Thus, many research findings and research-informed therapeutic approaches or strategies are not covered in the book. However, there are many excellent texts available, some of which I have referenced so that readers can find them more easily.

References

Agnew, R.M., Harper, H., Shapiro, D.A., & Barkham, M. (1994). Resolving a challenge to the therapeutic relationship: A single-case study. *British Journal of Medical Psychology*, *67*, 155–170.

Ahn, H., & Wampold, B.E. (2001). Where oh where are the specific ingredients: A meta-analysis of component studies in counseling and psychotherapy. *Journal of Counseling Psychology*, *48*(3), 251–257.

Ainsworth, M.D.S. (1989). Attachment beyond infancy. *American Psychologist*, *44*, 709–716.

Allen, L.B., McHugh, R.K., & Barlow, D.H. (2008). Emotional disorders: A unified protocol. In D.H. Barlow (ed.), *Clinical Handbook of Psychological Disorders: A Step-by-step Treatment Manual* (4th edition) (pp. 216–249). New York: Guilford Press.

American Psychiatric Association (2001). *Diagnostic and Statistical Manual of Mental Disorders* (4th edition). Text revision. Washington, DC: American Psychiatric Association.

American Psychiatric Association (2003). Practice Guidelines for the Assessment and Treatment of Patients with Suicidal Behaviours. *American Journal of Psychiatry*, Supplement, November.

Anderson, S.K. & Kitchener, K.S. (1998). Nonsexual post-therapy relationships: A conceptual framework to assess ethical risks. *Professional Psychology: Research and Practice*, *29*, 91–99.

Antony, M.M., Federici, A., & Stein, M.B. (2009). Overview and introduction to anxiety disorders. In M.M. Antony & M.B. Stein (eds), *Oxford Handbook of Anxiety and Related Disorders* (pp. 3–18). New York: Oxford University Press.

Antony, M.M. & Stein, M.B. (eds) (2009). *Oxford Handbook of Anxiety and Related Disorders*. New York: Oxford University Press.

Arkowitz, H., Westra, H.A., Miller, W.R., & Rollnick, S. (eds) (2008). *Motivational Interviewing in the Treatment of Psychological Problems*. New York: Guilford Press.

Arnkoff, D.B., Glass, C.R., & Shapiro, S.J. (2002). Expectations and preferences. In J.C. Nocross (ed.), *Psychotherapy Relationships that Work: Therapist Contributions and Responsiveness to Patients* (pp. 335–356). New York: Oxford University Press.

Asay, T.P. & Lambert, M.J. (1999). The empirical case for the common factors in therapy: Quantitative findings. In M.A. Hubble, B.L. Duncan, & S.D. Miller (eds), *The Heart and Soul of Change: What Works in Therapy* (pp. 23–55). Washington, DC: American Psychological Association.

Babor, T.F. & Del Boca, F.K. (eds) (2003). *Treatment Matching in Alcoholism*. Cambridge: Cambridge University Press.

Bambling, M., King, R., Raue, P., Schweitzer, R., & Lambert, E.W. (2006). Clinical supervision: Its influence on client-rated working alliance and client symptom reduction in the brief treatment of major depression. *Psychotherapy Research*, *16*(3), 317–331.

Bandura, A. (1977). *Social Learning Theory*. New York: General Learning Press.

Barber, J.P. & Crits-Christoph, P. (eds) (1995). *Dynamic Therapies for Psychiatric Disorders (Axis 1)*. New York: Basic Books.

Barkham, M., Margison, F., Leach, C., Lucock, M., & Mellor-Clark, J. (2001). Service profiling and outcomes benchmarking using the CORE-OM: Toward practice-based evidence in the psychological therapies. *Journal of Consulting and Clinical Psychology*, *69*(2), 184–196.

Barlow, D.H. (2002). *Anxiety and Its Disorders* (2nd edition). New York: Guilford Press.

Barlow, D.H (ed.) (2008). *Clinical Handbook of Psychological Disorders: A Step-by-step Treatment Manual* (4th edition). New York: Guilford Press.

Barlow, D.H., & Craske, M. (2007). *Mastery of Your Anxiety and Panic: Worksheet* (4th edition). New York: Oxford University Press.

Barlow, D.H., Gorman, J.M., Shear, K.M., & Woods, S.W. (2000). Cognitive-behavioral therapy, imipramine, or their combination for panic disorder. *JAMA (Journal of American Medical Association)*, *283*(19): 2529–2536.

Barrett-Lennard, G.T. (1998). *Carl Rogers' Helping System: Journey and Substance*. London: Sage.

Barrett-Lennard, G.T. (1986). The relationship inventory now: issues and advances in theory, method and use. In L.S. Greenberg and W.M. Pinsof (eds), *The Psychotherapeutic Process: A Research Handbook* (pp. 439–476). New York: Guilford Press.

Barrowclough, C. & Lobban, F. (2008). Family interventions. In K.T Mueser & D.V. Jeste (eds), *Clinical Handbook of Schizophrenia* (pp. 214–225). New York: Guilford Press.

Bartholomew, K. (1997). Adult attachment processes: Individual and couple perspectives. *British Journal of Medical Psychology*, *70*, 249–263.

Bartholomew, K., Kwong, M.J., & Hart, S.D. (2001). Attachment. In W.J. Livesley (ed.), *Handbook of Personality Disorders* (pp. 196–230). New York: Guilford Press.

Basco, M.R., Merlock, M., & McDonald, N. (2004). Treatment compliance. In S.L. Johnson & R.L. Leahy (eds), *Psychological Treatment of Bipolar Disorder* (pp. 245–264). New York: Guilford Press.

Bateman, A.W. & Fonagy, P. (2001). Treatment of borderline personality disorder with psychoanalytically oriented partial hospitalization: An 18-month follow-up. *American Journal of Psychiatry*, *158*, 36–42.

Bateman, A.W. & Fonagy, P. (2004). *Psychotherapy for Borderline Personality Disorder – Mentalization-based Treatment*. Oxford: Oxford University Press.

Bateman, A.W. & Holmes, J. (1995). *Introduction to Psychoanalysis*. London: Routledge.

Battle, C.G., Imber, S.D., Hoehn-Saric, R., Stone, A.R., Nash, E.R., & Frank, J.D. (1966). Target complaints as criterion for improvement. *American Journal of Psychotherapy*, *20*, 184–192.

Beach, S.R.H. & Jones, D.J. (2002). Marital and family therapy for depression in adults. In I.H. Gotlib & C.L. Hammen (eds), *Handbook of Depression* (pp. 422–440). New York: Guilford Press.

Bebbington, P. & Kuipers, E. (2008). Psychosocial factors. In K.T. Mueser & D.V. Jeste (eds), *Clinical Handbook of Schizophrenia* (pp. 74–81). New York: Guilford Press.

Beck, A.T. & Alford, B.A. (2008). *Depression: Causes and Treatment* (2nd edition). Philadelphia: University of Pennsylvania Press.

Beck, A.T., Rush, A.J., Shaw, B.F., & Emery, G. (1979). *Cognitive Therapy of Depression*. New York: Guilford Press.

Beck, A.T., Steer, R.A., & Garbin, M.G. (1988). Psychometric properties of the Beck Depression Inventory: Twenty-five years of evaluation. *Clinical Psychology Review*, *8*, 77–100.

Becker, D.R. (2008). Vocational rehabilitation. In K.T. Mueser & D.V. Jeste (eds), *Clinical Handbook of Schizophrenia* (pp. 261–267). New York: Guilford Press.

Beitman, B., Blinder, B., Thase, M.E., Riba, M.B., & Safer, D.L. (eds) (2003). *Integrating Psychotherapy and Pharmacotherapy: Dissolving the Mind–Brain Barrier*. New York: W.W. Norton.

Bellack, A.S., Mueser, K.T., Gingerich, S., & Agresta, J. (2004). *Social Skills Training for Schizophrenia: A Step-by-step Guide*. New York: Guilford Press.

Benjamin, L.S. (1996). *Interpersonal Diagnosis and Treatment of Personality Disorders* (2nd edition). New York: Guilford Press.

Bennett-Levy, J., Butler, G., Fennell, M.J.V., Hackmann, A., Mueller, M., & Westbrook, D. (eds) (2004). *The Oxford Guide to Behavioural Experiments in Cognitive Therapy*. Oxford: Oxford University Press.

Bentall, R.P. (2003). *Madness Explained*. London: Penguin.

Bentall, R.P. (2009). *Doctoring the Mind*. London: Allen Lane.

Berg, I.K. & Miller, S.D. (1992). *Working with the Problem Drinker: A Solution-focused Approach*. New York: W.W. Norton.

Bergin, A.E. & Richards, P.S. (1997). *A Spiritual Strategy for Counseling and Psychotherapy*. Washington, DC: American Psychological Association.

Beutler, L.E., Castonguay, L.G., & Follette, W.C. (2006). Integration of therapeutic factors in dysphoric disorders. In L.G. Castonguay & L.E. Beutler (eds), *Principles of Therapeutic Change that Work* (pp. 111–120). New York: Oxford University Press.

Beutler, L.E., Clarkin, J.F., & Bongar, B. (2000). *Guidelines for the Systematic Treatment of the Depressed Patient*. New York: Oxford University Press.

Beutler, L.E. & Harwood, T.M. (2000). *Prescriptive Psychotherapy: A Practical Guide to Systematic Treatment Selection*. New York: Oxford University Press.

Beutler, L.E., Machado, P.P., & Allstetter-Neufeldt, S. (1994). Therapist variables. In S.A.E. Bergin & L. Garfield (eds), *Handbook of Psychotherapy and Behavior Change* (4th edition) (pp. 229–269). New York: John Wiley.

Beutler, L.E., Malik, M., Alimohamed, S., Harwood, T.M., Talebi, H., Noble, S., et al. (2004). Therapist variables. In M.J. Lambert (ed.), *Bergin's and Garfield's Handbook of Psychotherapy and Behavior Change* (5th edition) (pp. 227–306). New York: John Wiley.

Birmaher, B., Brent, D.A., Kolko, D., Baugher, M., Bridge, J., Holder, D. et al. (2000). Clinical outcome after short-term psychotherapy for adolescents with major depressive disorder. *Archives of General Psychiatry*, *57*, 29–36.

Bishop, S.R. et al. (2004). Mindfulness: A proposed operational definition. *Clinical Psychology: Science and Practice*, *11*, 230–240.

Blatt, S.J. (2008). *Polarities of Experience*. Washington, DC: American Psychological Association.

Blatt, S.J., Shahar, G., & Zuroff, D.C. (2002). Anaclitic/sociotropic and introjective/autonomous dimensions. In J.C. Norcross (ed.), *Psychotherapy Relationships that Work: Therapist Contributions and Responsiveness to Patients* (pp. 315–334). New York: Oxford University Press.

Blatt, S.J., Zuroff, D.C., Bondi, C.M., Sanislow III, C.A., & Pilkonis, P.A. (1998). When and how perfectionism impedes the brief treatment of depression: Further analyses of the National Institute of Mental Health Treatment of Depression Collaborative Research Program. *Journal of Consulting and Clinical Psychology*, 66(2), 423–428.

Bohart, A.C., Elliott, R., Greenberg, L.S., & Watson, J.C. (2002). Empathy. In J.C. Nocross (ed.), *Psychotherapy Relationships that Work: Therapist Contributions and Responsiveness to Patients* (pp. 89–108). New York: Oxford University Press.

Bohart, A.C. & Greenberg, L.S. (eds) (1997). *Empathy Reconsidered: New Directions in Psychotherapy*. Washington, DC: American Psychological Association.

Bohart, A.C. & Rosenbaum, R. (1995). The dance of empathy: Empathy, diversity, and technical eclecticism. *The Person-Centered Journal*, *2*(1), 5–29.

Bohart, A.C. & Tallman, K. (1999). *How Clients Make Therapy Work*. Washington, DC: American Psychological Association.

Bond, T. (1993). *Standards and Ethics for Counselling in Action*. London: Sage.

Bond, T. (2000). *Standards and Ethics for Counselling in Action* (2nd edition). London: Sage.

Bond, T. & Mitchels, B. (2008). *Confidentiality and Record Keeping in Counselling and Psychotherapy*. London: Sage.

Bongar, B. (2002). *The Suicidal Patient: Clinical and Legal Standards of Care* (2nd edition). Washington, DC: American Psychological Association.

Book, H.E. (1997). *How to Practice Brief Psychodynamic Psychotherapy: The Core Conflictual Relationship Theme Method*. Washington, DC: American Psychological Association.

Bordin, E. (1979). The generalizability of the psychoanalytic concept of the working alliance. *Psychotherapy*, *16*, 252–260.

Boren, J.J., Leventhal, A., & Pigott, H.E. (2009). Just how effective are antidepressant medications? Results of a major new study. *Journal of Contemporary Psychotherapy*, *39*, 93–100.

Borkovec, T.D. & Costello, E. (1993). Efficacy of applied relaxation and cognitive-behavioral therapy in the treatment of generalized anxiety disorder. *Journal of Consulting and Clinical Psychology*, *61*(4), 611–619.

Borys, D.S. & Pope, K.S. (1989). Dual relationships between therapist and client: A national study of psychologists, psychiatrists, and social workers. *Professional Psychology: Research and Practice*, *20*(5), 283–293.

Bowlby, J. (1988). *A Secure Base: Parent-Child Attachment and Healthy Human Development*. London: Basic Books.

Brantley, J. (2003). *Calming Your Anxious Mind: How Mindfulness and Compassion Can Free You from Anxiety, Fear and Panic*. Oakland, CA: New Harbinger Publications.

Brewin, C.R., Andrews, B., & Valentine, J.D. (2000). Meta-analysis of risk factors for post traumatic stress disorder in trauma-exposed adults. *Journal of Consulting and Clinical Psychology*, *68*, 748–766.

British Association for Counselling and Psychotherapy (2010). *Ethical Framework for Good Practice in Counselling and Psychotherapy*. Lutterworth: BACP.

Brown, T.A., Di Nardo, P.A., & Barlow, D.H. (1994). *Anxiety Disorders Interview Schedule for DSM–IV (ADIS–IV)*. San Antonio, TX: Psychological Corporation/Graywind Publications Inc.

Brown, T.A., O'Leary, T.A., & Barlow, D.H. (2001). Generalized anxiety disorder. In D.H. Barlow (ed.), *Clinical Handbook of Psychological Disorders: A Step-by-step Treatment Manual* (3rd edition) (pp. 154–208). New York: Guilford Press.

Bulik, C.M. (2002). Anxiety, depression and eating disorders. In C.G. Fainburn & K.D. Brownell (eds), *Eating Disorders and Obesity* (pp. 193–197). New York: Guilford Press.

Burke, B.L., Arkowitz, H., & Dunn, C. (2002). The efficacy of motivational interviewing and its adaptations. In W.R. Miller & S. Rollnick (eds), *Motivational Interviewing* (pp. 217–250). New York: Guilford Press.

Cain, D.J. (2002). Defining characteristics, history, and evolution of humanistic psychotherapies. In D.J. Cain & J. Seeman (eds), *Humanistic Psychotherapies: Handbook of Research and Practice* (pp. 3–54). Washington, DC: American Psychological Association.

Cain, D.J. & Seeman, J. (eds) (2002). *Humanistic Psychotherapies: Handbook of Research and Practice*. Washington, DC: American Psychological Association.

Canadian Counselling Association (1999). *Code of Ethics*. Ottowa: CCA.

Casement, P. (1999). *On Learning from the Patient*. London: Routledge.

Castle, D.J. & Morgan, V. (2008). Epidemiology. In K.T. Mueser & D.V. Jeste (eds), *Clinical Handbook of Schizophrenia* (pp. 14–24). New York: Guilford Press.

Castonguay, L.G. & Beutler, L.E. (eds) (2006). *Principles of Therapeutic Change that Work*. New York: Oxford University Press.

Castonguay, L.G. et al. (2005). Cognitive-behavioral assimilative integration. In J.C. Norcross & M.R. Goldfried (eds), *Handbook of Psychotherapy Integration* (2nd edition) (pp. 241–262). New York: Oxford University Press.

Centers for Disease Control and Prevention (CDC) (2007). Web-based Injury Statistics Query and Reporting System (WISQARS) [Online]. National Center for Injury Prevention and Control, CDC (producer). Available at: URL: www.cdc.gov/injury/wisqars/index.html (accessed 14/6/2010).

Chesley, K. & Loring-McNulty, N.E. (2003). Process of suicide: Perspective of the suicide attempter. *Journal of American Psychiatric Nurses' Association*, *9*, 41–45.

Clarkin, J.F. & Levy, K.N. (2004). The influence of client variables on psychotherapy. In M.J. Lambert (ed.), *Bergin's and Garfield's Handbook of Psychotherapy and Behavior Change* (5th edition) (pp. 194–226). New York: John Wiley.

Cloninger, C.R. (1987). A systematic method for clinical description and classification of personality variants: a proposal. *Archives of General Psychiatry*, *44*(6), 573–588.

Coccaro, E.F. (2001). Biological and treatment correlates. In W.J. Livesley (ed.), *Handbook of Personality Disorders* (pp. 124–135). New York: Guilford Press.

Cohen, P., Chen, H., et al. (2008). Socioeconomic background and the developmental course of schizotypal and borderline personality disorder symptoms. *Development and Psychopathology*, *20*, 633–650.

Connolly Gibbons, M.B., Crits-Christoph, P., Barber, J.P., & Schamberger, M. (2007). Insight in psychotherapy: A review of empirical literature. In L.G. Castonguay & C.E. Hill (eds), *Insight in Psychotherapy* (pp. 143–166). Washington, DC: American Psychological Association.

Cooper, M. (2003). *Existential Therapies*. London: Sage.

Cooper, M. (2008a). *Essential Findings in Counselling and Psychotherapy*. London: Sage.

Cooper, M. (2008b). Existential psychotherapy. In J. LeBow (ed.), *Twenty-first Century Psychotherapies: Contemporary Approaches to Theory and Practice* (pp.237–276). London: John Wiley.

Cornelius, R.R. (2001). Crying and catharsis. In J.J.M. Vingerhoets & R.R. Cornelius (eds), *Adult Crying* (pp. 199–212). Hove: Brunner-Routledge.

Cornell, A.W. (1996). *The Power of Focusing: A Practical Guide to Emotional Self-Healing*. Oakland, CA: New Harbinger Publications.

Corsini, R.J. & Wedding, D. (2007). *Current Psychotherapies* (8th edition). Belmont, CA: Brooks Cole.

Craske, M.G. (2010). *Cognitive-Behavioral Therapy*. Washington, DC: American Psychological Association.

Craske, M.G., Antony, M.M., & Barlow, D.H (2006). *Mastery of Your Fears and Phobias*. New York: Oxford University Press.

Craske, M.G. & Barlow, D.H. (2001). Panic disorder and agoraphobia. In D.H. Barlow (ed.), *Clinical Handbook of Psychological Disorders: A Step-by-step Treatment Manual* (3rd edition) (pp. 1–59). New York: Guilford Press.

Craske, M.G. & Barlow, D.H. (2007). *Mastery of Your Anxiety and Panic: Therapist Guide* (4th edition). New York: Oxford University Press.

Craske, M.G. & Barlow, D.H. (2008). Panic disorder and agoraphobia. In D.H. Barlow (ed.), *Clinical Handbook of Psychological Disorders: A Step-by-step Treatment Manual* (4th edition) (pp. 1–65). New York: Guilford Press.

Critchfield, K.I. & Smith Benjamin, L. (2006). Integration of therapeutic factors in personality disorders. In L.G. Castonguay & L.E. Beutler (eds), *Principles of Therapeutic Change that Work* (pp. 253–274). New York: Oxford University Press.

Crits-Christoph, P. & Barber, J.P. (2007). Psychosocial treatments for personality disorders. In P.E. Nathan & J.M. Gorman (eds), *A Guide to Treatments that Work* (3rd edition) (pp. 641–658). New York: Oxford University Press.

Crits-Christoph, P. & Connolly-Gibbons, M.B. (2002). Relational interpretations. In J.C. Nocross (ed.), *Psychotherapy Relationships that Work: Therapist Contributions and Responsiveness to Patients* (pp. 285–302). New York: Oxford University Press.

Crits-Christoph, C., Crits-Christoph, K., Wolf-Palacio, D., Fichter, M., & Rudick, D. (1995). Brief supportive-expressive psychodynamic therapy for generalized anxiety disorder. In J.P. Barber & P. Crits-Christoph (eds), *Dynamic Therapies for Psychiatric Disorders (Axis 1)* (pp. 43–83). New York: Basic Books.

Crits-Christoph, P. & Luborsky, L. (1990). Changes in CCRT pervasiveness during psychotherapy. In L. Luborsky & P. Crits-Christoph, *Understanding Countertransference: The Core Conflictual Relationship Theme Method* (pp. 133–146). New York: Basic Books.

Crits-Christoph, P., Siqueland, L., Blaine, J., Frank, A., Luborsky, L., Onken, L.S., et al. (1999). Psychosocial treatment for cocaine dependence. *Archives of General Psychiatry*, *56*, 493–502.

Cuijpers, P. (1997). Bibliotherapy in unipolar depression: A meta-analysis. *Journal of Behavioural Therapy and Experimental Psychiatry*, *28*, 139–147.

Curtis, J.T. & Silberschatz, G. (2007). The plan formulation method. In T. Eells (ed.), *Handbook of Psychotherapy Case Formulation* (2nd edition) (pp. 198–220). New York: Guilford Press.

Curtis, J.T., Silberschatz, G., Sampson, H., & Weiss, J. (1994). The plan formulation method. *Psychotherapy Research*, *4*(3&4), 197–207.

Dale, P., Allen, J., & Measor, L. (1998). Counselling adults who were abused as children: Clients' perceptions of efficacy, client-counsellor communication, and dissatisfaction. *British Journal of Guidance and Counselling*, *26*, 141–157.

Daley, D.C. & Marlatt, G.A. (2005). Relapse prevention. In J.H. Lowinson, P. Ruiz, R.B. Millman, & J.G. Langrod (eds), *Substance Abuse* (4th edition) (pp. 772–785). Philadelphia: Lippincott Williams & Wilkins.

Daley, D.C., Mercer, D., & Carpenter, G. (2002). *Drug Counseling for Cocaine Addiction: The Collaborative Cocaine Treatment Study Model.* National Institute of Health publication. No. 02–4381, USA, 124 pp. Available online at: http://archives.drugabuse.gov/PDF/Manual 4.pdf (accessed 14/6/2010).

Davis, A.M. & Timulak, L. (2008, November). *Religion and Spirituality in 'Secular' Psychotherapy: The Story So Far.* Paper presented at the 38th Annual Conference, Psychological Society of Ireland, Carlow.

De Moor, M.H., Boomsma, D.I., et al. (2008). Testing causality in the association between regular exercise and symptoms of anxiety and depression. *Archives of General Psychiatry, 65*, 897–905.

Denison, S.J. (2005). Substance use disorders in individuals with co-occurring psychiatric disorders. In J.H. Lowinson, P. Ruiz, R.B. Millman, & J.G. Langrod (eds), *Substance Abuse* (4th edition) (pp. 904–912). Philadelphia: Lippincott Williams & Wilkins.

Depue, R.A. & Lenzenweger, M.F. (2001). A neurobehavioral model dimensional model. In W.J. Livesley (ed.), *Handbook of Personality Disorders* (pp. 136–176). New York: Guilford Press.

DeRubeis, R.J. & Beck, A.T. (1988). Cognitive therapy. In K.S. Dobson (ed.), *Handbook of Cognitive-behavioral Therapies*. New York: Guilford Press.

DiClemente, C.C. & Prochaska, J.O. (1982). Self change and therapy change of smoking behavior: A comparison of processes of change in cessation and maintenance. *Addictive Behaviors*, 7, 133–142.

Dimidjian, S., Hollon, S.D., et al. (2006). Randomized trial of behavioral activation, cognitive therapy, and antidepressant medication in the acute treatment of adults with major depression. *Journal of Consulting and Clinical Psychology*, 74(4), 658–670.

Dimidjian, S., Martell, C.R., Addis, M.E., & Herman-Dunn, R. (2008). Behavioral activation for depression. In D.H Barlow (ed.), *Clinical Handbook of Psychological Disorders: A Step-by-step Treatment Manual* (4th edition) (pp. 328–364). New York: Guilford Press.

Dobson, K.S. & Block, L. (1988). Historical and philosophical bases of the cognitive behavioral therapies. In K. Dobson (ed.), *Handbook of Cognitive-Behavioral Therapies* (pp. 3–39). New York: Guilford Press.

Dobson, K.S. & Dozois, D.J.A. (2010). Historical and philosophical bases of the cognitive-behavioral therapies. In K. Dobson (ed.), *Handbook of Cognitive-Behavioral Therapies* (3rd edition) (pp. 3–38). New York: Guilford Press.

Dobson, K.S., Hollon, S.D., et al. (2008). Randomized trial of behavioral activation, cognitive therapy, and antidepressant medication in the prevention of relapse and recurrence in major depression. *Journal of Consulting and Clinical Psychology*, 76, 468–477.

Doherty, W.J. (1995). *Soul Searching: Why Psychotherapy Must Promote Moral Responsibility*. New York: Basic Books.

Dolder, C.R. (2008). Side effects of antipsychotics. In K.T. Mueser & D.V. Jeste (eds), *Clinical Handbook of Schizophrenia* (pp. 168–177). New York: Guilford Press.

Dolhanty, J. & Greenberg, L.S. (2009). Emotion-focused therapy in a case of anorexia nervosa. *Clinical Psychology and Psychotherapy, 16*(4), 366–382.

Downar, J. & Kapur, S. (2008). Biological theories. In K.T. Mueser & D.V. Jeste (eds), *Clinical Handbook of Schizophrenia* (pp. 25–34). New York: Guilford Press.

Dryden, W. & Ellis, A. (1988). Ratonal-emotive therapy. In K. Dobson (ed.), *Handbook of Cognitive-Behavioral Therapies* (pp. 214–272). New York: Guilford Press.

Duncan, B.L., Miller, S.D., Sparks, J.A., & Claud, D.A. (2003). The Session Rating Scale: Preliminary psychometric properties of a 'working' alliance measure. *Journal of Brief Therapy, 3*, 3–12.

Eames, V. & Roth, A. (2000). Patient attachment orientation and the early working alliance: A study of patient and therapist reports of alliance quality and ruptures. *Psychotherapy Research, 10*, 421–434.

Eells, T.D. (ed.) (2007). *Handbook of Psychotherapy Case Formulation* (2nd edition). New York: Guilford Press.

Egan, G. (2002). *The Skilled Helper: A Problem Management Approach to Helping* (7th edition). Pacific-Grove, CA: Brooks Cole.

Elkin, I., Shea, M.T., Klett, C.J., Imber, S.D., Sotsky, S.M., Collins, J.F., et al. (1989). National Institute of Mental Health Treatment of Depression Collaborative Research Program: General effectiveness of treatments. *Archives of General Psychiatry, 46*, 971–982.

Elliott, R. (1984). A discovery-oriented approach to significant events in psychotherapy: Interpersonal process recall and comprehensive process analysis. In L. Rice and L. Greenberg (eds), *Patterns of Change* (pp. 249–286). New York: Guilford Press.

Elliott, R. (1985). Helpful and nonhelpful events in brief counseling interviews: An empirical taxonomy. *Journal of Counseling Psychology, 32*, 307–322.

Elliott, R., Greenberg, L.S., & Lietaer, G. (2004). Research on experiential psychotherapies. In M.J. Lambert (ed.), *Bergin's and Garfield's Handbook of Psychotherapy and Behavior Change* (5th edition) (pp. 493–539). New York: John Wiley.

Elliott, R., Mack, C., & Shapiro, D.A. (1999). *Simplified Personal Questionnaire Procedure*. Unpublished Manuscript: University of Toledo.

Elliott, R. & Shapiro, D.A. (1992). Client and therapist as analysts of significant events. In S.G. Toukmanian & D.L. Rennie (eds), *Psychotherapy Process Research: Paradigmatic and Narrative Approaches* (pp. 163–186). Newbury Park, CA: Sage.

Elliott, R., Shapiro, D.A., Firth-Cozens, J., Stiles, W.B., Hardy, G.E., Llewelyn, S.P., & Margison, F. (1994). Insight in interpersonal-dynamic therapy: A comprehensive process analysis. *Journal of Counseling Psychology, 41*, 449–463.

Elliott, R., Slatick, E., & Urman, M. (2001). Qualitative change process research on psychotherapy: Alternative strategies. *Psychologische Beiträge, 43*(3), 69–111.

Elliott, R., Watson, J.C., Goldman, R., & Greenberg, L.S. (2004). *Learning Emotion-focused Therapy: The Process-experiential Approach*. Washington, DC: American Psychological Association.

Emmelkamp, P.M.G. (2004). Behavior therapy with adults. In M.J. Lambert (ed.), *Bergin and Garfield's Handbook of Psychotherapy and Behavior Change* (5th edition) (pp. 393–446). New York: John Wiley.

Evans, C., Mellor-Clark, J., Margison, F., Barkham, M., Audin, K., Connell, J., & McGrath, G. (2000). CORE: Clinical Outcomes in Routine Evaluation. *Journal of Mental Health, 9*(3), 247–255.

Fairburn, C.G. (2008). *Cognitive-Behavioural Therapy and Eating Disorders*. New York: Guilford Press.

Fairburn, C.G., Cooper, Z., & Shafran, R. (2003). Cognitive behaviour therapy for eating disorders: A 'transdiagnostic' theory and treatment. *Behaviour Research and Therapy, 41*, 509–528.

Fairburn, C.G., Cooper, Z., Shafran, R., & Wilson, G.T. (2008). Eating disorders: A transdiagnostic protocol. In D.H. Barlow (ed.), *Clinical Handbook of Psychological Disorders: A Step-by-step Treatment Manual* (4th edition) (pp. 579 – 614). New York: Guilford Press.

Farber, B.A. & Lane, J.S. (2002). Positive regard. In J.C. Norcross (ed.), *Psychotherapy Relationships that Work: Therapist Contributions and Responsiveness to Patients* (pp. 175–194). New York: Oxford University Press.

Ferster, C.B. (1973). A functional analysis of depression. *American Psychologist*, *28*, 857–870.

Finney, J.W. & Moos, R.H. (2007). Psychosocial treatments for alcohol use disorders. In P.E. Nathan & J.M. Gorman (eds), *A Guide to Treatments that Work* (3rd edition) (pp. 157–168). New York: Oxford University Press.

First, M.B., Spitzer, R.L., Gibbon, M., & Williams, J.B.W. (1996). *Structured Clinical Interview for DSM–IV Axis I Disorders*. New York: New York State Psychiatric Institute.

Fisher, J.E. & O'Donohue, W.T. (eds) (2007). *Evidence-Based Psychotherapy*. New York: Springer.

Floyd, M. (2003). Bibliotherapy as an adjunct to psychotherapy for depression in older adults. *Journal of Clinical Psychology*, *59*(2), 187–195.

Floyd, M., Scogin, F., McKendree-Smith, N., Floyd, D., & Rokke, P.D. (2004). Cognitive therapy for depression: A comparison of individual psychotherapy and bibliotherapy for depressed older adults. *Behavior Modification*, *28*(2), 297–318.

Foa, E.B., Hembree, E.A., & Rothbaum, B.O. (2007). *Prolonged Exposure Therapy for PTSD: Emotional Processing of Traumatic Experiences*. New York: Oxford University Press.

Fox, C. & Hawton, K. (2004). *Deliberate Self-harm in Adolescence*. London: Jessica Kingsley.

Frank, E. & Schwartz, H.A. (2004). Interpersonal and social rhythm therapy. In S.L. Johnson & R.L. Leahy (eds), *Psychological Treatment of Bipolar Disorder* (pp. 162–183). New York: Guilford Press.

Frank, J.D. & Frank, J.B. (1991). *Persuasion and Healing: A Comparative Study of Psychotherapy* (3rd edition). Baltimore, M.D: Johns Hopkins University Press.

Franklin, M.E. & Foa, E.B. (2007). Cognitive behavioural treatment of obsessive-compulsive disorder. In P.E. Nathan & J.M. Gorman (eds), *A Guide to Treatments that Work* (2nd edition) (pp. 431–446). New York: Oxford University Press.

Franklin, M.E. & Foa, E.B. (2008). Obsessive compulsive disorder. In D.H. Barlow (ed.), *Clinical Handbook of Psychological Disorders* (4th edition) (pp. 164–215). New York: Guilford Press.

Franko, D.L. & Rolfe, S. (1996). Countertransference in the treatment of patients with eating disorders. *Psychiatry*, *59*, 108–116.

Freeman, M.S. & Hayes, G. (2002). Clients changing counselors: An inspirational journey. *Counseling and Values*, *47*, 13–21.

Freud, S. (2007/1900). *Interpretation of Dreams*. London: Nuvision Publishing.

Fried, D., Crits-Christoph, P., & Luborsky, L. (1990). The parallel of narratives about the therapist with the CCRT for other people. In L. Luborsky & P. Crits-Christoph (eds), *Understanding Transference: The CCRT Method* (pp. 147–157). New York: Basic Books.

Fujimura, L.E., Weis, D.M., & Cochran, J.R. (1985). Suicide: dynamics and implications for counselling. *Journal of Counselling and Development*, *63*, 612–615.

Gabbard, G.O. & Horowitz, M.J. (2009). Insight, transference interpretation, and therapeutic change in dynamic psychotherapy of borderline personality disorder. *American Journal of Psychiatry*, *166*, 517–521.

Gardner, E.L. (2005). Brain-reward mechanisms. In J.H. Lowinson, P. Ruiz, R.B. Millman & J.G. Langrod (eds), *Substance Abuse* (pp. 48–96). Philadelphia: Lippincott Williams & Wilkins.

Garfield, S.L. (1994). Research on client variables in psychotherapy. In A.E. Bergin & S.L. Garfield (eds), *Handbook of Psychotherapy and Behavior Change* (4th edition) (pp. 190–228). New York: John Wiley.

Geldard, K. & Geldard, D. (2008). *Counselling Children* (3rd edition). London: Sage.

Gelso, C.J. & Hayes, J.A. (1998). *The Psychotherapy Relationship*. New York: Wiley.

Gelso, C.J. & Hayes, J.A. (2002). The management of countertransference. In J.C. Nocross (ed.), *Psychotherapy Relationships that Work: Therapist Contributions and Responsiveness to Patients* (pp. 267–283). New York: Oxford University Press.

Gelso, C.J. & Hayes, J.A. (2007). *Countertransference and the Therapist's Inner Experience*. Mahwah, NJ: Lawrence Erlbaum Associates.

Gendlin, E.T. (1964). A theory of personality change. In P. Worchel & D. Byrne (eds), *Personality Change* (pp. 100–148). New York: John Wiley and Sons.

Gendlin, E.T. (1968). The experiential response. In E. Hammer (ed.), *The Use of Interpretation in Treatment*. New York: Grune and Stratton, Inc.

Gendlin, E.T. (1978). *Focusing*. New York: Everest House.

Gendlin, E.T. (1981). *Focusing*. New York: Bantam.

Gendlin, E.T. (1984). The client's client: the edge of awareness. In R.L. Levant & J.M. Shlien (eds), *Client-centered Therapy and the Person-Centered Approach: New Directions in Theory, Research and Practice* (pp. 76–107). New York: Praeger.

Gendlin, E.T. (1996). *Focusing-oriented Psychotherapy: A Manual of the Experiential Method*. New York: Guilford Press.

Gerson, J. & Stanley, B. (2002). Suicidal and self-injurious behavior in personality disorder: Controversies and treatment directions. *Current Psychiatry Reports*, *4*, 30–38.

Gilbert, P. (2007). *Psychotherapy and Counselling for Depression* (3rd edition). London: Sage.

Giovacchini, P.L. (1989). *Countertransference: Triumphs and Catastrophes*. Northvale, NJ: Jason Aronson.

Gotlib, I.H. & Hammen, C.L. (2002). Introduction. In I.H. Gotlib & C.L. Hammen, *Handbook of Depression* (pp. 1–20). New York: Guilford Press.

Grafanaki, S. & McLeod, J. (1999). Narrative processes in the construction of helpful and hindering events in experiential psychotherapy. *Psychotherapy Research*, *9*, 289–303.

Grant, A., Townend, M., Mills, J., & Cockx, A. (2008). *Assessment and Case Formulation in Cognitive Behavioural Therapy*. London: Sage.

Grant, B.F., Stinson, F.S., Dawson, D.A., et al. (2004a). Co-occurrence of 12-month alcohol and drug use disorders and personality disorders in the United States: Results from the National Epidemiologic Survey on Alcohol and Related Conditions. *Archives of General Psychiatry*, *61*, 361–368.

Grant, B.F., Stinson, F.S., Dawson, D.A., et al. (2004b). Prevalence and co-occurrence of substance use disorders and independent mood and anxiety disorders: Results from the National Epidemiologic Survey on Alcohol and Related Conditions. *Archives of General Psychiatry*, *61*, 807–816.

Gratz, K.L. (2001). Measurement of deliberate self-harm: Preliminary data on the Deliberate Self-Harm Inventory. *Journal of Psychopathology and Behavioral Assessment*, *23*(4), 253–263.

Grawe, K. (1996). Understanding change. In U. Esser, H. Pabst, & G.-W. Speierer (eds), *The Power of the Person-centered Approach: New Challenges, Perspectives, Answers* (pp. 139–156). Köln: GwG.

Grawe, K. (1997). Research-informed psychotherapy. *Psychotherapy Research*, 7, 1–19.

Grawe, K. (2004). *Psychological Therapy*. Göttingen: Hogfrege & Huber Publ.

Greenberg, L.S. (1984). Task analysis: the general approach. In L.N. Rice & L.S. Greenberg (eds), *Patterns of Change* (pp. 124–148). New York: Guilford Press.

Greenberg, L.S. (2002). *Emotion-focused Therapy: Coaching Clients to Work Through Their Feelings*. Washington, DC: American Psychological Association.

Greenberg, L.S. (2006, December). Emotion-focused Therapy: Transforming Power of Affect. Lecture. Dublin, Ireland.

Greenberg, L.S. (2007). *Emotion-focused Therapy for Depression*. DVD. Washington, DC: American Psychological Association.

Greenberg, L.S. (2009). *Emotion-focused Institute*. The Training Programme Lecture, October. Toronto: Canada.

Greenberg, L.S., Auszra, L., & Herrmann, I. (2007). The relationship between emotional productivity, emotional arousal and outcome in experiential therapy of depression. *Psychotherapy Research*, *17*(2), 57–66.

Greenberg, L.S. & Elliott, R. (1997). Varieties of empathic responding. In A. Bohart & L.S. Greenberg (eds), *Empathy Reconsidered: New Directions in Psychotherapy* (pp. 167–186). Washington, DC: American Psychological Association.

Greenberg, L.S. & Foerster, F. (1996). Resolving unfinished business: The process of change. *Journal of Consulting and Clinical Psychology*, *64*, 439–446.

Greenberg, L.S. & Goldman, R. (2007). Case formulation in emotion-focused therapy. In T. Eells (ed.), *Handbook of Psychotherapy Case Formulation* (2nd edition) (pp. 379–411). New York: Guilford Press.

Greenberg, L.S. & Goldman, R. (2008). *Emotion-Focused Couples Therapy: The Dynamics of Emotion, Love and Power*. Washington, DC: American Psychological Association.

Greenberg, L.S. & Johnson, S. (1988). *Emotionally Focused Therapy for Couples*. New York: Guilford Press.

Greenberg, L.S. & Paivio, S. (1997). *Working with Emotions in Psychotherapy*. New York: Guilford Press.

Greenberg, L.S., Rice, L.N., & Elliott, R. (1993). *Facilitating Emotional Change: The Moment-by-moment Process*. New York: Guilford Press.

Greenberg, L.S., & Safran, J.D. (1989). Emotion in psychotherapy. *American Psychologist*, *44*, 19–29.

Greenberg, L.S. & Van Balen, R. (1998). The theory of experience-centered therapies. In L.S. Greenberg, J.C. Watson, & G. Lietaer (eds), *Handbook of Experiential Psychotherapy* (pp. 28–57). New York: Guilford Press.

Greenberg, L.S., Warwar, S.H., & Malcolm, W.M. (2008). Differential effects of emotion-focused therapy and psychoeducation in facilitating forgiveness and letting go of emotional injuries. *Journal of Counseling Psychology*, *55*(2), 185–196.

Greenberg, L.S. & Watson, J.C. (2006). *Emotion-focused Therapy for Depression*. Washington, DC: American Psychological Association.

Greenberger, D. & Padesky, C.A. (1995). *Mind over Mood: Change How You Feel by Changing the Way You Think*. New York: Guilford Press.

Gross, S. (2001). On integrity. *Psychodynamic Practice*, 7, 207–216.

Guidano, V.F. & Liotti, G. (1988). A systems process-oriented approach to cognitive therapy. In Dobson, K. (ed.), *Handbook of Cognitive-Behavioral Therapies*. New York: Guilford Press.

Guthrie, E., Margison, F., Mackay, H., Chew-Graham, C., Moorey, J., & Sibbald, B. (2004). Effectiveness of psychodynamic interpersonal therapy training for primary care counsellors. *Psychotherapy Research*, *14*, 161–175.

Haffner, H. & An Der Heiden, W. (2008). Course and outcome. In K.T. Mueser & D.V. Jeste (eds), *Clinical Handbook of Schizophrenia* (pp. 100–116). New York: Guilford Press.

Halmi, K.A. (2003). From Giacometti to Botero: Images of eating disorders under investigation. *American Journal of Psychiatry*, *160*, 205–207.

Haw, C., Hawton, K., Houston, K., & Townsend, E. (2001). Psychiatric and personality disorders in deliberate self-harm patients. *British Journal of Psychiatry*, *178*, 48–54.

Hawton, K. & James, A. (2005). Suicide and deliberate self-harm in young people. *British Medical Journal*, *330*, 891–894.

Hawton, K.J., Rodham, K., Evans, E., & Wheatherhall, R. (2002). Deliberate self-harm in adolescents: Self report survey in schools in England. *British Medical Journal*, *325*, 1207–1211.

Hazlett-Stevens, H., Pruitt, L.D., & Collins, A. (2009). Phenomenology of generalized anxiety disorder. In M.M. Antony & M.B. Stein (eds), *Oxford Handbook of Anxiety and Related Disorders* (pp. 47–55). New York: Oxford University Press.

Heaton, K.J., Hill, C.E., Petersen, D., Rochlen, A.B., & Zack, J. (1998). A comparison of therapist-facilitated and self-guided dream interpretation sessions. *Journal of Counseling Psychology*, *45*, 115–122.

Hendricks, M. (2002). Focusing-oriented/experiential psychotherapy. In D. Cain & J. Seeman (eds), *Humanistic Psychotherapies: Handbook of Research and Practice*. Washington, DC: American Psychological Association.

Hesse, E. (1999). The adult attachment interview: Historical and current perspectives. In J. Cassidy & P. Shavers (eds), *Handbook of Attachment: Theory, Research, and Clinical Applications* (pp. 395–433). New York: Guilford Press.

Higgins, S.T., Sigmon, S.C., & Heil, S.H. (2008). Drug abuse and dependence. In D.H. Barlow (ed.), *Clinical Handbook of Psychological Disorders: A Step-by-step Treatment Manual* (4th edition) (pp. 547–577). New York: Guilford Press.

Hill, C.E. (1996). *Working with Dreams in Psychotherapy*. New York: Guilford Press.

Hill, C.E. (ed.) (2004). *Dream Work in Therapy: Facilitating Exploration, Insight, and Action*. Washington, DC: American Psychological Association.

Hill, C.E. (2009). *Helping Skills: Facilitating Exploration, Insight, and Action*. (3rd edition). Washington, DC: American Psychological Association.

Hill, C.E., Diemer, R., & Heaton, K.J. (1997). Dream interpretation sessions: Who volunteers, who benefits, and what volunteer clients view as most and least helpful. *Journal of Counseling Psychology*, *44*, 53–62.

Hill, C.E., Kellems, I.S., Kolchakian, M.R., Wonnell, T.L., Davis, T.L., & Nakayama, E.Y. (2003). The therapist experience of being the target of hostile versus suspected unasserted client anger: Factors associated with resolution. *Psychotherapy Research*, *13*, 475–491.

Hill, C.E. & Knox, S. (2002). Self-disclosure. In J.C. Norcross (ed.), *Psychotherapy Relationships that Work* (pp. 255–265). New York: Oxford.

Hill, C.E. & O'Brien, K. (1999). *Helping Skills: Facilitating Exploration, Insight, and Action*. Washington, DC: American Psychological Association.

Hobson, R.F. (1985). *Forms of Feeling: The Heart of Psychotherapy*. London: Tavistock.

Hoek, H.W. (2002). Distribution of eating disorders. In C.G. Fainburn & K.D. Brownell (eds), *Eating Disorders and Obesity* (pp. 233–237). New York: Guilford Press.

Hoek, H.W. & van Hoeken, D. (2003). Review of the prevalence and incidence of eating disorders. *The International Journal of Eating Disorders*, *34*(4), 383–396.

Høglend, P., Amlo, S., et al. (2006). Analysis of the patient–therapist relationship in dynamic psychotherapy: An experimental study of transference interpretations. *American Journal of Psychiatry*, *163*, 1739–1746.

Holmes, J. (2001). *The Search for the Secure Base*. New York: Brunner-Routledge.

Hollon, S.D. & Beck, A.T. (2004). Cognitive and cognitive behavioral therapies. In M.J. Lambert (ed.), *Garfield and Bergin's Handbook of Psychotherapy and Behavior Change* (5th edition) (pp. 447–492). New York: John Wiley.

Hopko, D.R., Lejuez, C.W., LePage, J.P., Hopko, S.D., & McNeil, D.W. (2003). A brief behavioral activation treatment for depression: A randomized pilot trial within an inpatient psychiatric hospital. *Behavior Modification*, *27*, 458–469.

Horowitz, M.J. & Eells, T.D. (2007). Configurational analysis. In T. Eells (ed.), *Handbook of Psychotherapy Case Formulation* (2nd edition) (pp. 136–163). New York: Guilford Press.

Horvath, A.O. & Bedi, R.P. (2002). The alliance. In J.C. Nocross (ed.), *Psychotherapy Relationships that Work: Therapist Contributions and Responsiveness to Patients* (pp. 37–69). New York: Oxford University Press.

Horvath, A.O. & Greenberg, L.S. (1989). The development and validation of the working alliance inventory. *Journal of Counseling Psychology*, *36*, 223–233.

Horvath, A.O. & Greenberg, L. (eds) (1994). *The Working Alliance: Theory, Research and Practice*. New York: John Wiley.

Horvath, A.T. (2005). Alternative support groups. In J.H. Lowinson, P. Ruiz, R.B. Millman, & J.G. Langrod (eds), *Substance Abuse* (4th edition) (pp. 599–608). Philadelphia: Lippincott Williams & Wilkins.

Hudson, J.L. & Rapee, R.M. (2009). Familial and social environments in the etiology and maintenance of anxiety disorders. In M.M. Antony & M.B. Stein (eds), *Oxford Handbook of Anxiety and Related Disorders* (pp. 173–189). New York: Oxford University Press.

Ingram, R.E. & Siegle, G.J. (2010). Cognitive science and the conceptual foundations of cognitive-behavior therapy. In K. Dobson (ed.), *Handbook of Cognitive-behavioral Therapies* (3rd edition) (pp. 74–93). New York: Guilford Press.

Jacobson, N.S., Dobson, K.S., Truax, P.A., Addis, M.E., Koerner, K., Gollan, J.K., et al. (1996). A component analysis of cognitive-behavioral treatment for depression. *Journal of Consulting and Clinical Psychology*, *64*, 295–304.

Jobes, D.A., Jacoby, A.M., Cimbolic, P., & Hustead, L.A.T. (1997). Assessment and treatment of suicidal clients in a university counseling center. *Journal of Counseling Psychology*, *44*(4), 368–377.

Johnson, B.D. & Golub, A. (2005). Sociocultural issues. In J.H. Lowinson, P. Ruiz, R.B. Millman, & J.G. Langrod (eds), *Substance Abuse* (4th edition) (pp. 107–120). Philadelphia: Lippincott Williams & Wilkins.

Johnson, S.M. (2004). *The Practice of Emotionally Focused Marital Therapy: Creating Connection* (2nd edition). New York: Brunner/Mazel.

Kabat-Zinn, J. (1996). *Full Catastrophe Living: How to Cope with Stress, Pain and Illness Using Mindfulness Meditation*. London: Piatkus.

Kaslow, F.W. (2004). Comprehensive Handbook of Psychotherapy (4 vols). New York: John Wiley.

Kazdin, A.E. (2004) Psychotherapy for children and adolescents. In M.J. Lambert (ed.), *Bergin and Garfield's Handbook of Psychotherapy and Behaviour Change* (pp. 543–589). New York: John Wiley and Sons.

Kessler, R.C. (2002). Epidemiology of depression. In I.H. Gotlib & C.L. Hammen, *Handbook of Depression* (pp. 23–42). New York: Guilford Press.

Khantzian, E.J., Dodes, L., & Brehm, N.M. (2005). Psychodynamics. In J.H. Lowinson, P. Ruiz, R.B. Millman, & J.G. Langrod (eds), *Substance Abuse* (4th edition) (pp. 97–106). Philadelphia: Lippincott Williams & Wilkins.

King, M., Sibbald, B., Ward, E., Bower, P., Lloyd, M., Gabbay, M., et al. (2000). Randomised controlled trial of non-directive counselling, cognitive-behaviour therapy and usual general practitioner care in the management of depression as well as mixed anxiety and depression in primary care. *Health Technology Assessment, 4*(19).

Kitchener, K.S. & Anderson, S.K. (2000). Ethical issues in counseling psychology: Old themes – new problems. In S.D. Brown & R.W. Lent (eds), *Handbook of Counseling Psychology* (3rd edition). New York: John Wiley.

Klein, M., Mathieu-Coughlan, P., Gendlin, E.T., & Kiesler, D.J. (1969). *The Experiencing Scales: A Research and Training Manual* (Vols 1 & 2). Madison, WI: Wisconsin University Press.

Klein, M.H., Kolden, G.G., Michels, J.L., & Chisholm-Stockard, S. (2002). Congruence. In J.C. Norcross (ed.), *Psychotherapy Relationships that Work: Therapist Contributions and Responsiveness to Patients* (pp. 195–216). New York: Oxford University Press.

Klerman, G.L., Weissman, M.M., Rounsaville, B.J., & Chevron, E.S. (1984). *Interpersonal Psychotherapy of Depression.* New York: Basic Books.

Knox, S., Hess, S.A., Petersen, D.A., & Hill, C.E. (1997). A qualitative analysis of client perceptions of the effects of helpful therapist self-disclosure in long-term therapy. *Journal of Counseling Psychology, 44*(3), 274–283.

Koeningsberg, H.V., Woo-Ming, A.M., & Siever, L.J. (2007). Psychopharmocological treatment of personality disorders. In P.E. Nathan & J.M. Gorman (eds), *A Guide to Treatments that Work* (3rd edition) (pp. 659–680). New York: Oxford University Press.

Koizumi, Y., Awata, S., et al. (2005). Association between social support and depression status in the elderly: Results of a one-year, community-based prospective cohort study in Japan. *Psychiatry and Clinical Neurosciences, 59*, 563–569.

Kolbasovsky, A. (2008). *A Therapist's Guide to Understanding Common Medical Conditions*. New York: W.W. Norton.

Koocher, G.P. & Keith-Spiegel, P. (2008). *Ethics in Psychology and Mental Health Professions: Standards and Cases* (3rd edition). New York: Oxford University Press.

Kopelowicz, A., Liberman, R.P., & Zarate, R. (2007). Psychosocial treatments of schizophrenia. In P.E. Nathan & J.M. Gorman (eds), *A Guide to Treatments that Work* (3rd edition) (pp. 243–270). New York: Oxford University Press.

Kratochvíl, S. (2002). *Základy psychoterapie* (4. aktualizované vydanie). Praha: Portál.

Kutscher, E.C. (2008). Antipsychotics. In K.T. Mueser & D.V. Jeste (eds), *Clinical Handbook of Schizophrenia* (pp. 159–167). New York: Guilford Press.

Ladany, N., O'Brien, K.M., Hill, C.E., Melincoff, D.S., Knox, S., & Petersen, D.A. (1997). Sexual attraction toward clients, use of supervision, and prior training: A qualitative study of predoctoral psychology interns. *Journal of Counseling Psychology, 44*(4), 413–424.

Lambert, M.J., Hansen, N.B., & Finch, A.E. (2001). Patient-focused research: Using patient outcome data to enhance treatment effects. *Journal of Consulting and Clinical Psychology, 69*(2), 159–172.

Lambert, M.J., Morton, J.J., Hatfield, D., Harmon, C., Hamilton, S., Redi, R., Shimokawa, K., Christopherson, C., & Burlingame, G. (2004). *Administration and Scoring Manual for the Outcome of Questionnaire 45.2*. Orem, UT: American Professional Credentialing Services.

Lampropoulos, G.K. (2001). Bridging technical eclecticism and theoretical integration: Assimilative integration. *Journal of Psychotherapy Integration*, *11*(1), 5–19.

Larson, D.G. & Hoyt, W.T. (2007). What has become of grief counselling? An evaluation of the empirical foundations of the new pessimism. *Professional Psychology: Research and Practice*, *38*, 347–355.

Leahy, R.L. (2003). *Cognitive Therapy Techniques: A Practitioner's Guide*. New York: Guilford Press.

Leahy, R.L. (2004). Cognitive therapy. In S.L. Johnson & R.L. Leahy (eds), *Psychological Treatment of Bipolar Disorder* (pp. 139–161). New York: Guilford Press.

Leahy, R. (2006) *The Worry Cure: Seven Steps to Stop Worry from Stopping You*. London: Piatkus Books.

Leijssen, M. (1998). Focusing microprocesses. In L.S. Greenberg, J.C. Watson, & G. Lietaer (eds), *Handbook of Experiential Psychotherapy* (pp. 121–154). New York: Guilford Press.

Levenson, H. & Strupp, H.H. (2007). Cyclical maladaptive patterns. In T. Eells (ed.), *Handbook of Psychotherapy Case Formulation* (2nd edition) (pp. 164–197). New York: Guilford Press.

Levitt, H.M. (2001). The sounds of silence in psychotherapy: Clients' experiences of pausing. *Psychotherapy Research*, *11*(3), 295–309.

Lewinsohn, P.M. (1974). A behavioral approach to depression. In R.J. Friedman & M. Katz (eds), *The Psychology of Depression: Contemporary Theory and Research* (pp. 157–178). Oxford: John Wiley.

Lietaer, G. (1993). Authenticity, congruence, and transparency. In D. Brazier (ed.), *Beyond Carl Rogers* (pp. 17–46). London: Constable

Lin, S.W. & Anthenelli, R.M. (2005). Genetic factors in the risk for substance use disorders. In J.H. Lowinson, P. Ruiz, R.B. Millman, & J.G. Langrod (eds), *Substance Abuse* (4th edition) (pp. 33–47). Philadelphia: Lippincott Williams & Wilkins.

Linehan, M.M. (1993). Cognitive Behavioral Treatment of Borderline Personality Disorder. New York: Guilford Press.

Linehan, M.M. (1996). *Suicide Behavior Questionnaire*. Washington, DC: University of Washington, Behavioral Research and Therapy Clinic, Department of Psychology.

Livesley, W.J. (2001). Conceptual and taxonomic issues. In W.J. Livesley (ed.), *Handbook of Personality Disorders* (pp. 3–38). New York: Guilford Press.

Low, G., Jones, D., Duggan, C., Power, M., & MacLeod, A. (2001). The treatment of deliberate self-harm in borderline personality disorder using dialectical behavior therapy: A pilot study in a high security hospital. *Behavioural and Cognitive Psychotherapy*, *29*, 85–92.

Lowinson, J.H., Ruiz, P., Millman, R.B., & Langrod, J.G. (eds) (2005). *Substance Abuse* (4th edition). Philadelphia: Lippincott Williams & Wilkins.

Luborsky, L. (1984). *Principles of Psychoanalytic Psychotherapy: A Manual for Supportive-expressive Treatment*. New York: Basic Books.

Luborsky, L., Barber, J.P., Binder, J., et al. (1993). Transference-related measures: A new class based on psychotherapy session. In N.E. Miller, L. Luborsky, J.P. Barber, & J.P. Docherty (eds), *Psychodynamic Treatment Research: A Handbook for Clinical Practice* (pp. 326–341). New York: Basic Books.

Luborsky, L. & Barrett, M.S. (2007). The core conflictual relationship theme. In T. Eells (ed.), *Handbook of Psychotherapy Case Formulation* (2nd edition) (pp. 105–135). New York: Guilford Press.

Luborsky, L. & Crits-Cristoph, P. (1990). *Understanding Transference: The Core Conflictual Relationships Method*. New York: Basic Books.

Luborsky, L. & Crits-Cristoph, P. (1998). *Understanding Transference: The Core Conflictual Relationships Method* (2nd edition). Washington, DC: American Psychological Association.

Luborsky, L. & Luborsky, E. (2006). *Research and Psychotherapy: The Vital Link*. Lanham, MD: Jason Aronson.

Luborsky, L., Mark, D., Hole, A.V., Popp, C., Goldsmith, B., & Cacciola, J. (1995). Supportive-expressive dynamic psychotherapy of depression: A time-limited version. In J.P. Barber & P. Crits-Christoph (eds), *Dynamic Therapies for Psychiatric Disorders (Axis I)* (pp. 13–42). New York: Basic Books.

Luborsky, L., Woody, G.E., Hole, A.V., & Velleco, A. (1995). Supportive-expressive dynamic psychotherapy for treatment of opiate drug dependence. In J.P. Barber & P. Crits-Christoph (eds), *Dynamic Therapies for Psychiatric Disorders (Axis I)* (pp. 131–160). New York: Basic Books.

Mahoney, M.J. (1974). *Cognitive and Behavior Modification*. Cambridge, MA: Ballinger.

Mahoney, M.J. (1988). The cognitive sciences and psychotherapy: Patterns in a developing relationship. In K.S. Dobson (ed.), *The Handbook of Cognitive-behavioral Therapies* (pp. 357–386). New York: Guilford Press.

Mahoney, M.J. (2003). *Constructive psychotherapy*. New York: Guilford Press.

Main, M. (1995). Attachment: Overview with implications for clinical work. In S. Goldberg, R. Muir, & J. Kerr (eds), *Attachment Theory: Social, Developmental, and Clinical Perspectives* (pp. 407–474). Hillsdale, NJ: Erlbaum.

Mansell, W. (2007). Reading about self-help books on cognitive-behavioural therapy for anxiety disorders. *The Psychiatrist*, *31*, 238–240.

Marks, I.M. Cavanagh, K., & Gega, L. (2007). *Hand-on Help: Computer-aided Psychotherapy*. Hove: Psychology Press.

Marrs, R.W. (1995). A meta-analysis of bibliotherapy studies. *American Journal of Psychology*, *23*, 843–870.

Martin, D.J., Garske, J.P., & Davies, M.K. (2000). Relation of the therapeutic alliance with outcome and other variables: A meta-analytic review. *Journal of Consulting and Clinical Psychology*, *68*, 438–450.

Mathews, C.A. (2009). Phenomenology of obsessive-compulsive disorder. In M.M. Antony & M.B. Stein (eds), *Oxford Handbook of Anxiety and Related Disorders* (pp. 56–64). New York: Oxford University Press.

Mattia, J.I. & Zimmerman, M. (2001). Epidemiology. In W.J. Livesley (ed.), *Handbook of Personality Disorders* (pp. 107–123). New York: Guilford Press.

McClintock, S.M., Ranginawala, N., & Hussain, M.M. (2008). Electroconvulsive therapy. In K.T. Mueser & D.V. Jeste (eds), *Clinical Handbook of Schizophrenia* (pp. 196–206). New York: Guilford Press.

McCrady, B.S. (2008). Alcohol use disorders. In D.H. Barlow (ed.), *Clinical Handbook of Psychological Disorders: A Step-by-step Treatment Manual* (4th edition) (pp. 492–546). New York: Guilford Press.

McCrady, B.S., Haaga, D.A.F., & Lebow, J. (2006). Integration of therapeutic factors in treating substance use disorders. In L.G. Castonguay & L.E. Beutler (eds), *Principles of Therapeutic Change that Work* (pp. 341–352). New York: Oxford University Press.

McLeod, J. (2009). *Introduction to Counselling.* (4th edition). London: Open University Press.

McMahon, M. (2008). Confidentiality, privacy, and health information managment. In R. Kennedy (ed.), *Allied Health Professionals and the Law* (pp. 108–130). Sydney: Federation Press.

McNally, R.J. (2007). Mechanisms of exposure therapy: How neuroscience can improve psychological treatments for anxiety disorders. *Clinical Psychology Review*, *27*(6), 750–759.

Meara, N.M., Schmidt, L.D., & Day, J.D. (1996). Principles and virtues: A foundation for ethical decisions, policies, and character. *The Counseling Psychologist*, *24*(1), 4–77.

Meichenbaum, D.H. (1977). *Cognitive-behavior Modification: An Integrative Approach.* New York: Plenum Press.

Mennin, D.S. (2004). An emotion regulation treatment for generalized anxiety disorder. *Clinical Psychology and Psychotherapy*, *11*, 17–29.

Mercer, D.E. & Woody, G.E. (1999). *Individual Drug Counseling.* National Institute of Health publication No. 99–4380, USA, 89 pp. Available online at: http://archives.drugabuse.gov/PDF/Manual3.pdf (accessed 14/6/2010).

Messer, S. (1992). A critical examination of belief structures in integrative and eclectic psychotherapy. In J. Norcross & M. Goldfried (eds), *Handbook of Psychotherapy Integration*. New York: Basic Books.

Meyer, B., Berger, T., Caspar, F., et al. (2009). Effectiveness of a novel integrative online treatment for depression (Deprexis): Randomized controlled trial. *Journal of Medical Internet Research*, *11*, e15.

Miklowitz, D.J. (2008). Bipolar disorder. In D.H. Barlow (ed.), *Clinical Handbook of Psychological Disorders: A Step-by-step Treatment Manual* (4th edition) (pp. 421–462). New York: Guilford Press.

Miklowitz, D.J. & Craighead, W.E. (2007). Psychosocial treatments for bipolar disorder. In P.E. Nathan & J.M. Gorman (eds), *A Guide to Treatments that Work* (3rd edition) (pp. 309–322). New York: Oxford University Press.

Miller, A.L. & Velligan, D.I. (2008). Treatment planning. In K.T. Mueser & D.V. Jeste (eds), *Clinical Handbook of Schizophrenia* (pp. 145–158). New York: Guilford Press.

Miller, N., Luborsky, L., Barber, J., & Docherty, J. (1993). *Psychodynamic Treatment Research*. New York: Basic Books.

Miller, R.B. (2004). *Facing Human Suffering*. Washington, DC: American Psychological Association.

Miller, S.D., Duncan, B.L., & Hubble, M.A. (2005). Outcome-informed clinical work. In J.C. Norcross & M.R. Goldfried (eds), *Handbook of Psychotherapy Integration* (2nd edition) (pp. 84–104). New York: Oxford University Press.

Miller, W.R. (1995). *Motivational Enhancement Therapy with Drug Abusers*. Bethesda: MD National Institute of Drug Abuse.

Miller, W.R. & Rollnick, S. (2002). *Motivational Interviewing: Preparing People to Change Addictive Behavior* (2nd edition). New York: Guilford Press.

Milton, J., Polmear, C., & Fabricius, J. (2004). *A Short Introduction to Psychoanalysis*. London: Sage.

Mineka, S. & Zinbarg, R. (2006). A contemporary learning theory perspective on the etiology of anxiety disorders: It's not what you thought it was. *American Psychologist*, *61*, 10–26.

Missirlian, T., Toukmanian, D., Warwar, S., & Greenberg, L. (2005) Emotional arousal, client perceptual processing, and the working alliance in experiential psychotherapy for depression. *Journal of Consulting and Clinical Psychology*, *73*, 861–871.

Mitchell, S. (1997). *Influence and Autonomy in Psychoanalysis*. Hillsdale, NJ: The Analytic Press.

Morrison, A.P. (2008). Cognitive-behavioral therapy. In K.T. Mueser & D.V. Jeste (eds), *Clinical Handbook of Schizophrenia* (pp. 226–239). New York: Guilford Press.

Morrison, A.P., Renton, J.C., Dunn, H., Williams, S., & Bentall, R.P. (2004). *Cognitive Therapy for Psychosis: A Formulation-based Approach*. London: Routledge.

Morrisson, J. (1999). *When Psychological Problems Mask Medical Disorder: A Guide for Psychotherapists*. New York: Guilford Press.

Mowrer, O.H. (1960). *Learning Theory and Behavior*. New York: John Wiley.

Moyers, T.B. & Martin, T. (2006). Therapist influence on client language during motivational interviewing sessions. *Journal of Substance Abuse*, *30*, 245–251.

Možný, P. & Praško, J. (1999). *Kognitivně-behaviorální terapie*. Praha: Triton.

Mueser, K.T. & Jeste, D.V. (eds) (2008). *Clinical Handbook of Schizophrenia*. New York: Guilford Press.

Mullen, P.E. & Purcell, R. (2007). Stalking therapists. In B. van Luyn, S. Akhtar, & J.W. Livesley (eds), *Severe Personality Disorders* (pp. 109–117). Cambridge: Cambridge University Press.

Nace, E.P. (2005). Alcoholics anonymous. In J.H. Lowinson, P. Ruiz, R.B. Millman, & J.G. Langrod (eds), *Substance Abuse* (4th edition) (pp. 587–598). Philadelphia: Lippincott Williams & Wilkins.

Najavits, L.M., Liese, B.S., & Harned, M.S. (2005). Cognitive and behavioral therapies. In J.H. Lowinson, P. Ruiz, R.B. Millman, & J.G. Langrod (eds), *Substance Abuse* (4th edition) (pp. 723–732). Philadelphia: Lippincott Williams & Wilkins.

Narrow, W.E., Rae, D.S., Robins, L.N., & Regier, D.A. (2002). Revised prevalence estimates of mental disorders in the United States using a clinical significance criterion to reconcile two survey's estimates. *Archives of General Psychiatry*, *59*, 115–123.

Nathan, P.E. & Gorman, J.M. (eds) (2007). *A Guide to Treatments that Work* (2nd edition). New York: Oxford University Press.

Nelson-Jones, R. (2009). *Introduction to Counselling Skills* (3rd edition). London: Sage.

Newman, M.G., Stiles, W.B., Janeck, A., & Woody, S.R. (2006). Integration of therapeutic factors in anxiety disorders. In L.G. Castonguay & L.E. Beutler (eds), *Principles of Therapeutic Change that Work* (pp. 187–202). New York: Oxford University Press.

Newton, M.S. & Ciliska, D. (2006). Internet-based innovations for the prevention of eating disorders: A systematic review. *Eating Disorders*, *14*(5), 365–384.

Norcross, J. (ed.). (2002). *Psychotherapy Relationships that Work: Therapist Contributions and Responsiveness to Patients*. New York: Oxford University Press.

Norcross, J.C. (2005). A primer on psychotherapy integration. In J.C. Norcross & M.R. Goldfried (eds), *Handbook of Psychotherapy Integration* (2nd edition) (pp. 3–23). New York: Oxford University Press.

Norcross, J.C., Beutler, L.E., & Levant, R.F. (eds) (2006). *Evidence-based Practices in Mental Health: Debate and Dialogue on the Fundamental Questions*. Washington, DC: American Psychological Association.

Norcross, J.C. & Goldfried, M.R. (eds) (2005). *Handbook of Psychotherapy Integration* (2nd edition). New York: Oxford University Press.

Norcross, J.C. & Guy, D. (2007). *Leaving It at the Office*. New York: Guilford Press.

Ohman, A. & Ruck, J. (2007). Four principles of fear and their implications for phobias. In J. Rottenberg & S.L. Johnson (eds), *Emotion and Psychopathology* (pp. 167–190). Washington, DC: American Psychological Association.

Orlinsky, D.E., Grawe, K., & Parks, B.K. (1994). Process and outcome in psychotherapy - *noch einmal*. In A.E. Bergin & S.L. Garfield (eds), *Handbook of Psychotherapy and Behavior Change* (4th edition) pp. 270–376). New York: John Wiley.

Orlinsky, D.E., Norcross, J.C., Ronnestad, M.H., & Wiseman, H. (2005). Outcomes and Impacts of Psychotherapists' Personal Therapy: A Research Review. In J.D. Geller, J.C. Norcross, & D.E. Orlinsky (eds), *The Psychotherapist's Own Psychotherapy Patient and Clinician Perspectives*. New York: Oxford University Press.

Orlinsky, D.E. & Ronnestad, M.H. (2005). *How Psychotherapists Develop: A Study of Therapeutic Work and Professional Growth*. Washington, DC: American Psychological Association.

Otto, M.W., Behar, E., Smith, J.A.J., & Hofmann, S.G. (2009). Combining pharmacological and cognitive behavioral therapy in the treatment of anxiety disorders. In M.M. Antony & M.B. Stein (eds), *Oxford Handbook of Anxiety and Related Disorders* (pp. 429–440). New York: Oxford University Press.

Paris, J. (2001). Psychosocial adversity. In W.J. Livesley (ed.), *Handbook of Personality Disorders* (pp. 231–241). New York: Guilford Press.

Paris, J. (2007). Managing suicidal crises in patients with severe personality disorders. In B. van Luyn, S. Akhtar, & J.W. Livesley (eds), *Severe Personality Disorders* (pp. 109–117). Cambridge: Cambridge University Press.

Pascual-Leone, A. & Greenberg, L.S. (2007) Emotional processing in experiential therapy: Why 'the only way out is through'. *Journal of Consulting and Clinical Psychology*, *75*(6), 875–887.

Patterson, J., Ari Albala, A., McCahill, M.E., & Edwards, T.M. (2006). *The Therapist's Guide to Psychopharmacology*. New York: Guilford Press.

Paulson, B.L. & Worth, M. (2002). Counseling for suicide: Client perspectives. *Journal of Counseling and Development*, *80*, 86–93.

Pavlov, I.P. (1927/1960). *Conditional Reflexes*. New York: Dover Publications.

Perls, F. (2008). The 'Case of Jane'. In D. Wedding & R.J. Corsini (eds), *Case Studies in Psychotherapy* (5th edition). Stamford, CA: Wadsworth.

Perls, F., Hefferling, R.F., & Goodman, P. (1951). *Gestalt Therapy: Excitement and Growth in the Human Personality*. New York: Delta Books.

Philips, J.P.N. (1986). Shapiro personal questionnaire and generalized personal questionnaire techniques: A repeated measures individualized outcome measurement. In L.S. Greenberg & W. Pinsof (eds), *The Psychotherapeutic Process: A research Handbook* (pp. 557–590). New York: Guilford Press.

Pomeroy, C. & Mitchell, J.E. (2002). Medical complications of anorexia nervosa and bulimia nervosa. In C.G. Fainburn & K.D. Brownell (eds), *Eating Disorders and Obesity* (pp. 278–285). New York: Guilford Press.

Pope, K.S., Keith-Spiegel, P., & Tabachnick, B. (1986). Sexual attraction to clients: The human psychologist and the (sometimes) inhuman training system. *American Psychologist*, *41*, 147–158.

Pope, K.S. & Vasquez, M.J.T. (2007) *Ethics in Psychotherapy and Counselling: A Practical Guide* (3rd edition). New York: John Wiley.

Pope, K.S. & Vetter, V.A. (1992). Ethical dilemmas encountered by members of the American Psychological Association: A national survey. *American Psychologist*, *47*, 397–411.

Power, M. & Brewin, C.R. (eds) (1997). *The Transformation of Meaning in Psychological Therapies*. Chichester: John Wiley.

Prochaska, J.O. & DiClemente, C.C. (1983). Stages and processes of self-change of smoking: Toward an integrative model of change. *Journal of Consulting and Clinical Psychology*, 51, 390–395.

Prochaska, J.O. & Norcross, J.C. (2002). Stages of change. In J.C. Norcross (ed.), *Psychotherapy Relationships that Work: Therapist Contributions and Responsiveness to Patients* (pp. 303–313). New York: Oxford University Press.

Prochaska, J.O. & Norcross, J.C. (2003). *Systems of Psychotherapy: A Transtheoretical Analysis* (5th edition). Pacific Grove, CA: Brooks Cole.

Proudfoot, J., Ryden, C., Everitt, B., et al. (2004). Clinical efficacy of computerised cognitive behavioural therapy for anxiety and depression in primary care. *British Journal of Psychiatry*, *185*, 46–54.

Prouty, G. (1994). *Theoretical Evolutions in Person-centered/Experiential Therapy: Applications to Schizophrenic Psychoses*. Westport, CT: Praeger.

Psychological Society of Ireland (2008). *The Code of Professional Ethics of the Psychological Society of Ireland*. Dublin: PSI.

Reich, J. (2003). The effect of Axis II disorders on the outcome of treatment of anxiety and unipolar depressive disorders: A review. *Journal of Personality Disorder*, *17*, 387–405.

Reis, B.F. & Brown, L.G. (1999). Reducing psychotherapy dropouts: Maximizing perspective convergence in the psychotherapy dyad. *Psychotherapy*, *36*(2), 123–136.

Rennie, D. (1990). Toward a representation of the client's experience of the psychotherapy hour. In G. Lietaer, J. Rombauts, & R. Van Balen (eds), *Client-centered and Experiential Psychotherapy in the Nineties* (pp. 155–172). Leuven: Leuven University Press.

Rennie, D. (1994). Client's deference in psychotherapy. *Journal of Counseling Psychology*, *41*, 427–437.

Rennie, D.L. (2002). Experiencing psychotherapy: Grounded theory studies. In D. Cain & J. Seeman (eds), *Humanistic Psychotherapies: Handbook of Research and Practice* (pp. 117–144). Washington, DC: American Psychological Association.

Resick, P.A. & Calhoun, K.S. (2001). Post-traumatic stress disorder. In D.H. Barlow (ed.), *Clinical Handbook of Psychological Disorders* (3rd edition) (pp. 60–113). New York: Guilford Press.

Resick, P.A., Monson, C.M., & Rizvi, S.L. (2008). Post-traumatic stress disorder. In D.H. Barlow (ed.), *Clinical Handbook of Psychological Disorders: A Step-by-step Treatment Manual* (4th edition) (pp. 65–122). New York: Guilford Press.

Rhodes, R.H., Hill, C.E., Thompson, B.J., & Elliott, R. (1994). Client retrospective recall of resolved and unresolved misunderstanding events. *Journal of Counseling Psychology*, *41*, 473–483.

Rice, L. & Greenberg, L. (1992). Humanistic approaches to psychotherapy. In D. Freedheim (ed.), *History of Psychotherapy: A Century of Change* (pp. 197–224). Washington, DC: American Psychological Association.

Rice, L.N. & Kerr, G.P. (1986). Measures of client and therapist vocal quality. In L.S. Greenberg & W. Pinsof (eds), *The Psychotherapeutic Process: A Research Handbook* (pp. 73–106). New York: Guilford Press.

Rice, L.N. & Saperia, E.P. (1984). Task analysis and the resolution of problematic reactions. In L.N. Rice & L.S. Greenberg (eds), *Patterns of Change* (pp. 29–66). New York: Guilford Press.

Ridgway, P. (2008). Supported housing. In K.T. Mueser & D.V. Jeste (eds), *Clinical Handbook of Schizophrenia* (pp. 287–297). New York: Guilford Press.

Rochlen, A.B., Ligiero, D.P., Hill, C.E., & Heaton, K.J. (1999). Effects of training in dream recall and dream interpretation skills on dream recall, attitudes, and dream interpretation outcome. *Journal of Counseling Psychology*, *46*, 27–34.

Rodham, K., Hawton, K., & Evans, E. (2004). Reasons for deliberate self-harm: Comparison of self-poisoners and self-cutters in a community sample of adolescents. *Journal of the American Academy of Child and Adolescent Psychiatry*, *43*, 80–87.

Rogers, C.R. (1942). *Counseling and Psychotherapy*. Boston: Houghton Mifflin.

Rogers, C.R. (1951). *Client-centered Therapy*. Boston: Houghton-Mifflin.

Rogers, C.R. (1957). The necessary and sufficient conditions of therapeuic personality change. *Journal of Consulting Psychology*, *21*, 95–103.

Rogers, C.R. (1958). A process conception of psychotherapy. *American Psychologist*, *13*, 142–149.

Rogers, C.R. (1959). A theory of therapy, personality and interpersonal relationships as developed in the client-centered framework. In S. Koch (ed.), *Psychology: A Study of a Science. Vol. 3: Formulations of the Person and the Social Context* (pp. 184–256). New York: McGraw-Hill.

Rogers, C.R. (1961). *On Becoming a Person: A Therapist's View of Psychotherapy*. Boston: Houghton Mifflin.

Rogers, C.R. (1980). *A Way of Being*. Boston: Houghton Mifflin.

Rogers, C.R. & Dymond, R. (eds) (1954). *Psychotherapy and Personality Change*. Chicago: University Press.

Roy-Byrne, P.P. & Cowley, D. (2007). Pharmacologic treatments for panic disorder, generalized anxiety disorders, specific phobia and social anxiety disorders. In P. E. Nathan & J.M. Gorman (eds), *A Guide to Treatments that Work* (3rd edition) (pp. 395–430). New York: Oxford University Press.

Ruiz-Sancho, A.M., Smith, G.W., & Gunderson, J.G. (2001). Psychoeducational approaches. In W.J. Livesley (ed.), *Handbook of Personality Disorders* (pp. 460–474). New York: Guilford Press.

Rush, A.J., Trivedi, M.H., Wisniewski, S.R., Nierenberg, A.A., et al. (2006). Acute and longer-term outcomes in depressed outpatients requiring one or several treatment steps: A STAR*D report. *American Journal of Psychiatry*, *163*, 1905–1917.

Ryle, A. (2005). Cognitive analytic therapy. In J.C. Norcross & M.R. Goldfried (eds), *Handbook of Psychotherapy Integration* (2nd edition) (pp. 196–220). New York: Oxford University Press.

Sachse, R. (1998). Goal-oriented, client-centered psychotherapy of psychosomatic disorders. In L. Greenberg, J. Watson, & G. Lietaer (eds), *Handbook of Experiential Psychotherapy* (pp. 295–327). New York: Guilford Press.

Sachse, R. & Elliott, R. (2002). Process–outcome research on humanistic therapy variables. In D. Cain & J. Seeman (eds), *Humanistic Psychotherapies: Handbook of Research and Practice* (pp. 83–116). Washington, DC: American Psychological Association.

Safran, J.D. & Muran, J.C. (1996). The resolutions of ruptures in the therapeutic alliance. *Journal of Consulting and Clinical Psychology*, *64*, 447–458.

Safran, J.D. & Muran, J.C. (2000). *Negotiating the Therapeutic Alliance*. New York: Guilford Press.

Samuels, J., Eaton, W.W., et al. (2002). Prevalence and correlates of personality disorders in a community sample. *British Journal of Psychiatry*, *180*, 536–542.

Satir, D.A., Thompson-Brenner, H., Boisseau, C.L., & Crisafulli, M.A. (2009). Countertransference reactions to adolescents with eating disorders: Relationships to clinician and patient factors. *International Journal of Eating Disorders*, *42*(6), 511–521.

Schmidt, U. (2002). Risk factors for eating disorders. In C.G. Fainburn & K.D. Brownell (eds), *Eating Disorders and Obesity* (pp. 247–250). New York: Guilford Press.

Schön, D.A. (1983). *The Reflective Practitioner.* New York: Basic Books.

Schultz, J.H. & Luthe, W. (1959) *Autogenic Training.* New York: Grune Stratton.

Scott, M.J. & Dryden, W. (1996). The cognitive-behavioral paradigm. In R. Woolfe & W. Dryden (eds), *Handbook of Counselling Psychology*. London: Sage.

Segal, Z.V., Williams, J.M.G., & Teasdale, J.D. (2002). *Mindfulness-based Cognitive Therapy for Depression.* New York: Guilford Press.

Sexton, T.L., Alexander, J.F., & Mease, A.L. (2004). Levels of evidence for the models and mechanisms of therapeutic change in family and couple therapy. In M.J. Lambert (ed.), *Bergin's and Garfield's Handbook of Psychotherapy and Behavior Change* (5th edition) (pp. 590–646). New York: John Wiley.

Shapiro, D.A., Barkham, M., Rees, A., Hardy, G.E., Reynolds, S., & Startup, M. (1994). Effects of treatment duration and severity of depression on the effectiveness of cognitive-behavioral and psychodynamic-interpersonal psychotherapy. *Journal of Consulting and Clinical Psychology*, *62*(3), 522–534.

Shedler, J. (2010). The efficacy of psychodynamic therapy. *American Psychologist*, *65*, 98–109.

Skinner, B.F. (1953). *Science and Human Behaviour.* New York: Free Press.

Skovholt, T.M. & Ronnestad, M.H. (1992). Themes in therapist and counselor development. *Journal of Counseling & Development*, *70*(4), 505–515.

Slife, B. (2004). Theoretical challenges to therapy practice and research: The constraint of naturalism. In M.J. Lambert (ed.), *Bergin's and Garfield's Handbook of Psychotherapy and Behavior Change* (5th edition) (pp. 44–83). New York: John Wiley.

Sperry, L. (2007). The Ethical and Professional Practice of Counseling and Psychotherapy. Boston: Allyn and Bacon.

Stedmon, J. & Dallos, R. (eds) (2009). *Reflective Practice in Psychotherapy and Counselling.* London: Routledge.

Stern, D.N. (1985). *The Interpersonal World of the Infant.* New York: Basic Books.

Stice, E., Ragan, J., & Randall, P. (2004). Prospective relations between social support and depression: Differential direction of effects for parent and peer support? *Journal of Abnormal Psychology*, *113*, 155–159.

Stiles, W.B. (2002). Assimilation of problematic experiences. In J.C. Norcross (ed.), *Psychotherapy Relationships that Work: Therapist Contributions and Responsiveness to Patients* (pp. 357–365). New York: Oxford University Press.

Stiles, W.B., Elliott, R., Llewelyn, S.P., Firth-Cozens, J.A., Margison, F.R., Shapiro, D.A., et al. (1990). Assimilation of problematic experiences by clients in psychotherapy. *Psychotherapy*, *27*, 411–420.

Stiles, W.B., Hanas-Webb, L., & Surko, M. (1998). Responsiveness in psychotherapy. *Clinical Psychology: Science and Practice*, *5*, 439–458.

Stinson, F.S., Grant, B.F. Dawson, D.A., et al. (2005). Comorbidity between DSM–IV alcohol and specific drug use disorders in the United States: Results from the National Epidemiologic Survey on Alcohol and Related Conditions. *Drug and Alcohol Dependence*, *80*, 105–116.

Stolberg, R.A., Clark, D.C., & Bongar, B. (2002). Epidemiology, assessment and management of suicide in depressed patients. In I.H. Gotlib & C.L. Hammen (eds), *Handbook of Depression* (pp. 581–601). New York: Guilford Press.

Stricker, G. & Gold, J. (2005). Assimilative psychodynamic therapy. In J.C. Norcross & M.R. Goldfried (eds), *Handbook of Psychotherapy Integration* (2nd edition) (pp. 221–240). New York: Oxford University Press.

Strohle, A. (2009). Physical activity, exercise, depression and anxiety disorders. *Journal of Neural Transmission*, *116*(6), 777–784.

Strupp, H.H. & Binder, J.L. (1984). *Psychotherapy in a New Key*. New York: Basic Books.

Substance Abuse and Mental Health Services Administration (2002). *Results from the 2001 National Household Survey on Drug Abuse: Vol. I. Summary of National Findings* (Office of Applied Studies, NHSDA Series H–17, DHHS Publication No. SMA 02–3758). Rockville, MD: SAMHSA.

Sullivan, P.F. (2002). Course and outcome of anorexia nervosa and bulimia nervosa. In C.G. Fainburn & K.D. Brownell (eds), *Eating Disorders and Obesity* (pp. 226–232). New York: Guilford Press.

Sussman, S., Skara, S., & Ames, S.L. (2008). Substance abuse among adolescents. *Substance Use & Misuse*, *43*, 1802–1828.

Tarrier, N. (2008). Schizophrenia and other psychotic disorders. In D.H. Barlow (ed.), *Clinical Handbook of Psychological Disorders: A Step-by-step Treatment Manual* (4th edition) (pp. 463–491). New York: Guilford Press.

Tarrier, N., Kinney, C., McCarthy, E., Humphreys, L, Wittkowski, A., & Morris, J. (2000). Two-year follow-up of cognitive-behavioral therapy and supportive counseling in the treatment of persistent symptoms in chronic schizophrenia. *Journal of Consulting and Clinical Psychology*, *68*, 917–922.

Tenhula, W.N. & Bellack, A.S. (2008). Social skills training. In K.T. Mueser & D.V. Jeste (eds), *Clinical Handbook of Schizophrenia* (pp. 240–248). New York: Guilford Press.

Teusch, L. & Bohme, H. (1999). Is the exposure principle really crucial in agoraphobia? The influence of client-centered 'nonprescriptive' treatment on exposure. *Psychotherapy Research*, *9*, 115–123.

Teusch, L. & Finke, J. (1996). Fundamental principles of a manual for client-centered therapy of panic and agoraphobia. In U. Esser, H. Pabst, & G.-W. Speierer (eds), *The Power of the Person-centered Approach: New Challenges, Perspectives, Answers*. Köln, Germany: GwG Verlag.

Thase, M.E. & Jindal, R.D. (2004). Combining psychotherapy and psychopharmacology for treatment of mental disorders. In M.J. Lambert (ed.), *Bergin's and Garfield's*

Handbook of Psychotherapy and Behavior Change (5th edition) (pp. 743–766). New York: John Wiley.

Timulak, L. (1999). Humility as an important attitude in overcoming a rupture in the therapeutic relationship. *The Person-Centered Journal*, *6*(2), 153–163.

Timulak L. (2001). *Significant Events in Psychotherapy*. Unpublished research report. Bratislava: Research Institute of Child Psychology.

Timulak, L. (2006). *Základy vedení psychoterapeutického rozhovoru*. Praha: Portál.

Timulak, L. (2007). Identifying core categories of client identified impact of helpful events in psychotherapy - a qualitative meta-analysis. *Psychotherapy Research*, *17*, 305–314.

Timulak, L. (2008). *Research in Psychotherapy and Counselling*. London: Sage.

Timulak, L., Belicova, A., & Miler, M. (2009). *Client-identified Significant Events in a Successful Therapy Case: The Link Between the Significant Events and Outcome*. Paper under review.

Timulak, L. & Elliott, R. (2003). Empowerment events in process-experiential psychotherapy of depression. *Psychotherapy Research*, *13*, 443–460.

Timulak, L. & Lietaer, G. (2001). Moments of empowerment: A qualitative analysis of positively experienced episodes in brief person-centred counselling. *Counselling and Psychotherapy Research*, *1*, 62–73.

Timulak, L. & McElvaney, R. (2009). Significant insight events in psychotherapy: A qualitative meta-analysis. Paper presented at BACP Research conference. Portsmouth, May.

Tjeltveit, A.C. (1999). *Ethics and Values in Psychotherapy*. London: Routledge.

Turk, C.L., Heimberg, R.H., & Magee, L. (2008). Social anxiety disorder. In D.H. Barlow (ed.), *Clinical Handbook of Psychological Disorders* (4th edition) (pp. 123–163). New York: Guilford Press.

Van Kessel, W. & Lietaer, G. (1998). Interpersonal processes. In L. Greenberg, G. Lietaer, & J. Watson (eds), *Handbook of Experiential Psychotherapy* (pp. 155–177). New York: Guilford Press.

Velligan, D.I. & Miller, A.L. (2008). Environmental supports. In K.T. Mueser & D.V. Jeste (eds), *Clinical Handbook of Schizophrenia* (pp. 207–213). New York: Guilford Press.

Wampold, B.E. (2001). *The Great Psychotherapy Debate: Models, Methods, and Findings*. Mahwah, NJ: Lawrence Erlbaum Associates.

Watson, J. (2002). Re-visioning empathy: Theory, research and practice. In D. Cain & J. Seeman (eds), *Handbook of Research and Practice in Humanistic Psychotherapy* (pp. 445–475). New York: American Psychological Association.

Watson, J.C., Goldman, R.N., & Greenberg, L.S. (2007). *Case Studies in Emotion-focused Treatment of Depression: Comparison of Good and Poor Outcome*. Washington, DC: American Psychological Association.

Watson, J., Goldman, R., & Vanaerschot, G. (1998). Empathic: A postmodern way of being? In L. Greenberg, J. Watson, & G. Lietaer (eds), *Handbook of Experiential Psychotherapy: Foundations and Differential Treatment* (pp. 61–81). New York: Guilford Press.

Weiss, J. (1993). *How Psychotherapy Works: Process and Technique*. New York: Guilford Press.

Weiss, J., Sampson, H., & Mount Zion Psychotherapy Research Group (1986). *The Psychoanalytic Process*. New York: Guilford Press.

Weissman, M.M., Markowitz, J.C., & Klerman, G.L. (2000). *Comprehensive Guide to Interpersonal Psychotherapy*. New York: Basic Books.

Wertz, F.J. (1985). Method and findings in a phenomenological psychological study of a complex life-event: Being criminally victimized. In A. Giorgi (ed.), *Phenomenology and Psychological Research* (pp. 155–216). Pittsburgh, PA: Duquesne University Press.

Westbrook, D., Kennerley, H., & Kirk, J. (2007). *An Introduction to Cognitive-behavioural Therapy: Skills and Applications*. London: Sage.

Westefeld, J.S., Werth, Jr., J.L., Range, L.M., Rogers, J.R., Maples, M.R., & Holdwick, Jr., D.J. (2000). Contemporary issues in suicidiology: A reply to Hoffman, Neimeyer, and Silverman. *The Counseling Psychologist*, *28*, 573–578.

Westen, D. (1998). The scientific legacy of Sigmund Freud: Toward a psychodynamically informed psychological science. *Psychological Bulletin*, *124*, 333–371.

Westen, D. & Gabbard, G. (1999). Psychoanalytic approaches to personality. In L. Pervin & O. John (eds), *Handbook of Personality: Theory and Research* (pp. 57–101). New York: Guilford Press.

Westen, D. & Morrison, K. (2001). A multidimensional meta-analysis of treatments for depression, panic, and generalized anxiety disorder: An empirical examination of the status of empirically supported therapies. *Journal of Consulting and Clinical Psychology*, *69*(6), 875–899.

Whipple, J.L., Lambert, M.J., Vermeersch, D.A., Smart, D.W., Nielsem, S.L., & Hawkins, E.J. (2003). Improving the effects of psychotherapy: The use of early identification of treatment failure and problem-solving strategies in routine practice. *Journal of Counseling Psychology*, *50*, 59–68.

Wiebe, R. & McCabe, S.B. (2002). Social perfectionism, dysphoria and aversive interpersonal behaviours. *Journal of Social and Clinical Psychology*, *21*, 67–90.

Wilfley, D.E., Welch, R.R., Stein, R.I., Spurell, E.B., Cohen, L.R., Saelens, B.E., et al. (2002). A randomized comparison of group cognitive-behavioral therapy and group interpersonal psychotherapy for treatment of overweight individuals with binge-eating disorder. *Archives of General Psychiatry*, *59*, 713–721.

Wilson, G.T. (2002). Eating disorders and addictive disorders. In C.G. Fainburn & K.D. Brownell (eds), *Eating Disorders and Obesity* (pp. 199–203). New York: Guilford Press.

Wilson, G.T. & Fairburn, C.G. (2007). Treatments for eating disorder. In P.E. Nathan & J.M. Gorman (eds), *A Guide to Treatments that Work* (2nd edition) (pp. 579–610). New York: Oxford University Press.

Winnick, C. & Norman, R.L. (2005). Epidemiology. In J.H. Lowinson, P. Ruiz, R.B. Millman, & J.G. Langrod (eds), *Substance Abuse* (pp. 15–20). Philadelphia: Lippincott Williams & Wilkins.

Wohlheiter, K. & Dixon, L. (2008). Assessing of co-occurring disorders. In K.T. Mueser & D.V. Jeste (eds), *Clinical Handbook of Schizophrenia* (pp. 125–134). New York: Guilford Press.

Wolpe, J. (1968). Psychotherapy by reciprocal inhibition. *Integrative Psychological and Behavioral Science*, *3*, 234–240.

Wolpe, J. & Lazarus, A.A. (1966). *Behavior Therapy Techniques: A Guide to the Treatment of Neuroses*. Oxford: Pergamon.

Wonderlich, S.A. (2002). Personality and eating disorders. In C.G Fainburn & K.D. Brownell (eds), *Eating Disorders and Obesity* (pp. 204–209). New York: Guilford Press.

Wonnell, T.L. & Hill, C.E. (2000). Effects of including the action stage in dream interpretation. *Journal of Counseling Psychology*, *47*(3), 372–379.

Woody, G.E., Luborsky, L., McLellan, A.T., O'Brien, C., Beck, A.T., Blaine, J., et al. (1983). Psychotherapy for opiate addicts: Does it help? *Archives of General Psychiatry*, *40*, 639–645.

Woody, S.R. & Ollendick, T.H. (2006). Technique factors in treating anxiety disorders. In L.G. Castonguay & L.E. Beutler (eds), *Principles of Therapeutic Change that Work* (pp. 167–186). New York: Oxford University Press.

World Health Organisation (WHO) (1992). *The ICD-10 Classification of Mental and Behavioural Disorders: Clinical Description and Diagnostic Guidelines*. Geneva: WHO.

Worthington, E.L. & Sandage, S.J. (2002). Religion and spirituality. In J.C. Norcross (ed), *Psychotherapy Relationships that Work: Therapist Contributions and Responsiveness to Patients* (pp. 383–400). New York: Oxford University Press.

Wright, J., Clum, G.A., Roodman, A., & Febbraro, G.A.M. (2000). A bibliotherapy approach to relapse prevention in individuals with panic attacks. *Journal of Anxiety Disorders*, *14*, 483– 499.

Wykes, D.R. (2008). Vocational rehabilitation. In K.T. Mueser & D.V. Jeste (eds), *Clinical Handbook of Schizophrenia* (pp. 261–267). New York: Guilford Press.

Yalom, I.D. & Leszcz, M. (2005). *The Theory & Practice of Group Psychotherapy* (5th edition). New York: Basic Books.

Yontef, G. & Jacobs, L. (2005). Gestalt therapy. In R.J. Corsini & D. Wedding (eds), *Current Psychotherapies* (pp. 328–367). Belmont, CA: Thomson/Brooks Cole.

Young, J.E., Rygh, J.L., Weinberger, A.D., & Beck, A.T. (2008). Cognitive therapy for depression. In D.H. Barlow (ed.), *Clinical Handbook of Psychological Disorders: A Step-by-step Treatment Manual* (4th edition) (pp.250–305). New York: Guilford Press.

Index